T0172752

# Big Data, Mining, and Analytics

## Components of
## Strategic Decision Making

# Big Data, Mining, and Analytics

## Components of Strategic Decision Making

Stephan Kudyba

Foreword by Thomas H. Davenport

## CRC Press
Taylor & Francis Group
Boca Raton London New York

CRC Press is an imprint of the
Taylor & Francis Group, an **informa** business

AN AUERBACH BOOK

CRC Press
Taylor & Francis Group
6000 Broken Sound Parkway NW, Suite 300
Boca Raton, FL 33487-2742

First issued in paperback 2019

© 2014 by Taylor & Francis Group, LLC
CRC Press is an imprint of Taylor & Francis Group, an Informa business

No claim to original U.S. Government works

ISBN-13: 978-1-4665-6870-9 (hbk)
ISBN-13: 978-0-367-37881-3 (pbk)

This book contains information obtained from authentic and highly regarded sources. Reasonable efforts have been made to publish reliable data and information, but the author and publisher cannot assume responsibility for the validity of all materials or the consequences of their use. The authors and publishers have attempted to trace the copyright holders of all material reproduced in this publication and apologize to copyright holders if permission to publish in this form has not been obtained. If any copyright material has not been acknowledged please write and let us know so we may rectify in any future reprint.

Except as permitted under U.S. Copyright Law, no part of this book may be reprinted, reproduced, transmitted, or utilized in any form by any electronic, mechanical, or other means, now known or hereafter invented, including photocopying, microfilming, and recording, or in any information storage or retrieval system, without written permission from the publishers.

For permission to photocopy or use material electronically from this work, please access www.copyright.com (http://www.copyright.com/) or contact the Copyright Clearance Center, Inc. (CCC), 222 Rosewood Drive, Danvers, MA 01923, 978-750-8400. CCC is a not-for-profit organization that provides licenses and registration for a variety of users. For organizations that have been granted a photocopy license by the CCC, a separate system of payment has been arranged.

**Trademark Notice:** Product or corporate names may be trademarks or registered trademarks, and are used only for identification and explanation without intent to infringe.

---

**Library of Congress Cataloging-in-Publication Data**

---

Big data, mining, and analytics : components of strategic decision making / editor, Stephan Kudyba.
    pages cm
  Includes bibliographical references and index.
  ISBN 978-1-4665-6870-9 (hardback)
  1. Strategic planning--Data processing. 2. Data mining. 3. Big data. 4. Business planning--Data processing. 5. Webometrics. 6. Data loggers. I. Kudyba, Stephan, 1963- editor of compilation.

HD30.28.B544 2014
658.4'012--dc23
2013049469

---

**Visit the Taylor & Francis Web site at**
**http://www.taylorandfrancis.com**

**and the CRC Press Web site at**
**http://www.crcpress.com**

*To my family, for their consistent support to pursue and complete these types of projects. And to two new and very special family members, Lauren and Kirsten, who through their evolving curiosity have reminded me that you never stop learning, no matter what age you are. Perhaps they will grow up to become analysts . . . perhaps not. Wherever their passion takes them, they will be supported.*

*To the contributors to this work, sincere gratitude for taking the time to share their expertise to enlighten the marketplace of an evolving era, and to Tom Davenport for his constant leadership in promoting the importance of analytics as a critical strategy for success.*

# Contents

# Foreword

Big data and analytics promise to change virtually every industry and business function over the next decade. Any organization that gets started early with big data can gain a significant competitive edge. Just as early analytical competitors in the "small data" era (including Capital One bank, Progressive Insurance, and Marriott hotels) moved out ahead of their competitors and built a sizable competitive edge, the time is now for firms to seize the big data opportunity.

As this book describes, the potential of big data is enabled by ubiquitous computing and data gathering devices; sensors and microprocessors will soon be everywhere. Virtually every mechanical or electronic device can leave a trail that describes its performance, location, or state. These devices, and the people who use them, communicate through the Internet—which leads to another vast data source. When all these bits are combined with those from other media—wireless and wired telephony, cable, satellite, and so forth—the future of data appears even bigger.

The availability of all this data means that virtually every business or organizational activity can be viewed as a big data problem or initiative. Manufacturing, in which most machines already have one or more microprocessors, is increasingly becoming a big data environment. Consumer marketing, with myriad customer touchpoints and clickstreams, is already a big data problem. Google has even described its self-driving car as a big data project. Big data is undeniably a big deal, but it needs to be put in context.

Although it may seem that the big data topic sprang full blown from the heads of IT and management gurus a couple of years ago, the concept actually has a long history. As Stephan Kudyba explains clearly in this book, it is the result of multiple efforts throughout several decades to make sense of data, be it big or small, structured or unstructured, fast moving or quite still. Kudyba and his collaborators in this volume have the knowledge and experience to put big data in the broader context of business and organizational intelligence.

If you are thinking, "I only want the new stuff on big data," that would be a mistake. My own research suggests that within both large non-online businesses (including GE, UPS, Wells Fargo Bank, and many other leading firms) and online firms such as Google, LinkedIn, and Amazon, big data is not being treated separately from the more traditional forms of analytics. Instead, it is being combined with traditional approaches into a hybrid capability within organizations.

There is, of course, considerable information in the book about big data alone. Kudyba and his fellow experts have included content here about the most exciting and current technologies for big data—and Hadoop is only the beginning of them. If it's goal to learn about all the technologies you will need to establish a platform for processing big data in your organization, you've come to the right place.

These technologies—and the subject of big data in general—are exciting and new, and there is no shortage of hype about them. I may have contributed to the hype with a coauthored article in the *Harvard Business Review* called "Data Scientist: The Sexiest Job of the 21st Century" (although I credit the title to my editors). However, not all aspects of big data are sexy. I remember thinking when I interviewed data scientists that it was not a job I would want; there is just too much wrestling with recalcitrant data for my skills and tastes.

Kudyba and his collaborators have done a good job of balancing the sexy (Chapter 1, for example) and the realistic (Chapter 5, for example). The latter chapter reminds us that—as with traditional analytics—we may have to spend more time cleaning, integrating, and otherwise preparing data for analysis than we do actually analyzing it. A major part of the appeal of big data is in combining diverse data types and formats. With the new tools we can do more of this combining than ever before, but it's still not easy.

Many of the applications discussed in this book deal with marketing—using Internet data for marketing, enhancing e-commerce marketing with analytics, and analyzing text for information about customer sentiments. I believe that marketing, more than any other business function, will be reshaped dramatically by big data and analytics. Already there is very strong demand for people who understand both the creative side of marketing and the digital, analytical side—an uncommon combination. Reading and learning from Chapters 6, 7, 10, and others will help to prepare anyone for the big data marketing jobs of the future.

Other functional domains are not slighted, however. For example, there are brief discussions in the book of the massive amounts of sensor data that will drive advances in supply chains, transportation routings, and the monitoring and servicing of industrial equipment. In Chapter 8, the role of streaming data is discussed in such diverse contexts as healthcare equipment and radio astronomy.

The discussions and examples in the book are spread across different industries, such as Chapter 12 on evolving data sources in healthcare. We can now begin to combine structured information about patients and treatments in electronic medical record systems with big data from medical equipment and sensors. This unprecedented amount of information about patients and treatments should eventually pay off in better care at lower cost, which is desperately needed in the United States and elsewhere. However, as with other industry and functional transformations, it will take considerable work and progress with big data before such benefits can be achieved.

In fact, the combination of hope and challenge is the core message of this book. Chapters 10 and 11, which focus on the mining and automated interpretation of textual data, provide an exemplary illustration of both the benefits from this particular form of big data analytics and the hard work involved in making it happen. There are many examples in these two chapters of the potential value in mining unstructured text: customer sentiment from open-ended surveys and social media, customer service requests, news content analysis, text search, and even patent analysis. There is little doubt that successfully analyzing text could make our lives and our businesses easier and more successful.

However, this field, like others in big data, is nothing if not challenging. Meta Brown, a consultant with considerable expertise in text mining, notes in Chapter 10, "Deriving meaning from language is no simple task," and then provides a description of the challenges. It is easy to suggest that a firm should analyze all the text in its customers' blogs and tweets, or that it should mine its competitors' patents. But there are many difficulties involved in disambiguating text and dealing with quintessentially human expressions like sarcasm and slang. As Brown notes, even the best automated text analysis will be only somewhat correct.

As we move into the age of big data, we'll be wrestling with these implementation challenges for many years. The book you're about to read is an excellent review of the opportunities involved in this revolution, but also a sobering reminder that no revolution happens without considerable effort, money, and false starts. The road to the Big Data Emerald City is paved with many potholes. Reading this book can help you avoid many of them, and avoid surprise when your trip is still a bit bumpy.

**Thomas H. Davenport**
*Distinguished Professor, Babson College*
*Fellow, MIT Center for Digital Business*
*Co-Founder, International Institute for Analytics*

# About the Author

**Stephan Kudyba, MBA, PhD,** is a faculty member in the school of management at New Jersey Institute of Technology (NJIT), where he teaches courses in the graduate and executive MBA curriculum addressing the utilization of information technologies, business intelligence, and information and knowledge management to enhance organizational efficiency and innovation. He has published numerous books, journal articles, and magazine articles on strategic utilization of data, information, and technologies to enhance organizational and macro productivity. Dr. Kudyba has been interviewed by prominent magazines and speaks at university symposiums, academic conferences, and corporate events. He has over 20 years of private sector experience in the United States and Europe, having held management and executive positions at prominent companies. He maintains consulting relations with organizations across industry sectors with his company Null Sigma Inc. Dr. Kudyba earned an MBA from Lehigh University and a PhD in economics with a focus on the information economy from Rensselaer Polytechnic Institute.

# Contributors

**Billie Anderson**
Bryant University
Smithfield, Rhode Island

**Steven Barber**
TIBCO StreamBase, Inc.
New York, New York

**Jerry Baulier**
SAS Institute
Cary, North Carolina

**Meta S. Brown**
Business consultant
Chicago, Illinois

**Thomas H. Davenport**
Babson College
Wellesley, Massachusetts

**J. Michael Hardin**
University of Alabama
Tuscaloosa, Alabama

**Ioannis Korkontzelos**
University of Manchester
Manchester, United Kingdom

**Stephan Kudyba**
New Jersey Institute of Technology
Newark, New Jersey

**Matthew Kwatinetz**
QBL Partners
New York, New York

**David Lubliner**
New Jersey Institute of Technology
Newark, New Jersey

**Viju Raghupathi**
Brooklyn College
City University of New York
New York, New York

**Wullianallur Raghupathi**
Fordham University
New York, New York

**Wayne Thompson**
SAS Institute
Cary, North Carolina

**Robert Young**
PHD, Inc.
Toronto, Ontario, Canada

# 1

# Introduction to the Big Data Era

*Stephan Kudyba and Matthew Kwatinetz*

## CONTENTS

By now you've heard the phrase "big data" a hundred times and it's intrigued you, scared you, or even bothered you. Whatever your feeling is, one thing that remains a source of interest in the new data age is a clear understanding of just what is meant by the concept and what it means for the realm of commerce. Big data, terabytes of data, mountains of data, no matter how you would like to describe it, there is an ongoing data explosion transpiring all around us that makes previous creations, collections, and storage of data merely trivial. Generally the concept of big data refers to the sources, variety, velocities, and volumes of this vast resource. Over the next few pages we will describe the meaning of these areas to provide a clearer understanding of the new data age.

The introduction of faster computer processing through Pentium technology in conjunction with enhanced storage capabilities introduced back in the early 1990s helped promote the beginning of the information economy, which made computers faster, better able to run state-of-the-art software devices, and store and analyze vast amounts of data (Kudyba, 2002). The creation, transmitting, processing, and storage capacities of today's enhanced computers, sensors, handheld devices, tablets, and the like, provide the platform for the next stage of the information age. These super electronic devices have the capabilities to run numerous applications, communicate across multiple platforms, and generate, process, and store unimaginable amounts of data. So if you were under the impression that big data was just a function of e-commerce (website) activity, think again. That's only part of the very large and growing pie.

When speaking of big data, one must consider the source of data. This involves the technologies that exist today and the industry applications that are facilitated by them. These industry applications are prevalent across the realm of commerce and continue to proliferate in countless activities:

- Marketing and advertising (online activities, text messaging, social media, new metrics in measuring ad spend and effectiveness, etc.)
- Healthcare (machines that provide treatment to patients, electronic health records (EHRs), digital images, wireless medical devices)
- Transportation (GPS activities)
- Energy (residential and commercial usage metrics)
- Retail (measuring foot traffic patterns at malls, demographics analysis)
- Sensors imbedded in products across industry sectors tracking usage

These are just a few examples of how industries are becoming more data intensive.

## DESCRIPTION OF BIG DATA

The source and variety of big data involves new technologies that create, communicate, or are involved with data-generating activities, which produce different types/formats of data resources. The data we are referring to isn't just numbers that depict amounts, or performance indicators or scale. Data also includes less structured forms, such as the following elements:

- Website links
- Emails
- Twitter responses
- Product reviews
- Pictures/images
- Written text on various platforms

What big data entails is structured and unstructured data that correspond to various activities. Structured data entails data that is categorized and stored in a file according to a particular format description, where unstructured data is free-form text that takes on a number of types, such as those listed above. The cell phones of yesteryear have evolved into smartphones capable of texting, surfing, phoning, and playing a host of software-based applications. All the activities conducted on these phones (every time you respond to a friend, respond to an ad, play a game, use an app, conduct a search) generates a traceable data asset. Computers and tablets connected to Internet-related platforms (social media, website activities, advertising via video platform) all generate data. Scanning technologies that read energy consumption, healthcare-related elements, traffic activity, etc., create data. And finally, good old traditional platforms such as spreadsheets, tables, and decision support platforms still play a role as well.

The next concept to consider when merely attempting to understand the big data age refers to velocities of data, where velocity entails how quickly data is being generated, communicated, and stored. Back in the beginning of the information economy (e.g., mid-1990s), the phrase "real time" was often used to refer to almost instantaneous tracking, updating, or some activities revolving around timely processing of data. This phrase has taken on a new dimension in today's ultra-fast, wireless world. Where real time was the goal of select industries (financial markets, e-commerce), the phrase has become commonplace in many areas of commerce today:

- Real-time communication with consumers via text, social media, email
- Real-time consumer reaction to events, advertisements via Twitter
- Real-time reading of energy consumption of residential households
- Real-time tracking of visitors on a website

Real time involves high-velocity or fast-moving data and fast generation of data that results in vast volumes of the asset. Non-real-time data
or sources of more slowly moving data activities also prevail today, where
the volumes of data generated refer to the storage and use of more historic
data resources that continue to provide value. Non-real time refers to measuring events and time-related processes and operations that are stored in
a repository:

- Consumer response to brand advertising
- Sales trends
- Generation of demographic profiles

As was mentioned above, velocity of data directly relates to volumes of
data, where some real-time data quickly generate a massive amount in a
very short time. When putting an amount on volume, the following statistic explains the recent state of affairs: as of 2012, about 2.5 exabytes of
data is created each day. A petabyte of data is 1 quadrillion bytes, which
is the equivalent of about 20 million file cabinets' worth of text, and an
exabyte is 1000 times that amount. The volume comes from both new data
variables and the amount of data records in those variables.

The ultimate result is more data that can provide the building blocks to
information generation through analytics. These data sources come in a
variety of types that are structured and unstructured that need to be managed to provide decision support for strategists of all walks (McAfee and
Brynjolfsson, 2012).

## BUILDING BLOCKS TO DECISION SUPPORT

You may ask: Why are there classifications of data? Isn't data simply data?
One of the reasons involves the activities required to manage and analyze
the resources that are involved in generating value from it. Yes, big data
sounds impressive and almost implies that value exists simply in storing it. The reality is, however, that unless data can help decision makers
make better decisions, enhance strategic initiatives, help marketers more
effectively communicate with consumers, enable healthcare providers to
better allocate resources to enhance the treatment and outcomes of their
patients, etc., there is little value to this resource, even if it is called big.

Data itself is a record of an event or a transaction:

A purchase of a product
A response to a marketing initiative
A text sent to another individual
A click on a link

In its crude form, data provides little value. However, if data is corrected for errors, aggregated, normalized, calculated, or categorized, its value grows dramatically. In other words, data are the building blocks to information, and information is a vital input to knowledge generation for decision makers (Davenport and Prusak, 2000). Taking this into consideration, the "big" part of big data can actually augment value significantly to those who use it correctly. Ultimately, when data is managed correctly, it provides a vital input for decision makers across industry sectors to make better decisions.

So why does big data imply a significant increase in the value of data? Because big data can provide more descriptive information as to why something has happened:

Why and who responded to my online marketing initiative?
What do people think of my product and potentially why?
What factors are affecting my performance metrics?
Why did my sales increase notably last month?
What led my patient treatment outcomes to improve?

## SOURCE OF MORE DESCRIPTIVE VARIABLES

Big data implies not just more records/elements of data, but more data variables and new data variables that possibly describe reasons why actions occur. When performing analytics and constructing models that utilize data to describe processes, an inherent limitation is that the analyst simply doesn't have all the pertinent data that accounts for all the explanatory variance of that process. The resulting analytic report may be missing some very important information. If you're attempting to better understand where to locate your new retail outlet in a mall and you don't have detailed shopper traffic patterns, you may be missing some essential descriptive information that affects your decision. As a result, you locate your store in what seems to be a strategically appropriate space, but for some reason, the traffic for your business just isn't there. You may want to know what the market thinks of your new product idea, but unfortunately you were only able to obtain 1000 responses to your survey of your target population. The result is you make decisions with the limited data resources you have. However, if you text your question to 50,000 of your target population, your results may be more accurate, or let's say, more of an indication of market sentiment.

As technology continues to evolve and become a natural part of everyone's lives, so too does the generation of new data sources. The last few years have seen the explosion of mobile computing: the smartphone may be the most headlining example, but the trend extends down to your laundry machine, sprinkler system, and the label on the clothing that you bought retail. One of the most unexpected and highest impact trends in this regard is the ability to leverage data variables that describe activities/processes. We all know that technology has provided faster, better computers—but now the trend is for technology to feed in the generation of never before seen data at a scale that is breathtaking. What follows are some brief examples of this.

The following illustrations depict the evolution of big data in various industry sectors and business scenarios. Just think of the new descriptive variables (data resources) that can be analyzed in these contemporary scenarios as opposed to the ancient times of the 1990s!

## INDUSTRY EXAMPLES OF BIG DATA

### Electioneering

In some recent political campaigns, politicians began to mobilize the electorate in greater proportion than ever before. Previously, campaign managers had relied unduly on door-to-door recruiting, flyering in coffee shops, rallies, and telemarketing calls. Now campaigns can be managed completely on the Internet, using social network data and implied geographic locations to expand connectivity between the like-minded. The focus is not just on generating more votes, but has extended to the ever-important fund-raising initiatives as well. Campaigners are able to leverage the power of big data and focus on micro-donations and the viral power of the Internet to spread the word—more dollars were raised through this vehicle than had been seen in history. The key function of the use of the big data allowed local supporters to organize other local supporters, using social networking software and self-identified zip code and neighborhood locations. That turned data resources *locational*, adding a new dimension of information to be exploited, polled, and aggregated to help determine where bases of support were stronger/weaker. Where will it go next? It is likely that in the not-so-distant future we will find voter registrations tagged to mobile devices, and the ability to circumvent statistical sampling polls with actual polls of the population, sorted by geography, demography, and psychographics. Democratic campaign managers estimate that they collected 13 million email addresses in the 2008 campaign, communicating directly with about 20% of the total votes needed to win. Eric Schmidt (former CEO of Google) says that since 2008, the game has completely changed: "In 2008 most people didn't operate on [Facebook and Twitter]. The difference now is, first and foremost, the growth of Facebook, which is much, much more deeply penetrated . . . you can run political campaigns on the sum of those tools [Facebook, YouTube and Twitter]" (quotes from *Bloomberg Business Week*, June 18–24, 2012; additional info from Tumulty, 2012).

## Investment Diligence and Social Media

"Wall Street analysts are increasingly incorporating data from social media and Internet search trends into their investment strategies" ("What the Experts Say," 2012). The use of social media data is generally called unstructured data. Five years ago, surveys showed that approximately 2% of investment firms used such data—today "that number is closer to 50 percent" (Cha, 2012). The World Economic Forum has now classified this type of data as an economic asset, and this includes monitoring millions of tweets per day, scanning comments on buyer sites such as Amazon, processing job offerings on TheLadders or Monster.com, etc. "Big data is fundamentally changing how we trade," said financial services consultant Adam Honore (adhonore, http://www.advancedtrading.com/Adam-Honore). Utilizing the number and trending features of Twitter, Facebook, and other media platforms, these investors can test how "sticky" certain products, services, or ideas are in the country. From this information, they can make investment choices on one product vs. another—or on the general investor sentiment. This information does not replace existing investment diligence, but in fact adds to the depth and quality (or lack thereof sometimes!) of analysis.

## Real Estate

Investment dollars in the capital markets are split between three main categories, as measured by value: bonds, stocks, and alternative assets, including real estate. Since bonds were traded, an informal network of brokers and market makers has been able to serve as gateways to information, given that many transactions go through centralized clearinghouses. In 1971, NASDAQ was the first stock market to go electronic, and as the information revolution continued, it soon allowed for any person around the world to sit at the hub of cutting-edge news, information, and share prices. After a particular tech-savvy Salomon Brothers trader left that company, he led the further digitization of data and constant updating of news to create a big data empire: Michael Bloomberg. Real estate, however, has been late to the game. To understand real estate prices in any given market has been more challenging, as many transactions are private, and different cities and counties can have significantly different reporting mechanisms and data structures. Through the late 1980s and 1990s, real estate was often tracked in boxes of files, mailed back and forth across the country. As cities began to go digital, a new opportunity was created. In the year 2000, Real Capital Analytics (http://www.rcanalytics.com) was founded by Robert White to utilize data mining techniques to aggregate data worldwide on real estate transactions, and make that data available digitally. Real estate research firms have many techniques to acquire data: programmatically scraping websites, taking feeds from property tax departments, polling brokerage firms, tracking news feeds, licensing and warehousing proprietary data, and more. All of these sources of data can be reviewed on an hourly basis, funneled through analysis, and then displayed in a user-friendly manner: charts, indices, and reports that are sorting hundreds of thousands of daily data points.

## Specialized Real Estate: Building Energy Disclosure and Smart Meters

Over 40% of energy use and carbon emissions in the United States come from existing buildings (http://www.eia.gov/consumption/commercial/index.cfm). To put this in perspective, if you combined the energy use and emissions output of all of the SUVs on the road in North America, this would be approximately 3%. So you can see that the use of energy by existing buildings is a very important piece of data. Until recently, this data has been held in many different databases for utilities across the country, with no central repository or easy means for reconciling these data sets. Today, three trends have picked up: (1) energy disclosure ordinances, (2) satellite heat map data, and (3) data warehousing aggregations based on smart meters. The amount of data needed here to control for effective information is staggering: any analysis must account for building size, use, geographic location, seasonality, climactic variation, occupancy, etc. In many of these cases, information is collected on a granularity of 1–15 minutes! That is for every building, in every city, in every state in the country: billions of data points *per day* (http://www.eebhub.org/).

## Commerce and Loyalty Data

When you walk into your favorite retail outlet—be it clothing, jewelry, books, or food—there is nothing quite as gratifying as being recognized, your tastes being understood, and receiving personal service ("The usual, please!"). In the distant past, this probably meant a neighborhood shop where you literally were known by the salesperson. In the 1990s this was transformed into a "loyalty program" craze in which large-scale (franchised, national, international) retailers were able to tag your shopping to a digital ID card that they enticed you to use by offering discounts. But Internet commerce, under the thought leadership of Amazon, transformed this experience entirely. Once you are online, not only can a retailer track your purchases, but it can track what products you look at, things you plan to buy (wish lists), items you buy for others (registry), and even what pages you spend time on and for how long. This provides retailers with a competitive advantage: they can tailor your shopping experience and suggest new products. Witness Netflix recommendations, Pandora's preference algorithms, and LinkedIn's suggestion of who you might next want to connect with or apply for a job from. Moreover, it is not just information from their own site that these online merchants can now pull from—the trend has now reclaimed the point-of-sale data from brick-and-mortar stores as well. Retailers integrate physical data with online point-of-sale data, and can also view what other sites you visit, where else you make purchases, who makes purchases for you, and what "like-minded shoppers" may be in your network.

## Crowd-Sourced Crime Fighting

In an effort to aid local policing efforts, policing has found a new ally: you! Over the last decade "hot spot" policing has become the effective leading strategy for reducing crime: take careful record of where crime occurs, measure density regions, and overwhelm the highest density regions with extremely quick and overpowering responses. However, this strategy still relies on actually being able to track all of the crime incidents—no small task, as the force's personnel have limited resources. Enter the crowd sourcing platforms. Some cities have created apps for mobile devices (or other interfaces) that allow individual citizens to upload information that indicates crimes they have witnessed (http://spotcrime.com/ga/augusta)! The upload contains the description of the crime, a geographic location, and a time stamp. As participation increases, so too do "eyes on the street," and the map is filled with the information needed to improve police performance.

## Pedestrian Traffic Patterns in Retail

Thanks to some recent controversies, you probably already know that your cell phone allows you to be tracked at nearly any time of day, provided it is powered on. While privacy laws currently still protect you from being identified with this feature (without your opting in), new technologies are available to identify unique movements. Cell tower "repeaters" in strategic locations in malls and downtowns can track "unique cell phones" and their walking patterns. As a result, a mall owner might want to know how many people take the elevator vs. the stairs—and of the ones who take the elevator, do they ever walk by the store on the other side of it? Further, if they find a patron lingering in the leather goods section of the store for more than 12 minutes, but that customer does not stop at the cash register, they will send a text message advertisement promotion to the customer's phone before he or she leaves the store, offering a discount on—you guessed it—leather goods. This is only the beginning of this technology. Expect to see it deployed in cities to track crime patterns, the safety of certain intersections, and more (http:// techcrunch.com/2007/12/14/path-intelligence-monitors-foot-traffic-in-retail-stores-by-pinging-peoples-phones/; http://allthingsd.com/20111103/ ex-googlers-raise-5-8-million-to-help-retailers-track-foot-traffic/).

### Intelligent Transport Application

New applications being developed for smartphones pool voluntarily offered information from unique sources into a real-time database providing an instant advantage from the use of big data. Uber, a mobile phone-based transportation application, connects drivers (of limousines, taxis) with potential passengers. As each driver "opts in" to uber from his or her phone, the phone sends a GPS signal update to the master Uber map. When a passenger is ready for a ride, the passenger turns on his or her Uber signal and effectively puts out an electronic thumb. Both passenger and driver receive an instant updated map with the potential matches to be found as moving dots across the map, with estimates of congestion (which influence pricing), as well as arrival information. In a similar fashion, Waze is a transport application for local drivers. When drivers get in their car, they turn on Waze, which utilizes the phone's GPS tracker, motion sensors, and built-in geographic road information (speed limits, lights, stop signs) to estimate the level of traffic you are experiencing while driving. Waze then merges your information with all other local drivers' information, creating a real-time picture of road traffic. The application also allows for the reporting of police presence, traffic, accidents, and not-to-miss sights! In essence, this application creates a virtual cloud of self-reported big data.

## DESCRIPTIVE POWER AND PREDICTIVE PATTERN MATCHING

As silos are broken down between traditional sources of data, aggregation of big data is allowing astounding predictive capabilities for the data scientist. One example comes from the MIT Media Lab, where a group used location data from mobile phones to estimate the number of shoppers at a particular department store on the biggest shopping day of the year: Black Friday. By combining this information with historical sales data, demographics of the trade region surrounding the department store, and other relevant factors (macroeconomic, weather, etc.), the team was able to predict retail sales on that day even before the department store itself could (McAfee and Brynjolfsson, 2012)! Another example of the same practice comes from Farecast.com (now owned by Microsoft and accessed through Bing). By aggregating pricing information from all airlines and comparing it to historical information as well as statistically correlated databases that signal pricing, Farecast is able to accurately predict whether the price of a specific airline ticket will go up or down in the near, mid, or short term. At one point it even offered insurance to guarantee the accuracy of its information (http:// www.upgradetravelbetter.com/2006/11/13/fare-guarantee-farecast-lets-you- insure-its-fare-predictions/)! Other examples of this approach include predicting housing price changes in the United States with publicly available web information (Wu and Brynjolfsson, 2009) and the Center for Disease Control (CDC) using tweets (twitter.com) to predict the spread of disease, such as cholera in Haiti. In development today is the Square Kilometre Array (SKA), a telescope that is being designed to crunch 300–1500 petabytes of data a year. Just how much data is that? "If you take the current global daily internet traffic and multiply it by two, you are in the range of the data set that the Square Kilometre Array radio telescope will be collecting every day," says IBM researcher Tom Engbersen. "This is big data analytics to the extreme" (Peckham, 2012).

Whatever way you may classify big data, whether it be new variable sources, larger volumes, closer to real-time activity, the mere availability of the resource doesn't necessarily imply greater value to organizations (http:// qz.com/81661/most-data-isnt-big-and-businesses-are-wasting-money- pretending-it-is/). A few key elements that have to be present in order for big data to have signification value is that the data must contain relevant information corresponding to a particular process or activity, and the data must have quality. As in the short examples mentioned above, one must realize that simply because new data sources are generated in a particular process, it doesn't imply that it provides descriptive information on the impacts to measuring that process's performance. As far as quality goes, new data variables or more volumes of data must be a reliable and consistent resource to making better decisions. The process of maintaining data quality, variable consistency, and the identification of variables that describe various activities is a daunting task and requires not only competent analysts, but also the inclusion of subject matter experts and data experts. This book will address the various activities that must be undertaken in order to fully leverage data to create true value for organizations. Remember, analytic techniques of all types are not self-generating methods for decision makers. Skilled professionals are essential to guide the process. Just consider some of the questions below regarding data that potentially describe processes:

- Do Twitter responses reflect accurate consumer sentiment toward events (was the tweet an overreaction or misinterpretation of the reported occurrence?)?
- Were survey questions interpreted correctly by responders?
- Do LinkedIn connections share the same business interests?
- Do Facebook friends share the same product interests?
- Do the demographics generated from credit card purchases truly reflect the profile of the consumer purchasing the product (did younger consumers borrow parents' credit cards?)?

## THE VALUE OF DATA

Simply crunching available data elements as they appear and drawing conclusions, whether it's big data or not, can yield suboptimal, even dangerous results to the decision-making process, and end up providing negative value to organizations rather than the assumed positive value. This last statement brings up a vital point to the realm of big data and value. When considering value, probably the most significant add to value that big data brings is the enhancement to the decision-making process to those who access it, manage it appropriately, and utilize it effectively. However, the concept of enhancing the decision-making process by leveraging data involves the widely encompassing realm of analytics and corresponding strategy. We use the phrase "widely encompassing" because the concept of analytics can include a vast variety of applications, depending on what you plan on doing with data. For simplicity's sake, this book will focus primarily on the incorporation of business intelligence and mining applications in leveraging data sources. In the next chapter we will describe a variety of analytic approaches and how they can be used to extract information from data to help decision makers better understand the marketplace with which they are dealing.

## CLOSING COMMENTS ON LEVERAGING DATA THROUGH ANALYTICS

Data resources can provide value to organizations from the information that can be extracted from them. This extraction process involves querying data resources for particular variables at particular levels of aggregation in a particular format, and then initiating some type of analytic process. However, before conducting any of these activities, one essential task that underpins the information creation initiative involves the creation of a conceptual model. In other words, whether you have terabytes of data or just a few thousand records, whether you are considering trends over the past few years or focusing on real-time data feeds, decision makers must determine what questions they are looking to answer with data and information. This process can be classified as a conceptual model. Consider using analytics to address the following scenario (e.g., what data variables and level of detail are needed to provide relevant information).

> As a hospital administrator, you are looking to analyze those factors that impact the patients' satisfaction metric that describes their experience while being treated at your hospital.

No matter what industry you operate in, the bottom line to the decision-making process is that individuals must rigorously deliberate over what they are looking to better understand. Once this has been established, the process of leveraging data resources can be undertaken. That process then entails extracting the relevant data variables at corresponding levels of detail and initiating an analytic framework. This concept will be addressed in greater detail in Chapter 5.

## ETHICAL CONSIDERATIONS IN THE BIG DATA ERA

Before we go any further in describing the process of leveraging data assets, it is important to stress the adherence to sound ethical practices regarding the various facets of data acquisition, storage, and utilization. Despite this book's focus on describing the various activities involved with extracting value from data, some important concepts should be kept in mind when dealing with data resources, with a particular emphasis on data that describes individuals.

This book does not promote or support heavy- or underhanded, controversial techniques in acquiring extensive personal data. Individuals should be made aware of how data is generated and gathered regarding their everyday activities, and privacy and security rules should be strictly adhered to. Ultimately, this book adheres to the notion that the management of data resources and analytics should be conducted to yield positive outcomes for processes and individuals who interact with them.

## REFERENCES

Cha, A.E. "Big Data" from Social Media, Elsewhere Online Redefines Trend-Watching. *Washington Post*, June 6, 2012.

Davenport, T., and Prusak, L. *Working Knowledge*. Harvard Business Review Press, Boston, Massachusetts, 2000.

Kudyba, S. *Information Technology, Corporate Productivity, and the New Economy*. Westport, Connecticut: Quorum Books. 2002.

McAfee, A., and Brynjolfsson, E. Big Data: The Management Revolution. *Harvard Business Review*, October 2012, pp. 60–62.

Peckham, M. IBM to Help Research and Develop 'Exascale' Supercomputing Telescope. *Time Magazine*, April 2, 2012. http://techland.time.com/2012/04/02/ibm-to-help-research-and-develop-exascale-supercomputing-telescope/.

Tumulty, K. Twitter Becomes a Key Real-Time Tool for Campaigns. *Washington Post*, April 26, 2012.

What the Experts Say: Twitter Guided Trading. *The Week*, June 14, 2012.

Wu, L., and Brynjolfsson, E. The Future of Prediction: How Google Searches Foreshadow Housing Prices and Quantities. In *ICIS 2009 Proceedings*, 2009, paper 147. http://aisel.aisnet.org/icis2009/147.

# 2

## Information Creation through Analytics

*Stephan Kudyba*

### CONTENTS

The primary initiative in leveraging the value of data resources lies in the realm of analytics. This term, however, encompasses a wide variety of methodologies that can provide descriptive, comparative, and predictive information for the end user. This chapter will provide a brief background and description of some noteworthy analytic approaches as applied to more historical, structured data and include references to big data issues

*17*

along the way. The area of big data and analytics will be addressed in greater detail in the real time and continuous analysis section at the end of this chapter and in Chapter 3.

Analytic methods can range from simple reports, tables, and graphics to more statistically based endeavors to quantitative-based methods. We provided some analytic approaches according to some commonly referred to categories below. Regardless of the techniques deployed, the end result of an analytic endeavor is to extract/generate information to provide a resource to enhance the decision-making process.

1. Spreadsheet applications (also facilitated by vendor software packages)
   a. Data/variable calculations, sorting, formatting, organizing
   b. Distribution analysis and statistics (max, min, average, median, percentages, etc.)
   c. Correlation calculation between variables
   d. Linear and goal programming (optimization)
   e. Pivot tables (an intro to online analytic processing (OLAP) and business intelligence)
2. Business intelligence
   a. Query and report creating
   b. Online analytic processing
   c. Dashboards
3. Multivariate analysis (also part of business intelligence)
   a. Regression (hypothesis approach)
   b. Data mining applications (data-driven information creation)
      - Neural networks
      - Clustering
      - Segmentation classification
      - Real-time mining
4. Analysis of unstructured data
   a. Text mining
5. Six Sigma
6. Visualization

The type of analytic approach is generally dictated by the objective of what the user of the analysis requires, and where the objective and overall initiative needs to be clearly defined to achieve the most effective and informative results. This problem definition process generally involves the selection of a performance metric and identification of variables that impact that metric. Once the scope of the analytic endeavor (problem definition) has been established, then corresponding data resources must be managed (variables selected at a particular level of detail) and analysis can begin. The steps to conducting a problem definition for analytics will be addressed in detail in Chapter 5. The remainder of this chapter will provide an overview of some of the analytic methods mentioned above.

# INTRODUCTION TO THE CONCEPT OF ANALYTICS

One of the initial stages of any analytic endeavor is the incorporation of an investigative study of a data resource. In other words, before a report is generated or quantitative modeling is conducted, an analyst needs to better understand what's in a data file. This investigative process involves conducting a distribution analysis of various data variables, perhaps calculating maximum, minimum, and variance metrics such as standard deviations. This provides a descriptive character of what the data variables are comprised of and renders additional analysis more robust, as it identifies the presence of such issues as data bias or skew, outliers, and even errors in data resources.

# BUSINESS INTELLIGENCE

## Reports

The focus of this book involves the utilization of business intelligence applications (e.g., OLAP, dashboards, mining) to extract actionable information from all types of data to enhance the decision-making process. One of the most basic levels of this approach is the creation of business reports that incorporate sequel-related queries of data resources to extract variables that describe a business scenario. The introduction of big data involves additional requirements to this process; namely, when devising the parameters of the report to be created, the decision maker now must consider new variables that impact that conceptual report. The volume of data that must be processed must also be considered, and finally, the currency of the report (e.g., how often a report must be updated to provide adequate information for the decision maker). However, as simple as the process of generating a report may be, creating one that provides essential information to those that receive it may be a quite complex task.

Consider a request by an Internet marketing department to produce an analytic report that depicts the performance of various Internet marketing tactics that drive traffic to a company's landing page. Although this initiative appears to be straightforward and simplistic in nature, one must consider all the variables that comprise the area to be analyzed, along with the needs of the user of the report.

Some dimensions and variables that could be included in this analysis would involve:

| Time | Performance Metric | Marketing Source | Source Traffic Location |
|------|-------------------|------------------|------------------------|
| Hour | Clicks | Paid, Generic search | Town |
| Day | Bounce | Mobile device | County |
| Month | Conversions | Banners | State |
| | Cost | Referral site | |

Platforms such as Google Analytics provide robust functionality to accomplish extensive report generation in the e-commerce spectrum. When conducting customized analytics (tailored analytics to a specific company's activities) data experts and analysts must apply due diligence to acquire that information that provides a strategic advantage in the marketplace. This involves the storage, processing, management, and ultimate analysis of data resources that describe a particular process.

Well-designed reports that incorporate all the pertinent and available variables that describe a business activity can be an important source of information to decision makers (see Figure 2.1). However, the limitation of information creation at the report level is that the user often scans a report, assimilates the information, and quickly thinks of alternative business scenarios that are essential to providing more robust information regarding a process or activity. The report is limited to its current level of data aggregation and variables depicted. The next step to analysis or business intelligence involves the application of OLAP, which gives users the flexibility to view and analyze multiple scenarios of a business process. Before we describe the application of OLAP functionality that leverages large data resources and addresses currency of data, consider the more simplistic spreadsheet application of Pivot Tables.

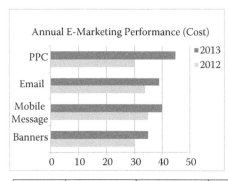
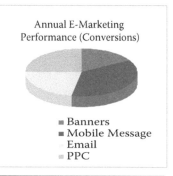

| Tactic | 2012 (cost) | 2013 (cost) | Change | Tactic | 2013 Conv |
|--------|-------------|-------------|--------|--------|-----------|
| PPC | 30,000 | 44,000 | 46% | PPC | 22% |
| Email | 34,000 | 39,000 | 15% | Email | 20% |
| Mobile | 35,000 | 40,000 | 14% | Mobile | 42% |
| Banner | 30,000 | 34,000 | 13% | Banner | 16% |

**FIGURE 2.1**
Annual report of e-marketing cost and conversions.

## Pivot Tables

A simplistic version of OLAP that many users can quickly relate to includes the use of pivot tables in a spreadsheet environment. Pivot tables leverage data in a flat, spreadsheet file to present alternative scenarios that describe a business activity. Through basic spreadsheet functionality, users can quickly generate a table view of relevant variables at a particular level of aggregation. For example, a spreadsheet of data that describes a software company's sales activities can include numerous rows according to corresponding variables. Hypothetical data recording national sales activities of branches across the country is illustrated in Table 2.1.

With a simple pivot function, Table 2.2 could be calculated with ease.

## Dynamic Reporting through OLAP

Pivot tables are similar to OLAP in that they provide a multidimensional view of an activity. Enterprise OLAP provides greater scale to the analytic process, as it provides the platform to address multiple levels of aggregation of data resources, can depict updated views as source data is updated, and can process extremely large volumes of data. With this flexibility OLAP can help decision makers investigate information addressing multiple descriptive scenarios regarding an operation's activity, therefore

**TABLE 2.1**

Hypothetical Data Recording National Sales Activities

| Salesperson | Product Category | City/Area | Customer Industry | Units | Sales |
|---|---|---|---|---|---|
| KDE | ETL | NY | Finance | 90 | $45,000 |
| SEF | Reporting | NY | Insurance | 80 | $24,000 |
| CHT | Analytics | Boston | Finance | 10 | $20,000 |
| HHT | Database | Phili | Retail | 55 | $41,250 |
| GGN | Database | Atlanta | Manufact | 65 | $48,750 |
| THT | ETL | DC | Retail | 18 | $9,000 |
| TTW | ETL | Phili | Retail | 42 | $21,000 |
| AHY | Analytics | Chicago | Retail | 30 | $60,000 |
| FDO | Reporting | San Fran | Manufact | 39 | $11,700 |
| JJT | Reporting | Chicago | Finance | 42 | $12,600 |
| GHI | ETL | NY | Transport | 32 | $16,000 |
| BDE | Analytics | DC | Transport | 71 | $142,000 |
| PEC | Reporting | NY | Finance | 26 | $57,045 |
| LYJ | Database | Chicago | Insurance | 52 | $39,000 |
| KIP | Analytics | San Fran | Insurance | 75 | $150,000 |
| OBN | Database | NY | Retail | 53 | $39,750 |
| ERB | Database | San Fran | Manufact | 93 | $69,750 |
| SEN | Reporting | LA | Retail | 17 | $5,100 |
| JJR | ETL | NY | Retail | 96 | $48,000 |
| WNS | ETL | Phili | Manufact | 32 | $16,000 |
| DHK | Reporting | Boston | Finance | 26 | $7,800 |
| TRN | Reporting | Boston | Transport | 30 | $9,000 |
| RGH | Database | Phili | Retail | 54 | $40,500 |
| MMR | Database | Atlanta | Retail | 46 | $34,500 |
| SJP | ETL | Atlanta | GPU | 80 | $40,000 |

enhancing the knowledge generation process and overall ability to generate effective strategic conclusions. The diversity of information views involves various dimensions of time, performance metrics, and descriptive variables.

**General Cube Inputs**

| Time | Descriptive Variables | Performance Metrics |
|---|---|---|
| Daily | Demographics | Sales |
| Weekly | Behavioral | Response rate |
| Monthly | Strategic | Operational |
| Quarterly | Process related | Units |

**TABLE 2.2**

Sales by Product Category by City

**ETL (Extract Transfer and Load)**

| | |
|---|---|
| New York | $61,000 |
| DC | $9,000 |
| Philadelphia | $37,000 |
| Atlanta | $40,000 |
| Total | $195,000 |

**Reporting**

| | |
|---|---|
| New York | $81,045 |
| San Francisco | $11,700 |
| Chicago | $12,600 |
| Boston | $16,800 |
| Los Angeles | $5,100 |
| Total | $127,245 |

These inputs must be organized to provide information (variables at levels of detail) that describes a business scenario in order to facilitate decision support for the end user. Consider the graphical view of a cube in Figure 2.2.

Figure 2.2 depicts an illustration of an OLAP cube that facilitates analytics of banner Internet marketing tactics. The cube presents a multidimensional view of the variables that describe the activities involved in banner advertising. The platform gives the analyst the ability to query data variables from different levels of detail and in different combinations, through both numeric data and visualization. The tabs at the top of the graphic depict the variables that are available to be analyzed. The scenario depicted illustrates the bounce rate (number of bounces) according to different types of referral sites where the various banner styles (static, animated, flash, and interactive) are displayed.

Users have the ability to change variable views from different perspectives, including:

Time (hourly, daily, quarterly)
Landing page (social media, home, custom landing design)
Banner type (static, animated, etc.)
Referral site (main hub, MSN, Yahoo; subhub, complementary site)
Position (banner position, top, middle, bottom)

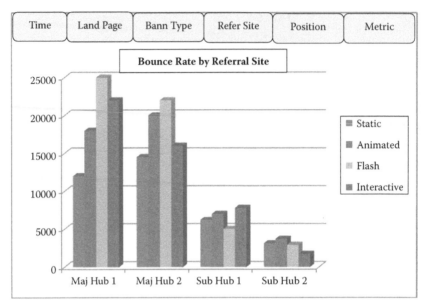

| Time | Land Page | Bann Type | Refer Site | Position | Metric |

| | Maj Hub 1 | Maj Hub 2 | Sub Hub 1 | Sub Hub 2 | Total |
|---|---|---|---|---|---|
| **Static** | 12000 | 14500 | 6200 | 3100 | 35800 |
| **Animated** | 18000 | 20000 | 7000 | 3700 | 48700 |
| **Flash** | 25000 | 22000 | 5000 | 2900 | 54900 |
| **Interactive** | 22000 | 16000 | 7800 | 1700 | 47500 |
| **Total** | 77000 | 72500 | 2000 | 11400 | 186900 |

**FIGURE 2.2**
**(See color insert.)** Banner performance multidimensional cube.

These perspectives can be analyzed according to predefined metrics, including bounce, views, click-throughs, and conversions. By navigating the different dimensions of the cube, the analyst can quickly identify strengths and weaknesses in different banner advertising initiatives. OLAP enhances the decision makers' ability to more fully understand the attributes that comprise the activities of banner advertising.

So what about big data, you say? Remember, big data entails not only volume of data but also the new variables (sources of data). Both these factors are considered when conducting analytics. In other words, a conceptual model must be generated that best describes the attributes of a desired process (entity to be better understood), and then data corresponding to those variables must be applied to that analytic framework. Big data adds complexity to the generation of the conceptual model as it introduces new descriptive variables that may not have been available or incorporated in the traditional structure of the particular process. The value of big data follows the basic concepts just mentioned; however, it can provide even greater value to the user by providing more robust models that provide greater descriptions and understanding of what affects process performance. In the banner ad scenario above, perhaps the new variable that must be added to provide more insightful information to decision makers regarding the effectiveness of their e-commerce advertising is the source of where traffic is coming from regarding the technological platform. In other words, is traffic coming from mobile devices, laptops, or tablets? When considering big volumes and velocities of data in an OLAP environment, methods such as parallel processing and map reduction of data resources must be considered. This topic will be addressed in greater detail in Chapter 3.

OLAP provides a robust source of business intelligence to decision makers, as it can leverage data resources including big data volumes and provides a platform that offers a flexible, accurate, and user-friendly mechanism to quickly understand what has happened and what is happening to a business process. The multidimensional framework will give users the power to view multiple scenarios of a given process, such as the following:

- What is the bounce rate if I utilize a specific type of landing page?
- Where are my highest conversion rates coming from?
- Is there seasonality according to day of the week or month of the year for my traffic?

The key to a valuable OLAP cube involves the combination of a few factors. One of these relates to the concept mentioned earlier, namely, that a cube must effectively describe a business scenario. The conceptual model that is used to build the cube must include noteworthy variables (relevant) with an appropriate detailed format that give users true business intelligence. The next major factor is filling the cube with accurate, current, and consistent data. Deficiencies in either of these areas can quickly render the analytic method useless for decision making.

## Analytics at a Glance through Dashboards

In today's ultra-fast, ultra-competitive information-based economy, it seems that the more senior a manager you may be, the less time that is available for investigation and drilling around multidimensional cubes.

Often the level of analytics is filtered down to a few insightful reports, ongoing insights absorbed in the marketplace, and the access to real-time dashboards that display key performance indicators relevant to a particular process. These dashboards are designed to provide decision makers with a feedback mechanism as to how an organization is performing. The key elements of dashboards are the delineation of relevant key performance indicators (KPIs) to a particular process, timeliness of their readings (currency of information), and finally, a user-friendly visual that provides the decision maker with a clear way of determining whether a process is operating successfully or not. The more traditional visual platform resembles that of an odometer in an automobile, where color schemes of performance reflect that of traffic lights (e.g., green, all is well; yellow, caution; and red, something is wrong and needs to be investigated). However, dashboard technology is quickly evolving where styles can include combinations of a variety of visuals (bar, line, pie charts) according to designated scales and are being utilized by decision makers at all levels in an organization.

The key to the effectiveness of a dashboard design involves its connection to the process at hand and use for decision making. Displays must be simple to understand and interpret. Just as a simple graphic display must adhere to design conventions (e.g., coherent color scheme, axis labeling, scale), so too must dashboard design, which adds complexity to the process as it combines various visual elements. The true key to a successful dashboard is evident by its effectiveness in providing timely, easy-to-understand decision support of a corresponding process. Dashboards that are too busy (include too many visuals), that are difficult to interpret, can quickly become omitted from an analyst's arsenal of decision support information.

Consider the dashboard example in Figure 2.3. The various graphic displays are clearly delineated from one another (separate sections) and are clearly labeled. Also, the design includes different visual displays, so the information presentation does not appear to overlap or include a blended view. Finally, complementary but distinctly different key performance indicators give the decision maker a well-rounded view of a human capital management application in this case.

## Robust BI and Drill-Down behind Dashboard Views

Dashboards provide an instantaneous mechanism to analyze the performance status of a process. Organizations with extensive analytic

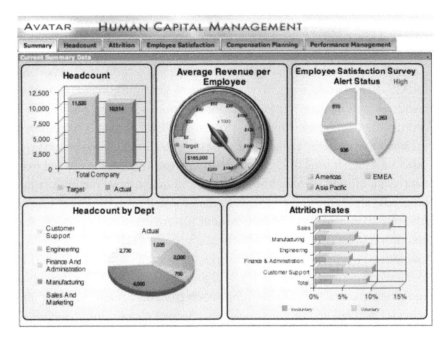

**FIGURE 2.3**
(**See color insert.**) Clearly designed employee analytic dashboard. (From http://www. dashboards-for-business.com/dashboards-templates/business-intelligence/business-intelligence-executive-dashboard; Domo, Inc., http://www.domo.com.)

capabilities through business intelligence applications can have OLAP cubes that can be quickly drilled into from a dashboard KPI that provides descriptive analytics of underlying variables that underpin the KPI. A prime example of an e-commerce-based KPI is the bounce rate on a landing page for an organization, especially when a new marketing initiative has been launched. Perhaps an organization has initiated an Internet marketing campaign with banners listed on various complementary referral sites. A red signal indicating a higher than acceptable bounce rate would provide decision makers with a timely analytic alert mechanism to investigate the source of the problem. A real-time cube or report could quickly depict which referral site may be the greatest source of misdirected traffic.

Not all dashboard displays need to be real time, where a simple refresh of data on an interim basis provides decision makers with an accurate indication of whether a process's performance is adequate. However, the big data era involving high velocity of streaming data resources often requires a real-time dashboard visual of a given process to provide users with a quick view of variable impacts on KPIs.

## DATA MINING AND THE VALUE OF DATA

As we've illustrated in the business intelligence section (e.g., reporting, OLAP, dashboards), a primary approach to generating value from data resources is to manage it into useful information assets (e.g., building conceptual models and viewing data according to level of details according to variables that describe a process). The next step in the valuation process is to generate a higher level of knowledge through the information created from data. Data mining involves the application of quantitative methods (equations and algorithms), along with forms of statistical testing that process data resources, which can identify reliable patterns, trends, and associations among variables that describe a particular process. Techniques such as segmentation classification, neural networks, logistic regression, and clustering, to name a few, incorporate the use of algorithms and code or mathematical equations to extract actionable information from data resources. Chapter 4 provides detailed descriptions and applications of major mining methods.

### Why Things Are Happening

Data mining can provide decision makers with two major sources of valuable information. The first refers to descriptive information, or the identification of why things may be occurring in a business process. This is done through the identification of recurring patterns between variables. Cross-sectional graphic displays can add significant information to decision makers to illustrate patterns between variables. Figure 2.4 provides a simple graphical view that illustrates an ad spend vs. dollar revenue elasticity curve as identified in the mining process. The figure depicts that a recurring pattern exists between the two variables, and that a direct relationship is prominent, where an increase in ad spend yields an increase in product revenue. Many non-mining-centric analysts would quickly raise the point that this information is not noteworthy, given the natural relationship between the two variables (e.g., the more spent on advertising, the more sales that are generated); however, this criticism is quickly dispelled when posing the question: If ad spend is increased by 5% from $200,000, what is the expected increase in revenue? That question is difficult to answer without the use of mining.

Mining methods can yield insightful patterns as to demographic and behavioral attributes of consumer response to marketing initiatives, the

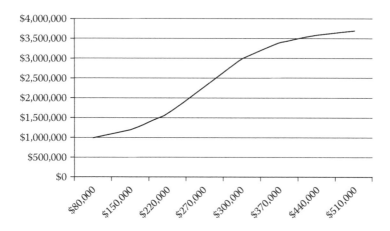

**FIGURE 2.4**
Advertising spend vs. revenue curve.

impacts of process components on performance metrics, and many more. Below are a few prominent applications where mining is often utilized:

- Consumer propensities
- Marketing and advertising effectiveness
- E-commerce initiatives
- Fraud detection
- Worker and team performance
- Pricing policies
- Process-related applications (throughput, workflow, traffic analysis)
- Healthcare-related areas (outcomes measurement, treatment effectiveness)
- Risk assessment

## What Is Likely to Happen

The other main source of information where mining provides value to decision makers is in the deployment of mining results. The patterns that have been identified are often embedded in an equation or algorithmic function, often referred to as the model, which can be used to perform a "what if" analysis or estimate future expected results based on inputs. In other words, if I market my product to a particular market segment defined by demographics, what is my expected response rate? Or, is a particular activity (e.g., credit card use) likely to be fraudulent? If the analysis is based on a time series approach, mining models can provide forecasts for product sales. The analyst in this case needs to make assumptions as to future input values.

## Real-Time Mining and Big Data

The evolution of the big data era has increased the utilization of the concept of real-time or streaming mining approaches. More traditional streaming mining involves the creation of models through analyzing a data sample or historical data of a given process. The resulting model then becomes a function that can be used to process streaming or real-time incoming data, and corresponding actionable outputs are generated in real time as well. Streaming mining addresses the big data concept of velocity and volume of data and is incorporated in processes where timely results are needed to improve strategies. Streaming mining applications are commonly applied in

- Website traffic analysis for real-time online marketing
- Fraud detection for online transactions
- Financial market risk and trading

The real time and continuous analytic section described later in this chapter along with Chapters 8 and 9 provide more detailed descriptions and applications in this area.

Some big data sources (e.g., sensor and satellite producing entities) with extreme velocity and volume sometimes render the ability to extract a sample that represents the entire data source as difficult, to say the least. In these instances, the ability to create optimized quantitative models to process this streaming data is limited. Techniques such as multisampling (Rajaraman and Ullman, 2011) and the implementation of self-optimizing quantitative techniques that learn as data is encountered have evolved to address this issue.

## Analysis of Unstructured Data and Combining Structured and Unstructured Sources

Up to this point, this chapter has dealt with analytics of structured data. The big data era, however, largely involves the incorporation of unstructured data resources that need to be analyzed in order to identify actionable information that enhances strategic initiatives. Text mining addresses the analytics of textual data (words, phrases, messages, emails, etc.). At a high level of description, text analytics seeks to create structure from unstructured sources. It does this by processing various unstructured forms and classifies them into particular categories. Processing is generally based in mathematics or linguistics.

In the realm of the vastly growing utilization of electronic communication, which includes texting, tweeting, leaving content on social media, emailing, etc., one can quickly see the possible value that exists in deploying analytic techniques to extract information that describes responses to marketing initiatives and product and service offerings, reactions to news and events, and general consumer behavior and sentiment.

An example involving the analysis of both structured and unstructured data for informative decision support is evident when examining patients' electronic health records (EHR) to better understand treatment outcomes and patient diagnosis.

More structured physiological data (e.g., blood sugar levels) can be combined with unstructured data (e.g., physician comments on treatment) to better understand a patient's status. Analytic techniques such as semantic mining can be applied in this situation to extract actionable information. The concept of mining unstructured data will be addressed in great detail in Chapters 4, 10, and 11.

## SIX SIGMA ANALYTICS

Still many other analytic approaches exist outside the realm of BI applications. More intensive user-generated analytics include Six Sigma-based initiatives. The core of Six Sigma is a philosophy and focus for reducing variability in process operations. It involves process definition and the incorporation of an array of statistical analytic methods to measure the performance of various attributes (Pande and Neuman, 2000). Classic Six Sigma is underpinned by the DMAIC methodology, which is an acronym for the following:

Define: Process attributes and project objectives.
Measure: Identify relevant data variables and measure performance of the process.
Analyze: Identification of sources of unacceptable variances.
Improve: Initiate strategic tactics to address causes of variance.

Control: Establish metrics to measure performance for ongoing feedback and take appropriate actions to address shortcomings of process.

The initial three steps to the methodology clearly depict classic analytics as they involve the definition of the problem objective and corresponding use of statistics and techniques to analyze the performance of the process. In the big data era, new sources of descriptive variables and volumes can enhance the application of Six Sigma across processes and industries. Consider the recent evolution of the healthcare industry that has involved an aggressive adoption of information technologies to underpin the vast processes that exist in a healthcare provider's operations in treating patients.

Activity time stamps are commonplace for many processes in healthcare organizations that simply record when an activity of a subprocess begins and ends. This data is available at the patient level of detail. This seemingly trivial data element yields great significance in its facilitation of conducting analytics. Consider the activity of a patient checking in to an emergency room.

The entire process of checking in to an ER to being diagnosed is comprised of various subcomponents (Table 2.3). Variability or breakdowns in throughput in any of these subcomponents can adversely increase waiting times for patients, which can result in poor customer satisfaction ratings and the subpar outcome of the patient's well-being. A DMAIC scenario is provided to illustrate the analytic initiative.

In the ER scenario provided, the process has been defined (e.g., tracking the time to patient disposition from checking in to an ER), and the [D]/define step for DMAIC has been addressed. The next step is to create data variables that describe the various subcomponents of the process and measure corresponding performance rates.

- Patient checks in to ER
- Patient is moved to triage, where nurse is assigned and patient is moved to bed
- Nurse collects patient information (medical history)
- Medical service exam (MSE) is performed by a physician and tests are ordered
- Test results are received and patient disposition (admitted to hospital or sent home) is conducted

Time stamps of corresponding subcomponents to the process are generated and stored, where duration of each of the subcomponents must be

**TABLE 2.3**

Subcomponents of ER Throughput

| Activity | Time | Duration | % Change | Alert |
|---|---|---|---|---|
| Check in at ER | 2:00 a.m. | | | |
| Move to Triage | 2:20 a.m. | 20 min. | 5% | |
| Information Collection | 2:28 a.m. | 8 min. | 10% | |
| MSE by Physician | 2:42 a.m. | 14 min. | 12% | |
| Disposition of Patient | 3:15 a.m. | 33 min. | 85% | XXX |

measured. In this case, the healthcare service provider has a historic perspective of measuring the process and has calculated the previous quarter's average duration for all the subcomponents. The next step is to analyze current performance (average for current month) to identify any significant changes to the baseline. Table 2.3 depicts a significant change (variance) in the duration of finishing the MSE to receiving lab results for patient disposition. Statistical techniques considering variance measurement are incorporated at the analytic stage to determine the level of significance, and therefore a need to implement the improve (I) stage. Here the analyst drills down into details of the process of ordering, conducting tests, and receiving results and communicating them back to the ER. At this stage, another, more detailed DMAIC study can be conducted to determine the factors that cause a high time duration from ordering to receiving test results to occur. Once this is accomplished, the decision maker can then formulate a strategic plan to address bottlenecks affecting the process (e.g., add radiology staff, adjust technology platform that communicates information in the test ordering process, implement an activity scheduling system). Once strategic initiatives have been implemented, the final step, control (C), follows to monitor effectiveness of the strategic endeavor and overall performance of the process (Kudyba and Radar, 2010).

The combination of available data (e.g., simple but voluminous sources of activity time stamps) in conjunction with a project and process definition and analytics enhances efficiency and organizational outcomes.

## AN OFTEN OVERLOOKED SECTOR OF ANALYTICS (POWER OF THE SIMPLE GRAPHIC)

Although many think of analytics as crunching numbers through an array of techniques and interpreting metrics to support decision making, analytics are greatly enhanced by the incorporation of an often taken for granted application of visual displays. Just think of having to analyze tables and columns of pure numbers when reviewing analytic reports. The process can quickly become mundane and even painful. In the host of analytic applications we described above and for numerous additional analytic methods, there is a common denominator to a successful endeavor, and that is the use of graphics to disseminate information. A simple view of a well-designed graphic can provide the decision maker with a clear presentation of extensive analytic results in a comprehendible manner.

In order to successfully leverage graphics, a few key points need to be considered. Before you become intrigued with robust colors and images that quickly draw you to generate dramatic conclusions about a particular process, take a step back and increase your understanding of what the information is actually portraying. In other words:

1. Analyze the titles and legends.
2. Take notice of the scale of the axis.
3. Understand the graphic/chart method used.

When you fully understand the variables that are depicted in the graphic, what the type of graphic focuses on, and the scale of the axis, only then can the analyst begin to generate effective interpretations. In the following section, a variety of graphical styles are listed with some simple descriptions of when they should be used. Keep in mind that when considering graphics in a big data era, the most significant elements are real-time graphics that provide analysts with a streaming view of processes. The real-time streaming visualization of data actually becomes a dashboard that analysts can monitor to observe variances in KPIs in relation to some event.

## Graphic Types

Figure 2.5 illustrates the classic pie chart that depicts how a whole unit is divided among some subcomponents (pieces of an established pie). Market share is a prime example for pie charts, where share can be delineated by product lines, regions, industry competitors, etc. Pie charts have limitations when considering negative values.

Despite the seemingly simplistic bar chart depicted in Figure 2.6, the visual actually incorporates a number of important elements in the realm of analytics. The graphic depicts a comparative view of a multicomponent

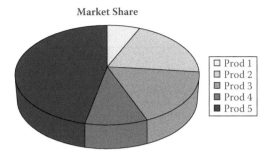

**FIGURE 2.5**
Pie chart depicting market share.

process (call centers in this case) in a time series setting (quarterly views). With a quick glance, the analyst can make inferences regarding relative performance (customer satisfaction) of three different call centers over time. Bar charts are more appropriate in depicting quantities or amounts of select variables.

Bar charts are also often used to illustrate variable distributions (percentages of ranges or categories of a given variable). Figure 2.7 depicts a categorical age variable and the amount of data that exists in selected ranges. This gives analysts a better understanding of the dimensions of a given data variable, and in this case enables them to determine if there is any age skew or bias (high percentage of one age range relative to the population).

**FIGURE 2.6**
Bar chart (comparative view of multi-component process).

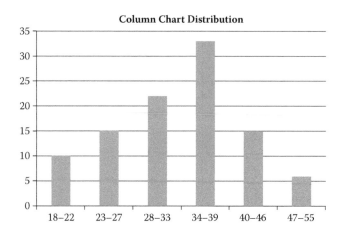

**FIGURE 2.7**
Age distribution chart.

In conducting market research, a variable distribution view enables the researcher to determine if a target market is included in a data resource.

Variable distribution analysis can often include visuals via line graphs that are useful in illustrating scenarios involving continuous variables. Figure 2.8 illustrates the continuous data variable of mall foot traffic for a given day according to retailers.

Time series line charts provide users with a visual of potential seasonality in processes. Figure 2.9 depicts the classic holiday effect in retail as is seen in the repetitive bump in sales in Q4.

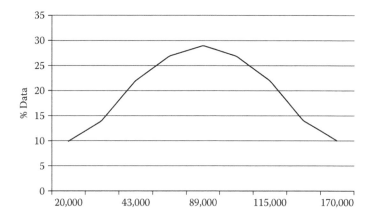

**FIGURE 2.8**
Line chart of continuous variable distribution of mall traffic.

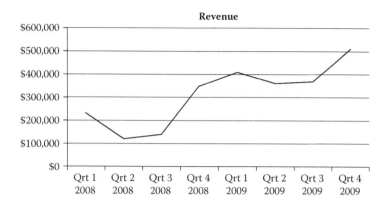

**FIGURE 2.9**
Time series line charts for seasonality.

Another type of chart involves the scatter plot that is commonly used to illustrate correlations between variables, where simple plots of individual data points are depicted. Figure 2.10 depicts data points depicting correlations between employee performance and training received.

A rather insightful chart style is the bubble chart. The bubble graphic enables analysts to depict three-dimensional scenarios in a coherent fashion by incorporating bubble size to illustrate variable attributes. Figure 2.11 depicts the multi-dimensional scenario of organizational team performance according to workload and team size.

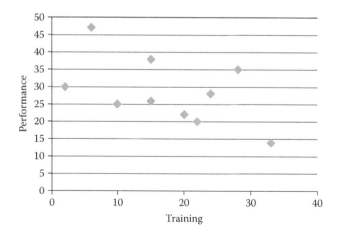

**FIGURE 2.10**
Scatterplot for correlations.

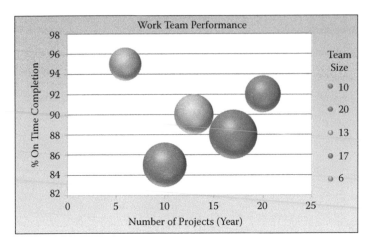

**FIGURE 2.11**
(**See color insert.**) Bubble chart depicting workforce team performance.

Yet another graphic style that has increased in importance over the evolution of the big data era is the use of maps. Map visuals are generally utilized when an analysis involving location is emphasized; however, location can also refer to a process location. Applications such as traffic analysis or population analytics are common examples. Traffic can refer to website activities, vehicular, consumer, or some type of designated activity. See Chapter 7 for more on heat maps for the web.

In a simple web traffic visual, a map can illustrate cross sections of time and area of a web page that are receiving high user traffic. This can provide strategists with actionable information to more effectively apply online marketing tactics (e.g., display banners in hot spots on a particular page at a particular time).

Civil engineering can leverage heat maps by incorporating GPS data to investigate hot areas of traffic incidents (congestion, accidents) and optimize new designs to alleviate existing trouble areas and in designing new roadways.

Figure 2.12 provides a standard heat map where "hot colors" depict more intense activity. In this case, the hotter areas depict areas where job vacancies are difficult to fill.

Map visuals are particularly applicable in the big data era, when real-time, high-velocity analytics and voluminous sources are involved. Applications that leverage big data include geovisualization that involves the analysis of geographic specific flows of data and bioinformatics and sensor output in the healthcare spectrum. For example, the healthcare industry is increasingly

Harder-to-fill jobs ■ ■ ▨ ▨ ▨ Easier-to-fill jobs ☐ Unavailable

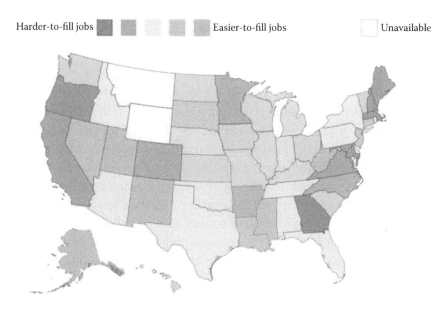

**FIGURE 2.12**
**(See color insert.)** Heat map that illustrates areas of hard-to-fill job vacancies. (From Wanted Analytics, http://www.wantedanalytics.com.)

utilizing streaming sensor data generated by various treatment and diagnostic technologies. For diagnosis (MRI), these data describe the characteristics of a patient. Visual displays of this source are essential to extract information on trouble areas for patients. Chapter 12 provides more detailed information corresponding to this concept. As big data sources emerge, the application of heat maps should become a common visual technique for providing analysts with a mechanism to enhance strategic initiatives.

This concludes our section on visual analytics. The following section provides a more technical description of data management and analytic concepts in a high volume, big data environment. Event stream processing (ESP) can be utilized for analyzing streaming big data in motion, where this technique is often utilized as a front end for historical analytics as well.

## REAL-TIME AND CONTINUOUS ANALYTICS*

Complex event processing (CEP) refers to systems that process or analyze events closer to the creation of those events, prior to storage. Some

---

* This section contributed by Jerry Baulier of SAS, Inc.

definitions refer to CEP events from the "event cloud" because it's not always defined where events will be published into CEP for processing and whether they will be ordered or not. This is very different than traditional analytics, or historical analytics, where data is first stored persistently (usually in a database) before it is analyzed or processed. Complex event processing systems reduce latency times of analyzing data, usually referred to as events, by analyzing or processing the data before it is stored. In fact, sometimes this form of analytics is done as a front end to historical analytics in order to aggregate (or reduce) raw data before storing it persistently for further analytics. This combination of complex event processing and front-ending historical analytics (as depicted in Figure 2.13) can be a very powerful, multistage approach to analyzing data for actionable intelligence and consequently acting on intelligence sooner than otherwise possible, which can sometimes create new business opportunities than otherwise possible.

The term *complex* in complex event processing sometimes creates confusion relative to what it refers to. Complex event processing systems analyze events that are published into them and create derived (or synthetic) events that represent some transformation of the events that were published into them. These derived events usually represent an aggregated view over time of many input events, and hence are referred to as complex events. While the name *complex event processing* is relatively new, the science of systems analyzing events in motion (before they are stored) has been around for some time. This science of analyzing events in motion consisted largely of two types of processing models. The first type was more rule based, both

Hybrid (Multi-Staged) Analytics:
Streaming Analytics Front-Ending Historical/Predictive Analytics

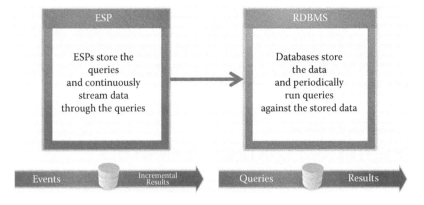

**FIGURE 2.13**
Event processing and front-ending historical analysis for faster decision making.

inference and event, condition, action (ECA). The second type of systems were based more on the concept of continuous queries, were mostly relational in nature, and they analyzed (or processed) events that were published into them as event streams. These systems tended to focus on processing high volumes of events in very low latencies, therefore creating new opportunities around leveraging actionable intelligence in very small time frames from the event occurrences. Systems that utilize continuous queries to analyze events in motion are referred to as event stream processing (ESP), even though many of these systems have product names that include complex event processing. So event stream processing can be viewed as a type of complex event processing system that utilizes continuous query models to analyze event streams in motion. Having made this initial distinction between rules-based and continuous query-based CEPs, there has been a blending of these approaches over time, and at least one rather prominent rules-based engine has focused on low-latency applications such as algorithmic trading in capital markets. The remainder of this section will focus on continuous query-based CEPs, which we will refer to as ESP.

As mentioned above, ESP systems are usually architected to handle large volumes of events with very low latencies, which is why a lot of these systems focused on capital markets, where front office trading, risk, and position management systems needed to make decisions in milliseconds, or more likely today, microseconds. These systems process financial market data from real-time financial feeds (such as trades, quotes, and orders) where the volumes could reach millions of events per second. ESP systems are being applied across many markets and applications, including personalized marketing, trading systems, operational predictive asset management, fraud prevention, and even cyber security.

The continuous annual growth of data, much of this being computer generated, has spawned the evolution of new methods to be able to analyze all of this data, and ESP helps fill that need by analyzing large volumes of raw data (or event streams) and looking for actionable intelligence. This actionable intelligence is usually aggregated events, and hence a significant level of data reduction by ESP systems can be done before it makes its way to the more traditional historical analytics. This form of multistage analytics helps keep up with the growth of data and enables actionable intelligence to be obtained in lower latencies, hence enabling opportunity. ESP systems will sometimes find patterns or other aggregations of events that are directly actionable, and other times they find aggregations of events that need to be analyzed further before they become actionable.

This multistage analytics approach is also very useful given that the type of analytics done by ESP is quite different than traditional statistical-based analytics. Historical analytics typically works on a static data set at rest and applies complex algorithms and searches that can be very statistical in nature. Event stream processing models, however, are much more additive and data transformational in nature. ESP models are often referred to as continuous queries because they essentially query data in motion, where the resultant set of the queries is continuously being updated. For this type of processing, it is important that the queries are additive in nature. In other words, when a new event comes in, these queries typically update the retained state of the queries without having to reread all the events already processed.

These continuous queries can be modeled as directed graphs where input event streams are published into the top of the graph, and each subsequent node in the graph performs transformations on the events it receives. The nodes of the graph can be thought of as windows with operators and retention policies. So each node performs a transformation on each event it gets, producing zero, one, or more resultant events that are retained in the window for a defined period of time or volume, and are passed on to the sibling nodes connected to that window. The nodes come in various forms, including relational, procedural, and rules. Relational nodes include all the primitives of Structured Query Language (SQL), such as joins, aggregates, projections, and filters. Most ESP systems also support pattern matching, which is a rule-based window that allows one to specify event patterns of a temporal nature. For example:

*Event-A* **Followed-by** (within 2 minutes) *Event-B*
**Followed-by** (within 1 minute) **Not** *Event-C*

where we are looking for an event pattern such that *Event-A* occurs, and that is followed within 2 minutes by *Event-B* occurring, which in turn is not followed by the occurrence of *Event-C* for the next minute.

Procedural nodes, or windows, typically allow one to write event stream handlers using some procedural language (like C++) to process the events from the event streams that are input into that node or window. So one can model continuous queries as one or more directed graphs of data transformation nodes that work in parallel to produce continuous results in very low latencies.

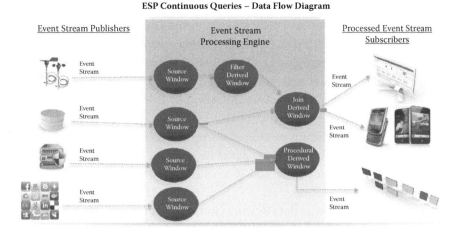

**FIGURE 2.14**
ESP continuous query.

Figure 2.14 is an example of a very simplistic ESP continuous query where event streams are published into the continuous query via source windows. Once each event is absorbed into the source window, it makes its way to any connected windows or subscribers. Every window type that is not a source window is referred to as a derived (or synthetic) window because they have an associated operator that transforms each event coming into it to zero, one, or more resultant events. In our simple example, we show window types filter, join, and procedural. The terminology (such as windows) is not standardized across ESP systems, but the basic concepts around continuous queries and their node types hold true. ESP continuous queries are data transformation models that continuously query event streams as they flow through the ESP where each window or operator in the flow could retain an event state that represents some period of recent events. One can model very powerful continuous queries that can reduce data into something immediately actionable or at least more relevant for further historical or predictive analytics.

## VALUE OF DATA AND ANALYTICS

We began this chapter by stressing the importance of analytics as an essential component to deriving value from data, where the era of big data adds intensity to the concept, as it adds new dimensions to the equation. Regardless of the source of data, its value is not realized unless it provides some resource to a strategic endeavor. Rarely does a decision maker reference a data source without first formulating a reason to do so. Once the conceptual need is defined, only then can data provide value.

The conceptual need involves the quest to better understand a process with the goal of enhancing its efficiency, productivity, or profitability. Simply analyzing random data and coming up with associations between variables may actually generate negative returns since the analytic process requires time and resources, and the result may not add meaningful information.

Consider the growing data resource in the area of sports. More variables (variety) and real-time downloads of various athletic activities at corresponding events (velocity and volume) may seemingly provide great value to understanding various attributes of different athletes and sports teams. However, in order to truly generate value for decision making, a conceptual model must be created. Consider the quest to better understand what leads a team to achieve a winning record. An analysis of corresponding data could yield the following result: a basketball team is more likely to win a game the more 3-point shots they make.

At first glance, this may seem to be very valuable information, but the revelation proves limited at best when looking to make a strategic decision. What does a coach do in leveraging this associative pattern—encourage players to take more shots from the 3-point zone? Does he change practice to intensify skills for increasing 3-point percentages for players? And if so, what happens to the team's performance from the 2-point zone, and does a reduction in 2-point conversions decrease the likelihood of winning a game despite an increase in 3-point shots? In the case at hand, does the variable of number of 3-point shots really add descriptive value to what leads to a team's success. Perhaps more appropriate variables that can provide strategic action could entail:

Team practice data (frequency, drills, duration)
Player descriptions (height, speed, position, age)
Type of offensive and defensive tactics

Identifying patterns among these types of variables empowers a coach (decision maker/strategist) to implement strategic initiatives that impact a performance metric or defined objective—winning.

## Efficiency, Productivity, and Profitability

The concept of value also extends to three often cited benchmarks in the realm of commerce: efficiency, productivity, and profitably. One should note that although the three terms appear synonymous, there are noteworthy differences among them, so when seeking to succeed in strategic endeavors, decision makers must clearly understand the entire initiative from the perspective of these three concepts.

Analytics of all types naturally address the quest for enhancing efficiencies of corresponding processes. Enhancing efficiency naturally leads to cost reduction for the defined process; however, simply increasing efficiency for a particular activity does not necessarily imply an increase in productivity and profitability at the organizational level. Consider a marketing department for a small retailer that depends on more traditional mail order initiatives to generate sales. The department could consistently achieve increased efficiency in the process of creating printed marketing materials, generating addresses, and mailing literature to the market. These efficiencies could be achieved by implementing new printing technologies, data-based endeavors, etc. However productivity as measured by response rate or increased product sales may not necessarily increase. Perhaps traditional mail is no longer the most effective marketing medium for the type of product given the evolution of e-marketing tactics and the adoption of smartphones and electronic communication by consumers, or perhaps the target market has changed its behavior and a different segment is actually more appropriate for the product. What may actually transpire for this endeavor is an efficient process that yields decreased productivity for the organization (deploying resources and achieving decreased returns).

Just as analytics were utilized to better understand what drives wasteful activities for the mail order marketing initiative, so too should they be utilized for such endeavors as better understanding overall marketing effectiveness and target marketing. Simply put, strategic endeavors must incorporate a bigger picture than simple processes, which provides a segue to the third concept of value, which involves profitability. Profitability must be included in any endeavor where productive and efficient strategies must make sense on a cost and revenue basis.

Investment in Internet advertising has grown dramatically over the past years, partially because of the cost-effectiveness of some tactics; however, the recent growth of this sector has also resulted in increased costs, a variable that needs to be monitored. A core tactic to e-marketing is search engine optimization for websites, an initiative that is ongoing and incurs costs of continuous management (verbiage of meta-tags, frequency of key phrases, reciprocal links). These costs must be considered in the overall spectrum of e-commerce initiatives. So when leveraging big data feeds involving site traffic relative to page layouts and cross-selling tactics, costs of an entire space need to be managed to understand profitability.

This introduces an important issue in the big data era. Big data is not free and involves technological infrastructure (servers, software) for data management along with labor resources (analytic and technical minds) to leverage this complex resource. Organizations must therefore fully understand how big data resources may impact their operations. Just because new volumes and velocities of data exist doesn't imply that the resource will be a value to every organization. An important concept to keep in mind to estimate this value is answering the question: Will new data resources help an organization better understand its process performance or marketplace?

With new resources come new ideas that leverage them. The evolving big data era in conjunction with new information technologies has introduced an opportunity for organizations to create new markets. Through analytics, big data is transformed into information that provides value by enhancing decision-making capabilities through knowledge generation. Organizations can better understand those processes essential to their operations. The concept of the creation and dissemination of information goes beyond value to organizations as it extends to individuals. Insightful information derived from big data generated from wireless sensor devices can be made available to consumers that may provide beneficial value to them. Consider a wireless device (body sensor) manufacturer that extracts information from users that may enable them to estimate and offer optimized fitness programs on a personalized basis, thus augmenting the value of the product device to existing consumers and adding value to new prospects. As the big data, analytic, and communication era continues to evolve, innovative initiatives that involve information creation in areas previously untapped can prove to be a bold new market.

The big data era requires the analyst to more intensely exhaust data resources that may provide descriptive elements of a given process as new varieties of data variables evolve. Analysts must also consider whether a process must be monitored in a real-time environment (velocity/volume) in order to uncover strategic insights in the information creation and decision-making process. There is little doubt that the job of analyst has become more important and also more complex. The remainder of this book should provide insights to help enlighten individuals as to some of the important concepts that are involved in this space.

## REFERENCES

Baulier, J. (contrib.). Real Time and Continuous Analytics. Cary, NC: SAS.

Kudyba, S., and Hoptroff, R. *Data Mining and Business Intelligence: A Guide to Productivity.* Hershey, Pennsylvania: IDEA Group Publishing, 2001.

Kudyba, S., and Radar, R. Enhancing Data Resources and Business Intelligence in Healthcare. In *Healthcare Informatics: Increasing Efficiency and Productivity.* Boca Raton, Florida: Taylor & Francis, 2010.

Pande, P., and Neuman, R. *The Six Sigma Way: How GE, Motorola, and Other Top Companies Are Honing Their Performance.* New York: McGraw Hill, 2000.

Rajaraman, A., and Ullman, J. Mining Data Streams. In *Mining of Massive Data Sets.* Cambridge: Cambridge University Press, 2011, pp. 129–132.

# 3

## *Big Data Analytics—Architectures, Implementation Methodology, and Tools*

*Wullianallur Raghupathi and Viju Raghupathi*

## CONTENTS

## OVERVIEW

With the storage and maintenance of very large or big data sets of structured and unstructured data, companies are starting to use big data analytics to analyze and gain insight to make informed decisions (Franks, 2012; Gobble, 2013; McAfee and Brynjolfsson, 2012). This chapter discusses big data analytics, followed by a description of the architecture, frameworks, and tools; an outline of an implementation methodology is then provided. This is followed by a discussion of the key challenges. The proposal for an ongoing big data analytics project in the mining of the unstructured information in cancer blogs is also described. Lastly, conclusions are offered.

## INTRODUCTION

The big data phenomenon has rapidly become pervasive across the spectrum of industries and sectors (Davenport, 2013; EIU, 2012; McAfee and Brynjolfsson, 2012). It typically describes the incredibly large volume of data that is collected, stored, and managed. This large volume of data is being analyzed to gain insight to make informed decisions (Manyika et al., 2011; Mehta, 2011; Russom, 2011). To this end, big data analytics is emerging as a subdiscipline of the field of business analytics involving the application of unique architectures and platforms, technologies, unique programming languages, and open-source tools. The key underlying principle is the utilization of distributed processing to address the large volume and simultaneous complexity and real-time nature of the analytics (Kumar et al., 2013; Oracle, 2012; Raden, 2012; SAP AG, 2012).

Very large data sets have existed for decades—the key difference is the emergence of the collection and storage of unstructured data primarily from social media, etc. The data gathered from unconventional sources such as blogs, online chats, email, sensors, tweets, etc., and information gleaned from nontraditional sources such as blogs, social media, email, sensors, pictures, audio and video multimedia utilizing web forms, mobile devices, scanners, etc., hold the potential of offering different types of analytics, such as descriptive, predictive, and prescriptive. From a comparative perspective, big data did exist in 1960s, 1970s, 1980s, and 1990s, but it was mostly structured data (e.g., numerical/quantitative) in flat files and relational databases. With the emergence of the Internet and the rapid proliferation of web applications and technologies there has been an exponential increase in the accumulation of unstructured data as well (Nair and Narayanan, 2012). This has led to an escalating and pressing opportunity to analyze this data for decision-making purposes.

For example, it is universal knowledge that Amazon, the online retailer, utilizes big data analytics to apply predictive and prescriptive analytics to forecast what products a customer ought to purchase. All of the visits, searches, personal data, orders, etc., are analyzed using complex analytics algorithms (Ohlhorst, 2012). Likewise, from a social media perspective, Facebook executes analytics on the data collected via the users' accounts. Google is another historical example of a company that analyzes a whole breadth and depth of data collected via the searches results tracking (Ohlhorst, 2012). Examples can be found not only in Internet-based companies, but also in industries such as banking, insurance, healthcare, and others, and in science and engineering (Connolly and Wooledge, 2013; Srinivasan and Nayar, 2012; White and Rowe, 2012). Recognizing that big data analytics is here to stay, we next discuss the primary characteristics.

## BIG DATA ANALYTICS

Like big data, the analytics associated with big data is also described by three primary characteristics: volume, velocity, and variety (http://www-01.ibm.com/software/data/bigdata/). There is no doubt data will continue to be created and collected, continually leading to incredible *volume* of data. Second, this data is being accumulated at a rapid pace, and in real time. This is indicative of *velocity*. Third, gone are the days of data being collected in standard quantitative formats and stored in spreadsheets or relational databases. Increasingly, the data is in multimedia format and unstructured. This is the *variety* characteristic. Considering volume, velocity, and variety, the analytics techniques have also evolved to accommodate these characteristics to scale up to the complex and sophisticated analytics needed (Russom, 2011; Zikopoulos et al., 2013). Some practitioners and researchers have introduced a fourth characteristic: *veracity* (Ohlhorst, 2012). The implication of this is data assurance. That is, both the data and the analytics and outcomes are error-free and credible.

Simultaneously, the architectures and platforms, algorithms, methodologies, and tools have also scaled up in granularity and performance to match the demands of big data (Ferguson, 2012; Zikopoulos et al., 2012). For example, big data analytics is executed in distributed processing across several servers (nodes) to utilize the paradigm of parallel computing and a divide and process approach. It is evident that the analytics tools for structured and unstructured big data are very different from the traditional business intelligence (BI) tools. The architectures and tools for big data analytics have to necessarily be of industrial strength. Likewise, the models and techniques such as data mining and statistical approaches, algorithms, visualization techniques, etc., have to be mindful of the characteristics of big data analytics. For example, the National Oceanic and Atmospheric Administration (NOAA) uses big data analytics to assist with climate, ecosystem, and environment, weather forecasting and pattern analysis, and commercial translational applications. NASA engages big data analytics for aeronautical and other types of research (Ohlhorst, 2012). Pharmaceutical companies are using big data analytics for drug discovery, analysis of clinical trial data, side effects and reactions, etc. Banking companies are utilizing big data analytics for investments, loans, customer demographics, etc. Insurance and healthcare provider and media companies are other big data analytics industries.

The 4Vs are a starting point for the discussion about big data analytics. Other issues include the number of architectures and platform, the dominance of the open-source paradigm in the availability of tools, the challenge of developing methodologies, and the need for user-friendly interfaces. While the overall cost of the hardware and software is declining, these issues have to be addressed to harness and maximize the potential of big data analytics. We next delve into the architectures, platforms, and tools.

## ARCHITECTURES, FRAMEWORKS, AND TOOLS

The conceptual framework for a big data analytics project is similar to that for a traditional business intelligence or analytics project. The key difference lies in how the processing is executed. In a regular analytics project, the analysis can be performed with a business intelligence tool installed on a stand-alone system such as a desktop or laptop. Since the big data is large by definition, the processing is broken down and executed across multiple nodes. While the concepts of distributed processing are not new and have existed for decades, their use in analyzing very large data sets is relatively new as companies start to tap into their data repositories to gain insight to make informed decisions. Additionally, the availability of open-source platforms such as Hadoop/MapReduce on the cloud has further encouraged the application of big data analytics in various domains. Third, while the algorithms and models are similar, the user interfaces are entirely different at this time. Classical business analytics tools have become very user-friendly and transparent. On the other hand, big data analytics tools are extremely complex, programming intensive, and need the application of a variety of skills. As Figure 3.1 indicates, a primary component is the data itself. The data can be from internal and external sources, often in multiple formats, residing at multiple locations in numerous legacy and other applications. All this data has to be pooled together for analytics purposes. The data is still in a raw state and needs to be transformed. Here, several options are available. A service-oriented architectural approach combined with web services (middleware) is one possibility. The data continues to be in the same state, and services are used to call, retrieve, and process the data. On the other hand, data warehousing is another approach wherein all the data from the different sources are aggregated and made ready for processing. However, the data is unavailable in real time. Via the steps of extract, transform, and load (ETL), the data from

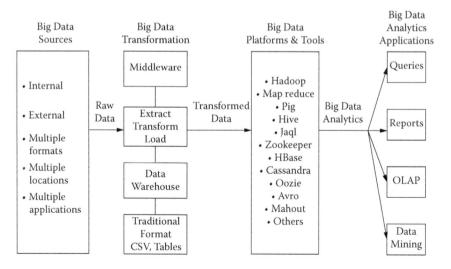

**FIGURE 3.1**
An applied conceptual architecture of big data analytics.

diverse sources is cleansed and made ready. Depending on whether the data is structured or unstructured, several data formats can be input to the Hadoop/MapReduce platform (Sathi, 2012; Zikopoulos et al., 2013).

In this next stage in the conceptual framework, several decisions are made regarding the data input approach, distributed design, tool selection, and analytics models. Finally, to the far right the four typical applications of big data analytics are shown. These include queries, reports, online analytic processing (OLAP), and data mining. Visualization is an overarching theme across the four applications. A wide variety of techniques and technologies have been developed and adapted to aggregate, manipulate, analyze, and visualize big data. These techniques and technologies draw from several fields, including statistics, computer science, applied mathematics, and economics (Courtney, 2013; HP 2012).

## Hadoop

The most significant platform for big data analytics is the open-source distributed data processing platform Hadoop (Apache platform), initially developed for routine functions such as aggregating web search indexes. It belongs to the class NoSQL technologies (others include CouchDB and MongoDB) that have evolved to aggregate data in unique ways. Hadoop has the potential to process extremely large amounts of data by mainly allocating partitioned data sets to numerous servers (nodes), which individually solve different parts of the larger problem and then integrate them back for the final result (Ohlhorst, 2012; Zikopoulos et al., 2012). It can serve in the twin roles of either as a data organizer or as an analytics tool. Hadoop offers a great deal of potential in enabling enterprises to harness the data that was, until now, difficult to manage and analyze. Specifically, Hadoop makes it possible to process extremely large volumes of data with varying structures (or no structure at all). However, Hadoop can be complex to install, configure, and administer, and there is not yet readily available individuals with Hadoop skills. Furthermore, organizations are not ready as well to embrace Hadoop completely.

It is generally accepted that there are two important modules in Hadoop (Borkar et al., 2012; Mone, 2013):

1. *The Hadoop Distributed File System (HDFS).* This facilitates the underlying storage for the Hadoop cluster. When data for the analytics arrives in the cluster, HDFS breaks it into smaller parts and

redistributes the parts among the different servers (nodes) engaged in the cluster. Only a small chunk of the entire data set resides on each server/node, and it is conceivable each chunk is duplicated on other servers/nodes.

2. *MapReduce.* Since the Hadoop platform stores the complete data set in small pieces across a connected set of servers/nodes in distributed fashion, the analytics tasks can be distributed across the servers/nodes too. Results from the individual pieces of processing are aggregated or pooled together for an integrated solution. MapReduce provides the interface for the distribution of the subtasks and then the gathering of the outputs (Sathi, 2012; Zikopoulos et al., 2012, 2013). MapReduce is discussed further below.

A major advantage of parallel/distributed processing is graceful degradation or capability to cope with possible failures. Therefore, HDFS and MapReduce are configured to continue to execute in the event of a failure. HDFS, for example, monitors the servers/nodes and storage devices continually. If a problem is detected, it automatically reroutes and restores data onto an alternative server/node. In other words, it is configured and designed to continue processing in light of a failure. In addition, replication adds a level of redundancy and backup. Similarly, when tasks are executed, MapReduce tracks the processing of each server/node. If it detects any anomalies such as reduced speed, going into a hiatus, or reaching a dead end, the task is transferred to another server/node that holds the duplicate data. Overall, the synergy between HDFS and MapReduce in the cloud environment facilitates industrial strength, scalable, reliable, and fault-tolerant support for both the storage and analytics (Zikopoulos et al., 2012, 2013).

In an example, it is reported that Yahoo! is an early user of Hadoop (Ohlhorst, 2012). Its key objective was to gain insight from the large amounts of data stored across the numerous and disparate servers. The integration of the data and the application of big data analytics was mission critical. Hadoop appeared to be the perfect platform for such an endeavor. Presently, Yahoo! is apparently one of the largest users of Hadoop and has deployed it on thousands on servers/nodes. The Yahoo! Hadoop cluster apparently holds huge "log files" of user-clicked data, advertisements, and lists of all Yahoo! published content. From a big data analytics perspective, Hadoop is used for a number of tasks, including correlation and cluster analysis to find patterns in the unstructured data sets.

Some of the more notable Hadoop-related application development-oriented initiatives include Apache Avro (for data serialization), Cassandra and HBase (databases), Chukka (a monitoring system specifically designed with large distributed systems in view), Hive (provides ad hoc Structured Query Language (SQL)-like queries for data aggregation and summarization), Mahout (a machine learning library), Pig (a high-level Hadoop programming language that provides a data flow language and execution framework for parallel computation), Zookeeper (provides coordination services for distributed applications), and others (Zikopoulos et al., 2012, 2013). The key ones are described below.

## MapReduce

MapReduce, as discussed above, is a programming framework developed by Google that supports the underlying Hadoop platform to process the big data sets residing on distributed servers (nodes) in order to produce the aggregated results. The primary component of an algorithm would *map* the broken up tasks (e.g., calculations) to the various locations in the distributed file system and consolidate the individual results (the *reduce step*) that are computed at the individual nodes of the file system. In summary, the data mining algorithm would perform computations at the server/node level and simultaneously in the overall distributed system to summate the individual outputs (Zikopoulos et al., 2012). It is important to note that the primary Hadoop MapReduce application programming interfaces (APIs) are mainly called from Java. This requires skilled programmers. In addition, advanced skills are indeed needed for development and maintenance.

In order to abstract some of the complexity of the Hadoop programming framework, several application development languages have emerged that run on top of Hadoop. Three popular ones are Pig, Hive, and Jaql. These are briefly described below.

### Pig and PigLatin

Pig was originally developed at Yahoo! The Pig programming language is configured to assimilate all types of data (structured/unstructured, etc.). Two key modules are comprised in it: the language itself, called PigLatin, and the runtime version in which the PigLatin code is executed (Borkar et al., 2012). According to Zikopoulos et al. (2012), the initial step in a Pig program is to *load* the data to be subject to analytics in HDFS. This is followed by a series of manipulations wherein the data is converted into a series of mapper and reducer tasks in the background. Last, the program *dumps* the data to the screen or stores the outputs at another location. The key advantage of Pig is that it enables the programmers utilizing Hadoop to focus more on the big data analytics and less on developing the mapper and reducer code (Zikopoulos et al., 2012).

## Hive

While Pig is robust and relatively easy to use, it still has a learning curve. This means the programmer needs to become proficient (Zikopoulos et al., 2012). To address this issue, Facebook has developed a runtime Hadoop support architecture that leverages SQL with the Hadoop platform (Borkar et al., 2012). This architecture is called Hive; it permits SQL programmers to develop Hive Query Language (HQL) statements akin to typical SQL statements. However, HQL is limited in the commands it recognizes. Ultimately, HQL statements are decomposed by the Hive Service into MapRaduce tasks and executed across a Hadoop cluster of servers/nodes (Zikopoulos et al., 2012). Also, since Hive is dependent on Hadoop and MapReduce executions, queries may have lag time in processing up to several minutes. This implies Hive may not be suitable for big data analytics applications that need rapid response times, typical of relational databases. Lastly, Hive is a read-based programming artifact; it is therefore not appropriate for transactions that engage in a large volume of write instructions (Zikopoulos et al., 2012).

## Jaql

Jaql's primary role is that of a query language for JavaScript Object Notational (JSON). However, its capability goes beyond LSON. It facilitates the analysis of both structured and nontraditional data (Zikopoulos et al., 2012). Pointedly, Jaql enables the functions of select, join, group, and filter of the data that resides in HDFS. In this regard, it is analogous to a hybrid of Pig and Hive. Jaql is a functional, declarative query language that is designed to process large data sets. To facilitate parallel processing, Jaql converts high-level queries into low-level queries consisting of MapReduce tasks (Zikopoulos et al., 2012).

## Zookeeper

Zookeeper is yet another open-source Apache project that allows a centralized infrastructure with various services; this provides for synchronization across a cluster of servers. Zookeeper maintains common objects required in large cluster situations (like a library). Examples of these typical objects include configuration information, hierarchical naming space, and others (Zikopoulos et al., 2012). Big data analytics applications can utilize these services to coordinate parallel processing across big clusters. As described in Zikopoulos et al. (2012), one can visualize a Hadoop cluster with >500 utility services. This necessitates a centralized management of the entire cluster in the context of such things as name services, group services, synchronization services, configuration management, and others. Furthermore, several other open-source projects that utilize Hadoop clusters require these types of cross-cluster services (Zikopoulos et al., 2012). The availability of these in a Zookeeper infrastructure implies that projects can be embedded by Zookeeper without duplicating or requiring constructing all over again. A final note: Interface with Zookeeper happens via Java or C interfaces presently (Zikopoulos et al., 2012).

## HBase

HBase is a column-oriented database management system that sits on the top of HDFS (Zikopoulos et al., 2012). In contrast to traditional relational database systems, HBase does not support a structured query language such as SQL. The applications in HBase are developed in Java much similar to other MapReduce applications. In addition, HBase does support application development in Avro, REST, or Thrift. HBase is built on concepts similar to how HDFS has a NameNode (master) and slave nodes, and MapReduce comprises JobTracker and TaskTracker slave nodes. A master node manages the cluster in HBase, and regional servers store parts of the table and execute the tasks on the big data (Zikopoulos et al., 2012).

## Cassandra

Cassandra, an Apache project, is also a distributed database system (Ohlhorst, 2012). It is designated as a top-level project modeled to handle big data distributed across many utility servers. Also, it provides reliable service with no particular point of failure (http://en.wikipedia.org/

wiki/Apache_Cassandra). It is also a NoSQL system. Facebook originally developed it to support its inbox search. The Cassandra database system can store 2 million columns in a single row. Similar to Yahoo!'s needs, Facebook wanted to use the Google BigTable architecture that could provide a column-and-row database structure; this could be distributed across a number of nodes. But BigTable faced a major limitation—its use of a master node approach made the entire application depend on one node for all read-write coordination—the antithesis of parallel processing (Ohlhorst, 2012). Cassandra was built on a distributed architecture named Dynamo, designed by Amazon engineers. Amazon used it to track what its millions of online customers were entering into their shopping carts. Dynamo gave Cassandra an advantage over BigTable; this is due to the fact that Dynamo is not dependent on any one master node. Any node can accept data for the whole system, as well as answer queries. Data is replicated on multiple hosts, creating stability and eliminating the single point of failure (Ohlhorst, 2012).

## Oozie

Many tasks may be tethered together to meet the requirements of a complex analytics application in MapReduce. The open-source project Oozie to an extent streamlines the workflow and coordination among the tasks (Zikopoulos et al., 2012). Its functionality permits programmers to define their own jobs and the relationships between those jobs. It will then automatically schedule the execution of the various jobs once the relationship criteria have been complied with.

## Lucene

Lucene is yet another widely used open-source Apache project predominantly used for text analytics/searches; it is incorporated into several open-source projects. Lucene precedes Hadoop and has been a top-level Apache project since 2005. Its scope includes full text indexing and library search for use within a Java application (Zikopoulos et al., 2012).

## Avro

Avro, also an Apache project, facilitates data serialization services. The data definition schema is also included in the data file. This makes it possible for an analytics application to access the data in the future since the schema is also stored along with. Versioning and version control are also added features of use in Avro. Schemas for prior data are available, making schema modifications possible (Zikopoulos et al., 2012).

### Mahout

Mahout is yet another Apache project whose goal is to generate free applications of distributed and scalable machine learning algorithms that support big data analytics on the Hadoop platform. Mahout is still an ongoing project, evolving to include additional algorithms (http://en.wikipedia.org/wiki/Mahout). The core widely used algorithms for classification, clustering, and collaborative filtering are implemented using the map/reduce paradigm.

### Streams

Streams deliver a robust analytics platform for analyzing data in real time (Zikopoulos et al., 2012). Compared to BigInsights, Streams applies the analytics techniques on data in motion. But like BigInsights, Streams is appropriate not only for structured data but also for nearly all other types of data—the nontraditional semistructured or unstructured data coming from sensors, voice, text, video, financial, and many other high-volume sources (Zikopoulos et al., 2012).

Overall, in summary, there are numerous vendors, including AWS, Cloudera, Hortonworks, and MapR Technologies, among others, who distribute open-source Hadoop platforms (Ohlhorst, 2012). Numerous proprietary options are also available, such as IBM's BigInsights. Further, many of these are cloud versions that make it more widely available. Cassandra, HBase, and MongoDB, as described above, are widely used for the database component. In the next section we offer an applied big data analytics methodology to develop and implement a big data project in a company.

## BIG DATA ANALYTICS METHODOLOGY

While several different methodologies are being developed in this rapidly emerging discipline, here a practical hands-on methodology is outlined. Table 3.1 shows the main stages of such a methodology. In stage 1, the

**TABLE 3.1**

Outline of Big Data Analytics Methodology

| | |
|---|---|
| Stage 1 | Concept design |
| | • Establish need for big data analytics project |
| | • Define problem statement |
| | • Why is project important and significant? |
| Stage 2 | Proposal |
| | • Abstract—summarize proposal |
| | • Introduction |
| |   • What is problem being addressed? |
| |   • Why is it important and interesting? |
| |   • Why big data analytics approach? |
| | • Background material |
| |   • Problem domain discussion |
| |   • Prior projects and research |
| Stage 3 | Methodology |
| | • Hypothesis development |
| | • Data sources and collection |
| | • Variable selection (independent and dependent variables) |
| | • ETL and data transformation |
| | • Platform/tool selection |
| | • Analytic techniques |
| | • Expected results and conclusions |
| | • Policy implications |
| | • Scope and limitations |
| | • Future research |
| | • Implementation |
| |   • Develop conceptual architecture |
| |     – Show and describe component (e.g., Figure 3.1) |
| |     – Show and describe big data analytic platform/tools |
| |   • Execute steps in methodology |
| |   • Import data |
| |   • Perform various big data analytics using various techniques and algorithms (e.g., word count, association, classification, clustering, etc.) |
| |   • Gain insight from outputs |
| |   • Draw conclusion |
| |   • Derive policy implications |
| |   • Make informed decisions |
| Stage 4 | • Presentation and walkthrough |
| | • Evaluation |

interdisciplinary big data analytics team develops a concept design. This is a first cut at briefly establishing the need for such a project since there are trade-offs in terms of cheaper options, risk, problem-solution alignment, etc. Additionally, a problem statement is followed by a description of project importance and significance. Once the concept design is approved in principle, one proceeds to stage 2, which is the proposal development stage. Here, more details are filled. Taking the concept design as input, an abstract highlighting the overall methodology and implementation process is outlined. This is followed by an introduction to the big data analytics domain: What is the problem being addressed? Why is it important and interesting to the organization? It is also necessary to make the case for a big data analytics approach. Since the complexity and cost are much higher than those of traditional analytics approaches, it is important to justify its use. Also, the project team should provide background information on the problem domain and prior projects and research done in this domain.

Both the concept design and the proposal are evaluated in terms of the 4Cs:

- *Completeness*: Is the concept design complete?
- *Correctness*: Is the design technically sound? Is correct terminology used?
- *Consistency*: Is the proposal cohesive, or does it appear choppy? Is there flow and continuity?
- *Communicability*: Is proposal formatted professionally? Does report communicate design in easily understood language?

Next, in stage 3, the steps in the methodology are fleshed out and implemented. The problem statement is broken down into a series of hypotheses. Please note these are not rigorous, as in the case of statistical approaches. Rather, they are developed to help guide the big data analytics process. Simultaneously, the independent and dependent variables are identified. In terms of analytics itself, it does not make a major difference to classify the variables. However, it helps identify causal relationships or correlations. The data sources as outlined in Figure 3.1 are identified; the data is collected (longitudinal data, if necessary), described, and transformed to make it ready for analytics. A very important step at this point is platform/tool evaluation and selection. For example, several options, as indicated previously, such as AWS Hadoop, Cloudera, IBM BigInsights, etc., are available. A major criterion is whether the platform is available on a desktop or on the cloud. The next step is to apply the various big data analytics techniques to the data. These are not different from the routine analytics. They're only scaled up to large data sets. Through a series of iterations and *what if* analysis, insight is gained from the big data analytics. From the insight, informed decisions can be made and policy shaped. In the final steps, conclusions are offered, scope and limitations are identified, and the policy implications discussed. In stage 4, the project and its findings are presented to the stakeholders for action. Additionally, the big data analytics project is validated using the following criteria:

- Robustness of analyses, queries, reports, and visualization
- Variety of insight
- Substantiveness of research question
- Demonstration of big data analytics application
- Some degree of integration among components
- Sophistication and complexity of analysis

The implementation is a staged approach with feedback loops built in at each stage to minimize risk of failure. The users should be involved in the implementation. It is also an iterative process, especially in the analytics step, wherein the analyst performs *what if* analysis. The next section briefly discusses some of the key challenges in big data analytics.

## CHALLENGES

For one, a big data analytics platform must support, at a minimum, the key functions necessary for processing the data. The criteria for platform evaluation may include availability, continuity, ease of use, scalability, ability to manipulate at different levels of granularity, privacy and security enablement, and quality assurance (Bollier, 2010; Ohlhorst, 2012). Additionally, while most currently available platforms are open source, the typical advantages and limitations of open-source platforms apply. They have to be shrink-wrapped, made user-friendly, and transparent for big data analytics to take off. Real-time big data analytics is a key requirement in many industries, such as retail, banking, healthcare, and others (SAP AG, 2012). The lag between when data is collected and processed has to be addressed. The dynamic availability of the numerous analytics algorithms, models, and methods in a pull-down type of menu is also necessary for large-scale adoption. The in-memory processing, such as in SAP's Hana, can be extended to the Hadoop/MapReduce framework. The various options of local processing (e.g., a network, desktop/laptop), cloud computing, software as a service (SaaS), and service-oriented architecture (SOA) web services delivery mechanisms have to be explored further. The key managerial issues of ownership, governance, and standards have to be addressed as well. Interleaved into these are the issues of continuous data acquisition and data cleansing. In the future, ontology and other design issues have to be discussed. Furthermore, an appliance-driven approach (e.g., access via mobile computing and wireless devices) has to be investigated. We next discuss big data analytics in a particularly industry, namely, healthcare and the practice of medicine.

## BIG DATA ANALYTICS IN HEALTHCARE

The healthcare industry has great potential in the application of big data analytics (Burghard, 2012; Fernandes et al., 2012; IBM, 2012; jStart, 2012; Raghupathi, 2010). From evidence-based to personalized medicine, from outcomes to reduction in medical errors, the pervasive impact of big data analytics in healthcare can be felt across the spectrum of healthcare delivery. Two broad categories of applications are envisaged: big data analytics in the business and delivery side (e.g., improved quality at lower costs) and in the practice of medicine (aid in diagnosis and treatment). The healthcare industry has all the necessary ingredients and qualities for the application of big data analytics—data intensive, critical decision support, outcomes based, improved delivery of quality healthcare at reduced costs (in this regard, the transformational role of health information technology such as big data analytics applications is recognized), and so on. However, one must keep in mind the historical challenges of the lack of user acceptance, lack of interoperability, and the need for compliance regarding privacy and security. Nevertheless, the promise and potential of big data analytics in healthcare cannot be overstated.

In terms of examples of big data applications, it is reported that the Department of Veterans Affairs (VA) in the United States has successfully demonstrated several healthcare information technology (HIT) and remote patent monitoring programs. The VA health system generally outperforms the private sector in following recommended processors for patient care, adhering to clinical guidelines, and achieving greater rates of evidence-based drug therapy. These achievements are largely possible because of the VA's performance-based accountability framework and disease management practices enabled by electronic medical records (EMRs) and HIT (Dembosky, 2012; Manyika et al., 2011). Another example is how California-based integrated managed care consortium Kaiser Permanente connected clinical and cost data early on, thus providing the crucial data set that led to the discovery of Vioxx's adverse drug effects and the subsequent withdrawal of the drug from the market (Manyika et al., 2011; Savage, 2012). Yet another example is the National Institute for Health and Clinical Excellence, part of the UK's National Health Service (NHS), pioneering use of large clinical data sets to investigate the clinical and cost effectiveness of new drugs and expensive existing treatments. The agency issues appropriate guidelines on such costs for the NHS and often negotiates prices and market access conditions with pharmaceutical and medical products (PMP) industries (Manyika et al., 2011). Further, the Italian Medicines Agency collects and analyzes clinical data on the experience of expensive new drugs as part of a national cost-effectiveness program. The agency can impose conditional imbursement status on new drugs and can then reevaluate prices and market access conditions in light of the results of its clinical data studies (Manyika et al., 2011).

## BIG DATA ANALYTICS OF CANCER BLOGS

In this section we describe our ongoing prototype research project in the use of the Hadoop/MapReduce framework on the AWS for the analysis of unstructured cancer blog data (Raghupathi, 2010). Health organizations and individuals such as patients are using blog content for several purposes. Health and medical blogs are rich in unstructured data for insight and informed decision making. While current applications such as web crawlers and blog analysis are good at generating statistics about the number of blogs, top 10 sites, etc., they are not advanced/useful or scalable computationally to help with analysis and extraction of insight. First, the blog data is growing exponentially (volume); second, they're posted in real time and the analysis could become outdated very quickly (velocity); and third, there is a variety of content in the blogs. Fourth, the blogs themselves are distributed and scattered all over the Internet. Therefore, blogs in particular and social media in general are great candidates for the application of big data analytics. To reiterate, there has been an exponential increase in the number of blogs in the healthcare area, as patients find them useful in disease management and developing support groups. Alternatively, healthcare providers such as physicians have started to use blogs to communicate and discuss medical information. Examples of useful information include alternative medicine and treatment, health condition management, diagnosis–treatment information, and support group resources. This rapid proliferation in health- and medical-related blogs has resulted in huge amounts of unstructured yet potentially valuable information being available for analysis and use. Statistics indicate health-related bloggers are very consistent at posting to blogs. The analysis and interpretation of health-related blogs are not trivial tasks. Unlike many of the blogs in various corporate domains, health blogs are far more complex and unstructured. The postings reflect two important facets of the bloggers and visitors: the individual patient care and disease management (fine granularity) to generalized medicine (e.g., public health).

Hadoop/MapReduce defines a framework for implementing systems for the analysis of unstructured data. In contrast to structured information, whose meaning is expressed by the structure or the format of the data, the meaning of unstructured information cannot be so inferred. Examples of data that carry unstructured information include natural language text and data from audio or video sources. More specifically, an audio stream has a well-defined syntax and semantics for rendering the stream on an audio device, but its music score is not directly represented. Hadoop/MapReduce is sufficiently advanced and sophisticated computationally to aid in the analysis and understanding of the content of health-related blogs. At the individual level (document-level analysis) one can perform analysis and gain insight into the patient in longitudinal studies. At the group level (collection-level analysis) one can gain insight into the patterns of the groups (network behavior, e.g., assessing the influence within the social group), for example, in a particular disease group, the community of participants in an HMO or hospital setting, or even in the global community of patients (ethnic stratification). The results of these analyses can be generalized (Raghupathi, 2010). While the blogs enable the formation of social networks of patients and providers, the uniqueness of the health/medical terminology comingled with the subjective vocabulary of the patient compounds the challenge of interpretation.

Discussing at a more general level, while blogs have emerged as contemporary modes of communication within a social network context, hardly any research or insight exists in the content analysis of blogs. The blog world is characterized by a lack of particular rules on format, how to post, and the structure of the content itself. Questions arise: How do we make sense of the aggregate content? How does one interpret and generalize? In health blogs in particular, what patterns of diagnosis, treatment, management, and support might emerge from a meta-analysis of a large pool of blog postings? How can the content be classified? What natural clusters can be formed about the topics? What associations and correlations exist between key topics? The overall goal, then, is to enhance the quality of health by reducing errors and assisting in clinical decision making. Additionally, one can reduce the cost of healthcare delivery by the use of these types of advanced health information technology. Therefore, the *objectives* of our project include the following:

1. To use Hadoop/MapReduce to perform analytics on a set of cancer blog postings from http://www.thecancerblog.com
2. To develop a parsing algorithm and association, classification, and clustering technique for the analysis of cancer blogs
3. To develop a vocabulary and taxonomy of keywords (based on existing medical nomenclature)
4. To build a prototype interface
5. To contribute to social media analysis in the semantic web by generalizing the models from cancer blogs

The following levels of development are envisaged: first level, patterns of symptoms, management (diagnosis/treatment); second level, glean insight into disease management at individual/group levels; and third level, clinical decision support (e.g., generalization of patterns, syntactic to semantic)—informed decision making. Typically, the unstructured information in blogs comprises the following:

Blog topic (posting): What issue or question does the blogger (and comments) discuss?

Disease and treatment (not limited to): What cancer type and treatment (and other issues) are identified and discussed?

Other information: What other related topics are discussed? What links are provided?

## What Can We Learn from Blog Postings?

Unstructured information related to blog postings (bloggers), including responses/comments, can provide insight into diseases (cancer), treatment (e.g., alternative medicine, therapy), support links, etc.

1. What are the most common issues patients have (bloggers/responses)?
2. What are the cancer types (conditions) most discussed? Why?
3. What therapies and treatments are being discussed? What medical and nonmedical information is provided?
4. Which blogs and bloggers are doing a good job of providing relevant and correct information?
5. What are the major motivations for the postings (comments)? Is it classified by role, such as provider (physician) or patient?
6. What are the emerging trends in disease (symptoms), treatment, and therapy (e.g., alternative medicine), support systems, and information sources (links, clinical trials)?

## What Are the Phases and Milestones?

This project envisions the use of Hadoop/MapReduce on the AWS to facilitate distributed processing and partitioning of the problem-solving process across the nodes for manageability. Additionally, supporting plug-ins are used to develop an application tool to analyze health-related blogs. The project is scoped to content analysis of the domain of cancer blogs at http://www.thecancerblog.com. Phase 1 involved the collection of blog postings from http://www.thecancerblog.com into a Derby application. Phase 2 consisted of the development and configuration of the architecture—keywords, associations, correlations, clusters, and taxonomy. Phase 3 entailed the analysis and integration of extracted information in the cancer blogs—preliminary results of initial analysis (e.g., patterns that are identified). Phase 4 involved the development of taxonomy. Phase 5 proposes to test the mining model and develop the user interface for deployment. We propose to develop a comprehensive text mining system that integrates several mining techniques, including association and clustering, to effectively organize the blog information and provide decision support in terms of search by keywords (Raghupathi, 2010).

## CONCLUSIONS

Big data analytics is transforming the way companies are using sophisticated information technologies to gain insight from their data repositories to make informed decisions. This data-driven approach is unprecedented, as the data collected via the web and social media is escalating by the second. In the future we'll see the rapid, widespread implementation and use of big data analytics across the organization and the industry. In the process, the several challenges highlighted above need to be addressed. As it becomes more mainstream, issues such as guaranteeing privacy, safeguarding security, establishing standards and governance, and continually improving the tools and technologies would garner attention. Big data analytics and applications are at a nascent stage of development, but the rapid advances in platforms and tools can accelerate their maturing process.

## REFERENCES

Bollier, D. *The Promise and Peril of Big Data*. Washington, DC: The Aspen Institute, Communications and Society Program, 2010.

Borkar, V.R., Carey, M.J., and C. Li. Big Data Platforms: What's Next? *XRDS*, 19(1), 44–49, 2012.

Burghard, C. *Big Data and Analytics Key to Accountable Care Success*. Framingham, MA: IDC Health Insights, 2012.

Connolly, S., and S. Wooledge. Harnessing the Value of Big Data Analytics. *Teradata*, January 2013.

Courtney, M. Puzzling Out Big Data. *Engineering and Technology*, January 2013, pp. 56–60.

Davenport, T.H., ed. *Enterprise Analytics*. Upper Saddle River, NJ: FT Press, Pearson Education, 2013.

Dembosky, A. Data Prescription for Better Healthcare. *Financial Times*, December 12, 2012, p. 19.

EIU. *Big Data—Lessons from the Leaders*. Economic Intelligence Unit, 2012.

Ferguson, M. *Architecting a Big Data Platform for Analytics*. Intelligent Business Strategies, October 2012.

Fernandes, L., O'Connor, M., and V. Weaver. Big Data, Bigger Outcomes. *Journal of AHIMA*, October 12, 2012, pp. 38–42.

Franks, B. *Taming the Big Data Tidal Wave*. New York: John Wiley & Sons, 2012.

Gobble, M. Big Data: The Next Big Thing in Innovation. *Research-Technology Management*, January–February, 2013, pp. 64–65.

HP. *Information Optimization—Harness the Power of Big Data*. December 2012.

IBM. *IBM Big Data Platform for Healthcare*. Solutions brief, June 2012.

jStart. *How Big Data Analytics Reduced Medicaid Re-admissions*. A jStart case study, 2012.

Kumar, A., Niu, F., and C. Re. Hazy: Making It Easier to Build and Maintain Big-Data Analytics. *Communications of the ACM*, 56(3), 40–49, 2013.

Manyika, J., Chui, M., Brown, B., Buhin, J., Dobbs, R., Roxburgh, C., and A.H. Byers. *Big Data: The Next Frontier for Innovation, Competition, and Productivity.* McKinsey Global Institute, 2011.

McAfee, A., and E. Brynjolfsson. Big Data: The Management Revolution. *Harvard Business Review*, October 2012, pp. 61–68.

Mehta, A. *Big Data: Powering the Next Industrial Revolution.* Tableau, April 2011.

Mone, G. Beyond Hadoop. *Communications of the ACM*, 56(1), 22–24, 2013.

Nair, R., and A. Narayanan. *Benefitting from Big Data Leveraging Unstructured Data Capabilities for Competitive Advantage.* Boozandco, 2012.

Ohlhorst, F. *Big Data Analytics: Turning Big Data into Big Money.* New York: John Wiley & Sons, 2012.

Oracle. *Oracle Information Architecture: An Architect's Guide to Big Data.* 2012.

Raden, N. *Big Data Analytics Architecture—Putting All Your Eggs in Three Baskets.* Hired Brains, 2012.

Raghupathi, W. Data Mining in Health Care. In *Healthcare Informatics: Improving Efficiency and Productivity*, ed. S. Kudyba. Boca Raton, FL: Taylor and Francis, 2010, pp. 211–223.

Russom, P. *Big Data Analytics.* TDWI Best Practices Report, 2011.

SAP AG. Harnessing the Power of Big Data in Real-Time through In-Memory Technology and Analytics. In *The Global Information Technology Report.* World Economic Forum, 2012, pp. 89–96.

Sathi, A. *Big Data Analytics.* MC Press Online LLC, 2012.

Savage, N. Digging for Drug Facts. *Communications of the ACM*, 55(10), 11–13, 2012.

Srinivasan, N., and R. Nayar. *Harnessing the Power of Big Data—Big Opportunity for Retailers to Win Customers.* Infosys, 2012.

White, D., and N. Rowe. *Go Big or Go Home? Maximizing the Value of Analytics and Big Data.* Aberdeen Group, 2012.

Zikopoulos, P.C., deRoos, D., Parasuraman, K., Deutsch, T., Corrigan, D., and J. Giles. *Harness the Power of Big Data—The IBM Big Data Platform.* New York: McGraw-Hill, 2013.

Zikopoulos, P.C., Eaton, C., deRoos, D., Deutsch, T., and G. Lapis. *Understanding Big Data—Analytics for Enterprise Class Hadoop and Streaming Data.* New York: McGraw-Hill, 2012.

# 4

# Data Mining Methods
# and the Rise of Big Data

*Wayne Thompson*

## CONTENTS

---

## BIG DATA

*Big data* is a popular term that describes the exponential growth, availability, and use of information, both structured and unstructured. Big data continues to gain attention from the high-performance computing niche of the information technology market. According to International Data Corporation (IDC), "in 2011, the amount of information created and replicated will surpass 1.8 zettabytes (1.8 trillion gigabytes), growing by a factor of nine in just five years. That's nearly as many bits of information in the digital universe as stars in the physical universe."

Big data provides both challenges and opportunities for data miners to develop improved models. Today's massively parallel in-memory analytical computing appliances no longer hinder the size of data you can analyze. A key advantage is you are able to analyze more of the population with a broad range of classical and modern analytics. The goal of data mining is generalization. Rather than rely on sampling, you can isolate hard-to-detect signals in the data, and you can also produce models that generalize better when deployed into operations. You can also more readily detect outliers that often lead to the best insights. You can also try more configuration options for a specific algorithm, for example, neural network topologies including different activation and combination functions, because the models runs in seconds or minutes instead of hours.

Enterprises are also moving toward creating large multipurpose analytical base tables that several analysts can use to develop a plethora of models for risk, marketing, and so on (Chu et al., 2007). Developing standardized analytical tables that contain thousands of candidate predictors and targets supports what is referred to as model harvesting or a model factory. A small team of analysts at Cisco Systems currently build over 30,000 propensity-to-purchase models each quarter. This seasoned team of analysts have developed highly repeatable data preparation strategies along with a sound modeling methodology that they can apply over and over. Customer dynamics also change quickly, as does the underlying snapshot of the historical modeling data. So the analyst often needs to refresh (retrain) models at very frequent intervals. Now more than ever, analysts need the ability to develop models in minutes, if not seconds, vs. hours or days (Figure 4.1).

Using several champion and challenger methods is critical. Data scientists should not be restricted to using one or two modeling algorithms. Model development (including discovery) is also iterative by nature, so

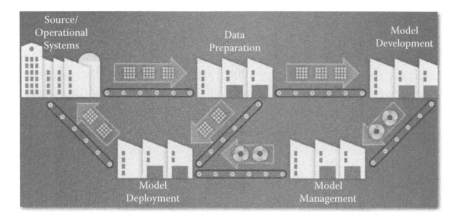

**FIGURE 4.1**
Analytics is moving out of research and more into operations.

data miners need to be agile when they develop models. The bottom line is that big data is only getting bigger, and data miners need to significantly reduce the cycle time it takes to go from analyzing big data to creating ready-to-deploy models.

Many applications can benefit from big data analytics. One of these applications is telematics, which is the transfer of data from any telecommunications device or chip. The volume of data that these devices generate is massive. For example, automobiles have hundreds of sensors. Automotive manufactures need scalable algorithms to predict vehicle performance and problems on demand. Insurance companies are also implementing pay-as-you-drive plans, in which a GPS device that is installed in your car tracks the distance driven and automatically transmits the information to the insurer. More advanced GPS devices that contain integrated accelerometers also capture date, time, location, speed, cornering, harsh braking, and even frequent lane changing. Data scientists and actuaries can leverage this big data to build more profitable insurance premium models. Personalized policies can also be written that reward truly safe drivers.

The smart energy grid is another interesting application area that encourages customer participation. Sensor systems called synchophasers monitor in real time the health of the grid and collect many streams per second. The consumption in very short intervals can be modeled during peak and off-peak periods to develop pricing plan models. Many customers are "peakier" than others and more expensive to service. Segmentation models can also be built to define custom pricing models that decrease usage in peak hours. Example segments might be "weekday workers," "early birds, home worker," and "late-night gamers."

There are so many complex problems that can be better evaluated now with the rise of big data and sophisticated analytics in a distributed, in-memory environment to make better decisions within tight time frames. The underlying optimization methods can now solve problems in parallel through co-location of the data in memory. The data mining algorithms are vastly still the same; they are just able to handle more data and are much faster.

## DATA MINING METHODS

The remainder of the chapter provides a summary of the most common data mining algorithms. The discussion is broken into two subsections, each with a specific theme: classical data mining techniques and machine learning methods. The goal is to describe algorithms at a high level so that you can understand how each algorithm fits into the landscape of data mining methods. Although there are a number of other algorithms and many variations of the techniques, these represent popular methods used today in real-world deployments of data mining systems.

### Classical Data Mining Techniques

Data mining methods have largely been contributed from statistics, machine learning, artificial intelligence, and database systems. By strict definition statistics are not data mining. Statistical methods were being used long before the term *data mining* was coined to apply to business applications. In classical inferential statistics, the investigator proposes some model that may explain the relationship between an outcome of interest (dependent response variable) and explanatory variables (independent variables). Once a conceptual model has been proposed, the investigator then collects the data with the purpose of testing the model. Testing typically involves the statistical significance of the parameters associated with the explanatory variables. For these tests to be valid, distributional assumptions about the response or the error terms in the model need to correct or not violate too severely. Two of the most broadly used statistical methods are multiple linear regression and logistic regression.

Multiple linear regression and logistic regression are also commonly used in data mining. A critical distinction between their inferential applications and their data mining applications is in how one determines suitability of the model. A typical data mining application is to predict an outcome, a target in data mining jargon, based on the explanatory variables, inputs, or features in data mining jargon. Because of the emphasis on prediction, the distributional assumptions of the target or errors are much less important.

Often the historical data that is used in data mining model development has a time dimension, such as monthly spending habits for each customer. The typical data mining approach to account for variation over time is to construct inputs or features that summarize the customer behavior for different time intervals. Common summaries are recency, frequency, and monetary (RFM) value. This approach results in one row per customer in the model development data table.

An alternative approach is to construct multiple rows for each customer, where the rows include the customer behavior for previous months. The multiple rows for each customer represent a time series of features of the customer's past behavior. When you have data of this form, you should use a repeated measures or time series cross-sectional model.

Predictive modeling (supervised learning) techniques enable the analyst to identify whether a set of input variables is useful in predicting some outcome variable. For example, a financial institution might try to determine whether knowledge of an applicant's income and credit history (input variables) helps predict whether the applicant is likely to default on a loan (outcome variable). Descriptive techniques (unsupervised learning) enable you to identify underlying patterns in a data set.

Model overfitting happens when your model describes random noise or error instead of the true relationships in the data. Albert Einstein once said, "Everything should be as simple as it is, but not simple." This is a maxim practice to abide by when you develop predictive models. Simple models that do a good job of classification or prediction are easier to interpret and tend to generalize better when they are scored. You should develop your model from holdout evaluation sources to determine whether your model overfits. Another strategy, especially for a small training data set, is to use $k$-fold cross-validation, which is a method of estimating how well your model fits based on resampling. You divide the data into $k$ subsets of approximately the same size. You train your model $k$ times, each time leaving out one of the subsets that is used to evaluate the model. You can then measure model stability across the $k$ holdout samples.

## *k*-Means Clustering

*k*-Means clustering is a descriptive algorithm that scales well to large data (Hartigan, 1975). Cluster analysis has wide application, including customer segmentation, pattern recognition, biological studies, and web document classification. *k*-Means clustering attempts to find *k* partitions (McQueen, 1967) in the data, in which each observation belongs to the cluster with the nearest mean. The basic steps for *k*-means are

1. Select *k* observations arbitrarily as initial cluster centroids.
2. Assign each observation to the cluster that has the closest centroid.
3. Once all observations are assigned, recalculate the positions of the *k* centroids.

Repeat steps 2 and 3 until the centroids no longer change (Figure 4.2). This repetition helps minimize the variability within clusters and maximize the variability between clusters. Note that the observations are divided into clusters so that every observation belongs to at most one cluster. Some software packages select an appropriate value of *k*. You should still try to experiment with different values of *k* that result in good homogeneous clusters that are relatively stable when they are applied to new data.

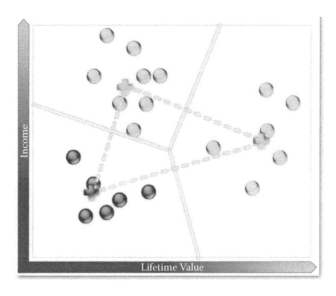

**FIGURE 4.2**
*k*-Means cluster analysis cross symbols represent the cluster centroids.

You should try to select input variables that are both representative of your business problem and predominantly independent. Outliers tend to dominate cluster formation, so consider removing outliers. Normalization is also recommended to standardize the values of all inputs from dynamic range into specific range. When using a distance measure, it is extremely important for the inputs to have comparable measurement scales. Most clustering algorithms work well with interval inputs. Most *k*-means implementations support several dimension encoding techniques for computing distances for nominal and ordinal inputs.

After you group the observations into clusters, you can profile the input variables to help further label each cluster. One convenient way to profile the clusters is to use the cluster IDs as a target variable, and then use a decision tree and candidate inputs to classify cluster membership.

After the clusters have been identified and interpreted, you might decide to treat each cluster independently. You might also decide to develop separate predictive models for each cluster. Other popular clustering techniques include hierarchical clustering and expectation maximization (EM) clustering.

## Association Analysis

Association analysis (also called affinity analysis or market basket analysis) identifies groupings of products or services that tend to be purchased at the same time or purchased at different times by the same customer. Association analysis falls within the descriptive modeling phase of data mining. Association analysis helps you answer questions such as the following:

- What proportion of people who purchase low-fat yogurt and 2% milk also purchase bananas?
- What proportion of people who have a car loan with a financial institution later obtain a home mortgage from that institution?
- What percentage of people who purchase tires and wiper blades also get automotive service done at the same shop?

At a minimum, the data for association analysis contains the transaction ID and an item (Table 4.1).

In the example data, let's assume that the transactions are from listeners of Pandora. The items represent the artist and the song. You can develop

**TABLE 4.1**

Sample Data Layout for Market Basket Analysis

| User ID | Artist Name | Song Title |
|---------|-------------|------------|
| WayneT223 | Black Eyed Peas | "Let's Get It Started" |
| WayneT223 | Coldplay | "Viva La Vida" |
| WayneT223 | Aerosmith | "Crazy" |
| Stephen707 | Black Eyed Peas | "Let's Get It Started" |
| Stephen707 | Amy Winehouse | "Valerie" |

rules that are based on listener preferences for artists or songs. Association rules are based on frequency counts of the number of times that items occur alone and in combination in the transaction record. Confidence and support are important measures that evaluate the strength of the associations (SAS® Enterprise Miner™ 12.1, 2012b). Using the rule A==>B, the confidence for the association rule is the conditional probability that a transaction contains item B, given that the transaction already contains item A. Confidence for the association rule A==>B can be expressed mathematically as the following ratio:

$$\frac{\text{transactions that contain both items A and B}}{\text{transactions that contain item A}}$$

The level of support indicates how often the association combination occurs within the transaction database. In other words, support quantifies the probability of a transaction that contains both item A and item B. Support for the association rule A==>B can be expressed mathematically as the following ratio:

$$\frac{\text{transactions that contain both items A and B}}{\text{all transactions}}$$

Expected confidence for the rule is another important evaluation criterion. It is the proportion of all transactions that contain item B. The difference between confidence and expected confidence is a measure of the change in predictive power due to the presence of item A in a transaction. Expected confidence indicates what the confidence would be if there were no relationship between the items. Expected confidence for the association rule A==>B can be expressed mathematically as the following ratio:

$$\frac{\text{transactions that contain item B}}{\text{all transactions}}$$

A final measure is lift, which is the ratio of the rule's confidence to the rule's expected confidence. In other words, lift is the factor by which the confidence exceeds the expected confidence. Larger lift ratios tend to indicate more interesting association rules. The greater the lift, the greater the influence item A in a transaction has on the likelihood that item B will be contained in the transaction.

You want to isolate interesting rules that have not only high confidence, but also reasonable support and lift values greater than 1. A rule might be: "If a user listens to the Black Eyed Peas, there is a 28% confidence that she will also listen to Coldplay." A support value of 1.5% indicates how frequently this combination of songs appears among all user listening transactions.

Association rules should not be interpreted as direct causation. Association rules define some affinity between two or more items. You can develop rules of a predefined chain length among the set of items. This example rule has a chain length of 2.

The network plot in Figure 4.3 displays rules for the various artists. The maximum number of artists in a rule (chain length) was set to 2. The plot

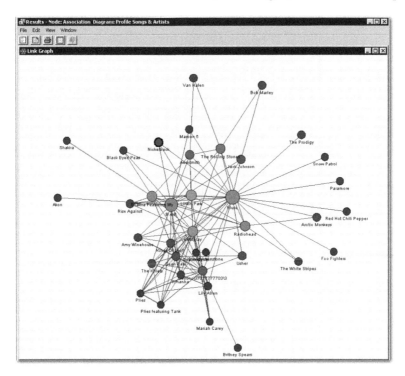

**FIGURE 4.3**
**(See color insert.)** Network plot of artist listening rules derived from market basket analysis.

has been filtered to include only rules that a have confidence of 2 and support of 1. Although they are a bit hard to see, the color and thickness of the lines indicate the confidence of a rule. The color and size of the nodes indicate the counts. There are some very nice clusters of artists based on genre, artist type, and artist hotness. For example, Beyoncé, Mariah Carey, and Britney Spears are connected. You can develop rules for a sample of historical transactions as done here, and then score future listeners to produce recommendations of artists (or songs) that a new user might want to hear.

Association discovery can be extended to sequence analysis for time stamps. An example sequence rule might be: "Of customers who purchased an iPhone, 15% of them will purchase an iPad Mini in the next 6 months."

## Multiple Linear Regression

Multiple linear regression models the relationship between two or more inputs (predictors) and a continuous target variable by fitting a learner model to the training data. The regression model is represented as

$$E(y) = \beta_0 + \beta_1 x_1 + \beta_2 x_2 + \cdots + \beta_k x_k$$

where $E(y)$ is the expected target values, $x$s represent the $k$ model inputs, $\beta_0$ is the intercept that centers the range of predictions, and the remaining $\beta$s are the slope estimates that determine the trend strength between each $k$ input and the target. Simple linear regression has one model input $x$.

The method of least squares is used to estimate the intercept and parameter estimates by the equation that minimizes the sums of squares of errors of the deviations of the observed values of $y$ from the predicted values of $\hat{y}$. The regression can be expressed as

$$\hat{y} = b_0 + b_1 x_1 + b_2 x_2 + \cdots + b_k x_k$$

where the squared error function is

$$\Sigma(Yi - \hat{Yi})^2.$$

Multiple linear regression is advantageous because of familiarity and interpretability. Regression models also generate optimal unbiased estimates for unknown parameters. Many phenomena cannot be described by linear relationships among the target variables and the input variables. You can use polynomial regression (adding power terms, including interaction effects) to the model to approximate more complex nonlinear relationships.

The adjusted coefficient of determination (adjusted $R^2$) is a commonly used measure of the goodness of fit of regression models. Essentially, it is the percentage of the variability that is explained by the model relative to the total variability, adjusted for the number of inputs in your model. A traditional $R^2$ statistic does not penalize the model for the number of parameters, so you almost always end up choosing the model that has the most parameters. Another common criterion is the root mean square error (RMSE), which indicates the absolute fit of the data to the actual values. You usually want to evaluate the RMSE on holdout validation and test data sources; lower values are better.

Data scientists almost always use stepwise regression selection to fit a subset of the full regression model. Remember that the key goal of predictive modeling is to build a parsimonious model that generalizes well on unseen data. The three stepwise regression methods are as follows:

- Forward selection enters inputs one at a time until no more significant variables can be entered.
- Backward elimination removes inputs one at a time until there are no more nonsignificant inputs to remove.
- Stepwise selection is a combination of forward selection and backward elimination.

Stepwise selection has plenty of critics, but it is sufficiently reasonable as long as you are not trying to closely evaluate the *p*-values or the parameter estimates. Most software packages include penalty functions, such as Akaike's information criterion (AIC) or the Bayesian information criterion (BIC), to choose a best subset of predictors. All possible subset regression combination routines are also commonly supported in data mining toolkits. These methods should be more computationally feasible for big data as high-performance analytical computing appliances continue to get more powerful.

Shrinkage estimators such as the least absolute shrinkage and selection operator (LASSO) (Tibshirani, 1996) are preferred over true stepwise selection methods. They use information from the full model to provide a hybrid estimate of the regression parameters by shrinking the full model estimates toward the candidate submodel.

Multicollinearity occurs when one input is relatively highly correlated with at least another input. It is not uncommon in data mining and is not a concern when the goal is prediction. Multicollinearity tends to inflate the standard errors of the parameter estimates, and in some cases the sign of the coefficient can switch from what you expect. In other cases, the coefficients can even be doubled or halved. If your goal is model interpretability, then you want to detect collinearity by using measures such as tolerances and variance inflation factors. At a minimum, you should evaluate a correlation matrix of the candidate inputs and choose one input over another correlated input based on your business or research knowledge. Other strategies for handling correlated inputs include centering the data or redefining the suspect variable (which is not always possible). You can also generate principal components that are orthogonal transformations of the uncorrelated variables and capture $p\%$ of the variance of the predictor. The components are a weighted linear combination of the original inputs. The uncorrelated principal components are used as inputs to the regression model. The first principal component explains the largest amount of variability. The second principal component is orthogonal to the first. You can select a subset of the components that describe a specific percentage of variability in the predictors (say 85%). Keep in mind that principal components handle continuous inputs.

Regression also requires complete case analysis, so it does not directly handle missing data. If one or more inputs for a single observation have missing values, then this observation is discarded from the analysis. You can replace (impute) missing values with the mean, median, or other measures. You can also fit a model using the input as the target and the remaining inputs as predictors to impute missing values. Software packages also support creating a missing indicator for each input, where the missing indicator is 1 when the corresponding input is missing, and 0 otherwise. The missing indicator variables are used as inputs to the model. Missing values trends across customers can be predictive.

Multiple linear regression is predominantly used for continuous targets. One of the best sources for regression modeling is made by Rawlings (1988). Other important topics addressed include residual diagnostics and outliers.

## Logistic Regression

Logistic regression is a form of regression analysis in which the target variable (response variable) is categorical. It is the algorithm in data mining that is most widely use to predict the probability that an event of interest will occur. Logistic regression can be used to estimate fraud, bad credit status, purchase propensity, part failure status, churn, disease incidence, and many other binary target outcomes. Multinomial logistic regression supports more than two discrete categorical target outcomes.

For logistic regression, the expected probability of the event outcome is transformed by a link function to restrict its value to the unit interval. A linear combination of the inputs produces a logit score (the log odds of the event). Maximum likelihood is used to estimate the values of the parameters. Figure 4.4 shows a partial listing of the maximum likelihood estimates along with the absolute regression effect estimates from a stepwise logistic regression that is classifying home equity loan applicants as good or bad.

Some of the candidate inputs that are selected by the stepwise model to classify bad debt status are occupational category (JOB), number of recent credit inquires (NINQ), value of current property (VALUE), amount of loan request (LOAN), and debt-to-income ratio (DEBTINC). Some of the inputs have missing values, so they were imputed (replaced) using either the mode (most frequently occurring value) or the median. These estimates have a prefix of *IMP* to indicate that they are imputed by the software. Logistic

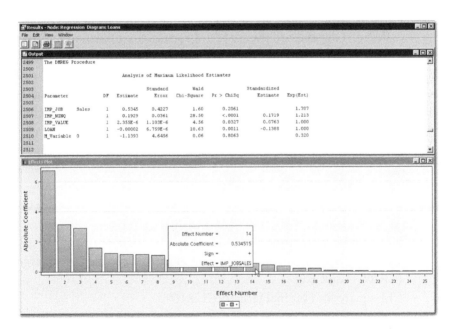

**FIGURE 4.4**
SAS Enterprise Miner logistic regression sample output.

regression also requires complete case analysis; otherwise, any observation that has one or more missing values is discarded from the analysis.

The exponential of a parameter estimate provides an odds ratio. The odds ratio can be thought of as the increase in the primary odds, with being a bad debt applicant associated with a change of one unit in each input. The absolute value indicates the magnitude or relevance of a model effect. For example, the absolute value of 0.535 for the JOB category SALES ranks 14th out of all model effects. The color indicates the sign of the coefficient.

## Decision Trees

A decision tree is another type of analytic approach developed independently in the statistics and artificial intelligence communities. The tree represents a segmentation of the data that is created by applying a series of simple rules. Each rule assigns an observation to a segment based on the value of one input. One rule is applied after another, resulting in a hierarchy of segments within segments. The hierarchy is called a tree, and each segment is called a node. The original segment contains the entire data set and is called the root node of the tree. A node with all its successors forms a branch of the node that created it. The final nodes are called leaves. For each leaf, a decision is made and applied to all observations in the leaf. The type of decision depends on the context. In predictive modeling, the decision is simply the predicted value or the majority class value.

The decision tree partitions the data by recursively searching for candidate input variable thresholds at which to split a node and choosing the input and split point that lead to the greatest improvement in the prediction. Classification and regression trees (Brieman et al., 1984), chi-square automatic interaction detector (Kass, 1980), and C5.0 are the most well-known decision tree algorithms. Each of these algorithms supports one of several splitting criteria, such as the following:

- Variance reduction for interval targets (CHAID)
- $f$-Test for interval targets (CHAID)
- Gini or entropy reduction (information gain) for a categorical target (CART™ and C5.0)
- Chi-square for nominal targets (CHAID)

These algorithms also offer control over how to handle missing values, the depth of tree, the leaf size, pruning, and many other options.

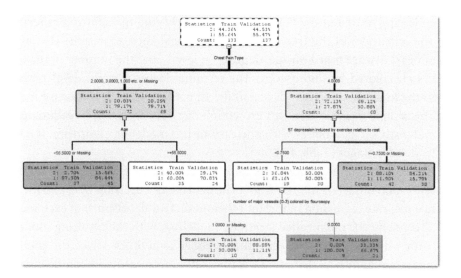

**FIGURE 4.5**
Illustration of a decision tree for classifying two types of heart disease.

The decision (classification) tree in Figure 4.5 displays the results of classifying patients as having one of two types of heart disease. The classification is based on data such as age, alcohol use, blood pressure, and maximum heart rate. For explanatory purposes, a very simple decision tree was grown by partitioning 50% of the data into a training source and 50% into a validation source. Decision trees, like other predictive modeling algorithms, can overfit the data. Validation data is incorporated by the algorithm to automatically prune the decision tree to a simpler fit.

The top-level root node shows that 55.64% of 133 patients in the training data have heart disease type 1 and 44% have type 2 heart disease. The heart disease incidence of patients in the training and validation data is approximately the same because a random sample that is stratified by the target is used prior to growing the tree. The initial split that best separates the two types of heart disease is based on the discrete predictor *chest pain type*. Patients with type 4 chest pain have a 72.13% incidence of type 2 heart disease. Otherwise, the patients tend to have type 1 heart disease. The nodes that result from the chest pain split have essentially the same distribution of chest pain types for both the training and validation data. Large differences in the target distribution indicate an unstable split, which is not the case here. If the training and validation numbers are out of sync, you should consider overriding the tree with a manual split by using one or more of the following methods: an interactive decision tree, collecting more representative data, and modifying the splitting criteria. The remainder of the tree shows the additional successive splits that are of heart disease based on age, depression levels, and the number of major vessels colored by fluoroscopy. The terminal leaves (unsplit data) result in the final classification (decision) for all patients in each respective leaf. This simple decision tree was grown interactively. Decision trees provide many advantages, but as with any easy-to-use modeling algorithm, it has its disadvantages (Table 4.2).

A common strategy for potentially enhancing the predictive ability of regression models is to first stratify the data using a decision tree, and then fit a separate regression model (or other predictive algorithms) in each leaf. This practice is often called stratified modeling, with the resulting model being a hybrid model. The stratified model sometimes solves the problem of nonadditivity. Dividing the population into segments can be more representative of the population. Typically, a small decision tree is grown interactively by the user. The algorithm can help suggest splits, or you can impose your business experience to define a splitting rule. Separate regression models are then developed in each leaf. For example, rather than continuing to grow a decision tree, you may want to define a single splitting rule, such as the chest pain split shown in Figure 4.5, and then use another modeling technique to model the observations in each node.

**TABLE 4.2**

Decision Tree Advantages and Disadvantages

| Advantages | Disadvantages |
| --- | --- |
| Enables interpretation of a model as a sequence of if-then-else rules, especially for smaller trees. | Large decision trees can be hard to interpret. |
| Handles missing values as separate new values or via surrogate (backup) splitting rules. | Can be unstable. Small changes in the underlying data can result in an entirely different decision tree. |
| Accounts for interaction effects. One tip is to export the node ID variable from a decision tree as an input to another model that represents interaction effects. | Uses a step function that can have large errors near boundaries. These errors can result in poor prediction performance for complex nonlinear patterns. |
| Works well with high-dimensional data. | Uses less data after each split (this can also be advantageous). |
| Often used for variable selection and easily ignores redundant variables. | |
| Supports categorical and continuous targets and inputs. | |

## Machine Learning

Machine learning (ML) algorithms are quantitative techniques used for applications that are focused on classification, clustering, and prediction and are generally used for large data sets. Machine learning algorithms also focus on automation, especially the newer methods that handle the data enrichment and variable selection layer. The algorithms commonly have built data handling features such as treating missing values, binning features, and preselecting variables. The term *data mining* has been around for at least two decades. Data mining is the application of statistics, machine learning, artificial intelligence, optimization, and other analytical disciplines to actual research or commercial problems. Many ML algorithms draw heavily from statistical learning research. Characterizing the distribution of variables and the errors from models was central in the works of Fisher, Karl Pearson, and the other seminal thinkers of statistics.

## Neural Networks

Artificial neural networks were originally developed by researchers who were trying to mimic the neurophysiology of the human brain. By combining many simple computing elements (neurons or units) into a highly interconnected system, these researchers hoped to produce complex phenomena such as intelligence. Although there is controversy about whether neural networks are really intelligent, they are without question very powerful at detecting complex nonlinear relationships in high-dimensional data.

The term *network* refers to the connection of basic building blocks called neurons (Bishop, 1995). The input units contain the values of the predictor variables. The hidden units do the internal, often highly flexible nonlinear computations. The output units compute predictions and compare these with the values of the target. A very simple network, such as that in Figure 4.6, has one input layer that is connected to a hidden unit, which is then connected to an output unit. You can design very complex networks—software packages naturally make this a lot easier—that contain perhaps several hundred hidden units. You can define hidden layers that enable you to specify different types of transformations.

The primary advantage of neural networks is that they are extremely powerful at modeling nonlinear trends. They are also useful when the

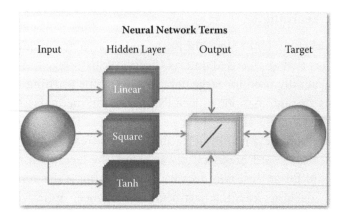

**FIGURE 4.6**

Simple neural network with one hidden layer and three hidden units.

relationship among the input variables (including interactions) is vaguely understood. You can also use neural networks to fit ordinary least squares and logistic regression models in their simplest form.

As with most predictive modeling algorithms, you should be careful not to overfit the training data, which is easy to do for neural networks. Choosing the number of hidden layers and neurons is hard, so it is best to start with simple networks. You should start with simple networks and progressively build and evaluate the benefit of more complex network topologies. Most neural network modeling packages support preliminary runs. Using preliminary runs is highly advisable because it prevents your network from converging to local minima instead of a global minimum. Local minimum is where the network gets trapped in a suboptimal solution instead of finding the true global minimum. A local minimum is analogous to if you start on the side of a mountain and walk downhill, you may find only the local low point, not necessarily the global low point (Figure 4.7).

Neural networks are also often referred to as black boxes; even though they are extremely good at prediction, they are often hard to understand. Like regression analysis, neural networks require you to first replace (impute) missing values before you train the network. The most popular machine learning algorithm today is deep learning neural networks. These new generation neural networks have highly deep and complex architectures that address the issue of local minima by adding unsupervised layer-wise pretraining of deep architectures.

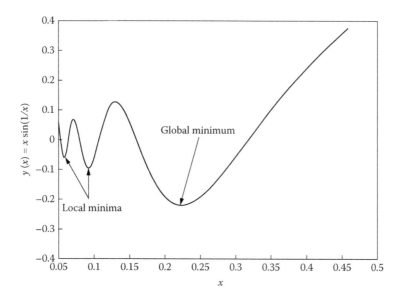

**FIGURE 4.7**
Example local vs. global minimum for a simple function.

## Support Vector Machines

Support vector machines (SVMs) are a powerful machine learning technique for classification and regression (Vapnik, 1995). They work by finding a hyperplane that best splits the target values. The gap (margin) is the largest distance between the borderline data points, or what are called the support vectors (see the points colored yellow) (Figure 4.8). New data

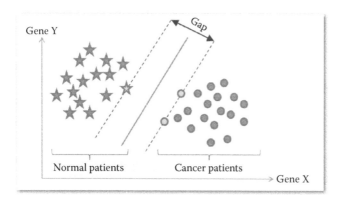

**FIGURE 4.8**
Support vector machines find the hyperplane that best separates the data classes.

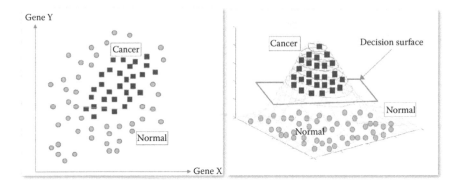

**FIGURE 4.9**
SVMs handle nonlinearity by mapping the data into a higher-dimensional space using kernel tricks.

points are scored based on their position in the decision on the boundary where only the support vectors values are needed.

Naturally, many data are not so easily separable. Patients might fall in the margin or the data may be very nonlinear. To handle nonlinearity, SVMs introduce a kernel trick, which maps the inputs to a higher-dimensional space to enable separation of the classes (Figure 4.9).

SVMs are good at classifying both simple and complex models. Unlike neural networks, they avoid local minima and overfitting.

## Ensemble Models

Ensemble models are now standard in data mining because they perform extremely well on large complex data and because they are automated. *Ensemble* stems from the French word together that means "all the parts considered." One ensemble approach is to use multiple modeling methods, such as a neural network and a decision tree, to obtain separate models from the same training data set. The component models from the complementary modeling methods are averaged to form the final model.

Ensemble models tend to work best when the individual models disagree with one another. Combining linear models often leads to the same model solution. Decision trees are weak learners and are very unstable when presented with new data, but they are excellent candidates for an ensemble model. *Bagging* (Breiman, 1996) is a common ensemble algorithm, in which you do the following:

1. Develop separate models on $k$ random samples of the data of about the same size.
2. Fit a classification or regression tree to each sample.
3. Average or vote to derive the final predictions or classifications.

*Boosting* (Freund and Schapire, 2012) goes one step further and weights observations that are misclassified in the previous models more heavily for inclusion into subsequent samples. The successive samples are adjusted to accommodate previously computed inaccuracies. *Gradient boosting* (Friedman, 2001) resamples the training data several times to generate results that form a weighted average of the resampled data set. Each tree in the series is fit to the residual of the prediction from the earlier trees in the series. The residual is defined in terms of the derivative of a loss function. For squared error loss and an interval target, the residual is simply the target value minus the predicted value. Because each successive sample is weighted according to the classification accuracy of previous models, this approach is sometimes called *stochastic gradient boosting.*

Random forests are my favorite data mining algorithm, especially when I have little subject knowledge of the application. You grow many large decision trees at random and vote over all trees in the forest. The algorithm works as follows:

1. You develop random samples of the data and grow $k$ decision trees. The size of $k$ is large, usually greater than or equal to 100. A typical sample size is about two-thirds of the training data.
2. At each split point for each tree you evaluate a random subset of candidate inputs (predictors). You hold the size of the subset constant across all trees.
3. You grow each tree as large as possible without pruning.

In a random forest you are perturbing not only the data, but also the variables that are used to construct each tree. The error rate is measured on the remaining holdout data not used for training. This remaining one-third of the data is called the out-of-bag sample. Variable importance can also be inferred based on how often an input was used in the construction of the trees.

## Model Comparison

It is very important to compare models that are developed from the same algorithm across challenger methods to help ensure that you select a sound model that is useful for scoring and also provides useful insights (Figure 4.10). It is important to incorporate the following three partitioned data sources into your model building efforts:

- Training data, which are used for preliminary model fitting
- Validation data, which are used to access the adequacy of the model. For example, validation data can be used to stop a neural network, determine the best subtree for a decision tree, or select the final subset of inputs from a stepwise regression.
- Test data, which are used to obtain a final, unbiased estimate of the generalization error of the model.

You should also develop stratified random samples to preserve the ratio of rare target events, such as fraud or other important strata variables, such as cluster codes, geography, and time.

Figure 4.11 provides model comparison statistics for a logistic regression, a decision tree, and a neural network model that is used to classify home equity loans as good or bad. The misclassification chart (see Figure 4.11, top left) displays how often the model correctly classified good applicants (0) and bad applicants (1) in the validation data. The misclassification chart (also called a confusion matrix) is often reported in table format. The decision tree is selected as the best model based on minimizing the

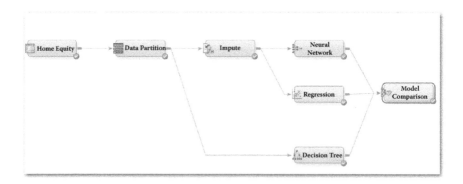

**FIGURE 4.10**

SAS Enterprise Miner process flow analysis. The model comparison node provides a common framework for comparing the predictions from modeling tools.

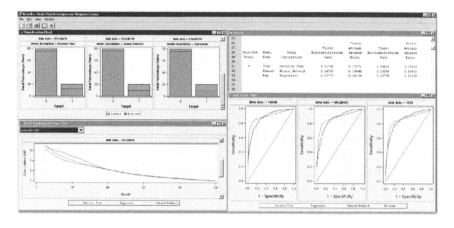

**FIGURE 4.11**
Misclassification chart, cumulative lift chart, fit statistics, and ROC chart for three classification models.

misclassification rate in the validation data. The overall misclassification rate for the decision tree is 11.74% in the validation data (see Figure 4.11, top right). The misclassification rate is also comparable in the test data set (not shown). The lift or gains chart (Figure 4.9, bottom left) shows the cumulative lift for each model using the validation data. Lift is calculated as the ratio between the results obtained with the predictive and using no model. You can also think of lift as how well the model captures the target event (bad credit applicants) across the ranked scored applicants relative to random model. The scores have been sorted from high to low and grouped into 10 deciles. We expect the random baseline model to capture 10% of the bad credit applications in each decile. The decision tree model captures about 35% more bad credit applicants in the second decile (35/10 = 3.5). The cumulative lift is comparable for all three models at about the fourth decile and beyond. Cumulative response and model lift are often used in targeted marketing campaigns to determine an appropriate depth of file for targeting customers.

All these comparison statistics are based on a default posterior probability of 0.5. Any applicant with a score above 0.5 is classified as a bad credit applicant. You might want to modify the cutoff (especially for rare events) to see how this modified cutoff affects the decisions. The receiver operating curve (ROC) (Figure 4.11, bottom right) displays sensitivity vs. 1 – specificity (the true positive rate vs. the positive rate for each model).

|  | **Predicted Nonevent** | **Predicted Event** |
|---|---|---|
| Nonevent (good applicant) | True negative (A) | False positive (B) |
| Event (bad applicant) | False negative (C) | True positive (D) |

- Sensitivity (true positive rate): $100*D/(C + D)$
- Specificity (true negative rate): $100*A/(A + B)$
- 1 – specificity (false positive rate): $100*B/(A + B)$

Because the true positive rate and false positive rate are both measures that depend on the selected cutoff value of the posterior probability, the ROC is calculated for all possible cutoff values. Each point on the curve represents cutoff probabilities. Points closer to the lower left represent higher cutoff probabilities. Points closer to the upper right correspond to lower cutoff points. The extreme points (1, 1) and (0, 0) represent rules in which each case is classified as a events (1) or a nonevent (0). Models that push upward and more to the left have stronger discriminatory power.

## Text Analytics

Text analytics encompasses tools, solutions, and processes for getting the most out of your unstructured text. That text may come from myriad sources—both informal sources such as online complaints, emails, and social media comments, and formal sources such as patent documents, inspection reports, and warranty claims. Regardless of origin, you want to understand and use both the global themes and patterns contained in the collection as a whole, as well as detect the isolated comment buried in a single phrase of a single document that is hidden within tens of thousands of documents.

Text analytics can be viewed from two perspectives. On the one hand, it may involve learning patterns across an entire collection of documents, so that we can apply these patterns to make decisions on new documents. This process is called text mining and requires an entire collection of data in order for the patterns to emerge. Another perspective of text analytics comes from realizing that we understand a lot about language and the way things are written. Given the right tool and the knowledge of what we are trying to identify, we can write rules based on the syntax and grammar of the sentences to extract key information and apply them to vast collections. We refer to this process as knowledge engineering.

In the end, both approaches are important and useful, and can be combined for great benefit to the business analyst. While many companies are just concerned with storing and preserving textual content, the savvy business analyst is looking to automatically leverage text analytics to improve business models and to gain insight that would not otherwise be apparent. The following list is not exhaustive but represents the kinds of projects many business analysts modeling with text accomplish:

1. Gain an understanding of what their customers are saying in email, chat rooms, social media, call center data, and surveys. This can occur with drill-down, as in learning what differences there may be between what your high-profit customers are writing and what your low-profit customers are saying.
2. Monitor patterns and trends in a textual warranty report in order to indicate when issues in the field or in a call center are becoming a serious problem and need intervention.
3. Build a statistical model using text, possibly in addition to other qualitative and quantitative variables, to predict fraud, churn, upsell opportunity, etc.
4. Determine public sentiment toward their new product or any aspects of their product.
5. Analyze your company in comparison with your competition by using public comments on social media sites.
6. Organize and classify your documents so that they are easily explored and found by your user base.

### Accessing the Documents

Text analytics requires several important aspects to enable the analyst to reach these goals. The first component is providing access to the documents. These documents may be contained within a directory on your computer's file system, in SAS data sets, other third-party databases, across the web on html pages, or other kinds of document management systems. In addition, the formats may be stored in a variety of ways, such as MS Word, PDF, html, xml, or plain text. Tools to reach this data and extract the relevant text for analysis are important. Once the documents are accessible, referenced by a table that perhaps contains additional metadata data about the documents, such as demographic information about the author and time stamps, the real text analytics can begin.

### Learning from the Collection: Text Mining

Text mining involves translating the unstructured text to a table form so that either a text-specific algorithm or any of the traditional data mining algorithms can be used.

### From Text to Data Set

The best approaches to text mining require complex language-specific functionality for creating features from text. The simplest approach is to tokenize the text and use terms as features for your data set, but more complex features extraction can also be important, such as using part-of-speech tags and other linguistic elements as features. In addition, users typically apply stop lists to eliminate noise terms and synonyms lists to map terms together that mean the same thing. Another nice technique is to use a statistical spelling correction feature that will help you assign improperly spelled terms to their intended spelling. The end result is a quantitative representation of the collection where each row of the data set represents a document and the extracted features become the variables for the data set. The entries in the cells of this data set are weighted frequencies of the feature counts within each document. See the original matrix in Figure 4.12 for an example.

### Dimension Reduction with Singular Value Decomposition

When the term by document matrix is created, it may have hundreds of thousands of variables, and it will be very sparse, since any one document contains very few of the features in the corpus. As a result, this augmented document goes by the term *data set*, which as input to traditional data mining algorithms needs to be reduced. This is accomplished with a matrix factorization approach known as the singular value decomposition (SVD). The SVD algorithm discovers a weight matrix, shown as weights in Figure 4.12, that allows any document to be projected into a much smaller dimensional space. In the example, the end result is a two-dimensional representation of each. The final reduced matrix for mining maintains the information in the original data set, but compresses it into a much smaller form.

### Exploratory Models

With text mining, you can use the patterns that are found across the collection to enhance exploratory analysis in the following ways:

Original Matrix

| | | Document | Error | Invalid | Message | File | Format | Unable | To | Open | Using | Path | Variable |
|---|---|---|---|---|---|---|---|---|---|---|---|---|---|
| 1 | d1 | | 1 | 1 | 1 | 1 | 1 | 0 | 0 | 0 | 0 | 0 | 0 |
| 2 | d2 | | 1 | 0 | 2 | 1 | 0 | 1 | 1 | 1 | 1 | 1 | 0 |
| 3 | d3 | | 1 | 0 | 0 | 0 | 1 | 1 | 1 | 0 | 0 | 0 | 1 |

Weights

| | $U_2$ | |
|---|---|---|
| Error | 43 | 0.30 |
| Invalid | 0.11 | 0.13 |
| Message | 0.55 | −0.37 |
| File | 0.33 | −0.12 |
| Format | 0.21 | 0.55 |
| Unable | 0.31 | 0.18 |
| To | 0.31 | 0.18 |
| Open | 0.22 | −0.25 |
| Using | 0.22 | −0.25 |
| Path | 0.22 | −0.25 |
| Variable | 0.09 | 0.42 |

Form
Dot
Products

| | | Document | SVD1 | SVD2 |
|---|---|---|---|---|
| 1 | d1 | | 1.63 | 49 |
| 2 | d2 | | 3.14 | −0.96 |
| 3 | d3 | | 1.35 | 1.64 |

Normalize

| | | Document | SVD1 | SVD2 |
|---|---|---|---|---|
| 1 | d1 | | 0.96 | 0.29 |
| 2 | d2 | | 0.96 | −0.29 |
| 3 | d3 | | 0.64 | 0.77 |

**FIGURE 4.12**
A data set representation of a document collection and the results of the singular value decomposition.

- Clustering: Document clustering separates your documents into mutually exclusive sets. There are many algorithms that can be used once the SVD has been applied. Two common approaches are hierarchical clustering, that shows relationships between clusters and subclusters, and a mixed Gaussian model approach that assumes a collection of Gaussian distributions generated the data. For both approaches, you can interpret the discovered clusters by reporting on the terms that characterize them.

- Topic modeling: Another approach that is similar to clustering is topic modeling. Topics are more flexible than clusters because they allow documents to contain or be associated with many topics. One approach to topic modeling rotates the SVD vectors of weights (described earlier in Figure 4.12) in order to more clearly distinguish what subset of terms contribute the most to each dimension. The terms associated with the highest weight become the automated label for the discovered topic. An example is shown in Figure 4.13. Another popular approach to topic models involves latent Dirichlet allocation. This approach assumes the topics were generated from a generative process, and the parameters of that generative process are then optimized to fit the training data.
- Trending and profiling: Another technique that is important in exploratory analysis is the ability to explore the relationships between the text in your documents and any other variable associated with your document. For instance, you might want to report on how complaints written by women differ from those written by men, or if a time stamp on your collection exists, you can indicate what terms are trending over time. Figure 4.14 profiles four different tweeters by reporting on the terms each tweeter tends to use.

### Predictive Models

With labeled textual training data, predictions can be made to do such things as automatically separate documents into categories, or predict an interval-valued variable such as profit. Once the SVD transformation is

Topics

| | | | Recalculate | |
|---|---|---|---|---|
| Topic | Category | Term Cutoff | Document Cutoff | |
| +team,+game,+play,+player,+hockey | Multiple | 0.112 | 0.643 | 253 |
| +program,+system,+problem,+version,+software | Multiple | 0.103 | 0.472 | 301 |
| gordon,+banks,n3jxp,skepticism,chastity | Multiple | 0.086 | 0.475 | 108 |

Terms

| Topic Weight | + | Term | Role | # Docs | Freq |
|---|---|---|---|---|---|
| 0.674 | + | team | Noun | 74 | 176 |
| 0.643 | + | game | Noun | 71 | 173 |
| 0.54 | + | play | Verb | 68 | 135 |
| 0.518 | + | player | Noun | 61 | 138 |

**FIGURE 4.13**
Detected topics and the term weights for the first topic.

**FIGURE 4.14**
Profile of terms commonly used by four tweeters.

done, these tasks can be done with standard data mining models such as regression models, decision trees, neural networks, and other models discussed in earlier sections.

In addition, models designed specifically for text can be applied. One example is an inductive rule learning algorithm. This approach has the benefit of learning rules that are interpretable and useful for categorizing documents. The rules are simply formed from the presence or absence of terms and are marked as significant based on a test such as the chi-square test. An example of such a rule might be "patriot" and "revolution" and not "football" and not "missile." This might be a good predictor that a document that satisfies this rule is about an American Revolution patriot and not a football team or a missile.

### *Digging Deeper with Natural Language: Knowledge Engineering*

While text mining attempts to leverage the entire collection to learn patterns, another important approach for text analytics is to have a domain specialist write linguistic rules for identifying and extracting important information from individual documents. The rules are not derived from a text collection, but rather are created by a specialist who understands the goals of the analysis. As a result, an analyst may write linguistic rules that empower a "classification engine" that automates the organization and retrieval of textual content for people in various divisions of your organization. An example of a tool that allows a user to create these rules is shown in Figure 4.15.

Sentiment analysis is a second goal that often benefits from this user-driven approach. The domain expert writes natural language rules in order to analyze the written sentiment directed toward such things as your company or your company's products or services. The solution helps you

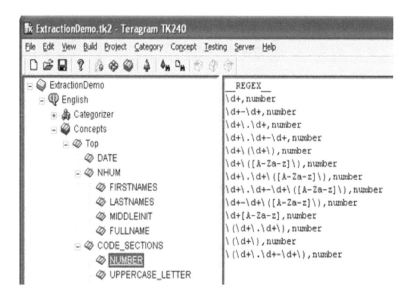

**FIGURE 4.15**
A tool for extracting content from natural language text.

to determine if the expressed attitudes are generally positive or negative, and helps to determine in what ways they are positive or negative.

### Combining Approaches

The best text analytics no doubt leverages both of these approaches. On the one hand, a domain expert may custom design a rule that then becomes an important feature in a statistically based text mining model. On the other hand, a statistical model may inform a domain specialist as to what rules he or she may write. The end result is more effective text analytics.

## REFERENCES

Bishop, C.M. (1995). *Neural networks for pattern recognition.* Oxford: Oxford University Press.

Breiman, L. (1996). Bagging predictors. *Machine Learning,* 24, 123–140.

Breiman, L., Friedman, J.H., Olshen, R.A., and Stone, C.J. (1984). *Classification and regression trees.* Belmont, CA: Wadsworth International.

Chu, R., Duling, D., and Thompson, W. (2007). Best Practices for Managing Predictive Models in a Production Environment. In *Proceedings of the SAS Global 2007 Conference.* Cary, NC: SAS Institute.

Friedman, J.H. (2001). Greedy function approximation: A gradient boosting machine. *Annals of Statistics,* 29, 1189–1232.

Hartigan, J.A. (1975). *Clustering algorithms.* New York: Wiley.

IDC digital universe study. Sponsored by EMC, June 2011.

Kass, G.V. (1980). An exploratory technique for investigating large quantities of categorical data. *Applied Statistics,* 29, 119–127. (Standard reference for the CHAID algorithm Kass described in his 1975 PhD thesis.)

McQueen, J. (1967). Some methods for classification and analysis of ultivariate observations. In *Proceedings of 5th Berkeley Symposium on Mathematical Statistics Probability,* vol. 1, pp. 281–297.

Neville, P. (1999). Growing trees for stratified modeling. *Computing Science and Statistics,* 30. (Extends the ideas of Sonquist et al. and Alexander and Grimshaw for more independent variables and more types of models.)

Rawlings, J.O. (1988). *Applied regression analysis: A research tool.* Belmont, CA: Wadsworth.

SAS Enterprise Miner 12.1. (2012). On-line reference help. Cary, NC: SAS Institute.

Schapire, R. E., and Freund, Y. (2012). *Boosting: Foundations and Algorithms.* Cambridge, MA: MIT Press.

Tibshirani, R. (1996). Regression shrinkage and selection via the lasso. *Journal of the Royal Statistical Society B* (*Methodological*), 267–288.

Vapnik, V. *The nature of statistical learning theory.* New York: Springer-Verlag, 1995.

# 5

## Data Management and the Model Creation Process of Structured Data for Mining and Analytics

*Stephan Kudyba*

### CONTENTS

This chapter provides some essential underpinnings that are required to manage data before analyzing it with mining and analytic techniques. Although emphasis is placed on data issues for directed mining models, many of the essential steps to model creation are applicable to directed analytic methods in general. Directed approaches refer to projects in which the analyst seeks to better understand a target or performance metric of a particular process. The chapter focuses on the selection, formatting, transformation, and normalization of available structured data resources. Emphasis is placed on the development of robust data models that provide decision support for strategic initiatives.

Simply put, do not underestimate the word *data* in data mining or in any analytic approach for that matter. The data preparation stage can sometimes involve 70 to 80% of the time required to conduct an effective analysis. A basic requirement to data is that it must

Be relevant
Be available
Be accurate
Be in a format that can be mined

Just because you have access to a data source doesn't mean that sophisticated mining techniques will uncover magical patterns that will provide a solution to your business conundrum. Data has to be relevant and contain information. In other words, the data source that you are accessing has to include variables that describe/underpin the process you are seeking to better understand. Whether it be the inclusion of demographic and behavioral variables when seeking to better understand customer propensities or general process inputs that describe a particular performance metric, your data resource has to contain relevant/descriptive information to your analysis.

The topic of relevancy does not end with just having the right variables, but data variables must be representative of the scenario the miner is addressing. This involves the issue of currency of data, or in other words, is your data resource a sound representation of the business problem you are addressing? A prime illustration follows:

> Using data resources that include consumer demographics and their response to marketing initiatives from mortgage providers from the year 2006 to estimate consumer propensities to respond to the same marketing initiatives in 2013 would provide little value. The significant change in economic activity and housing industry characteristics has most likely drastically changed consumer behavior in this space.

The above concept presents a reality check for the data mining spectrum. Analysts and decision makers should always be cognizant of the fact that as sophisticated as mining methods may seem, they remain analytic techniques that learn and extract information from the source they are provided with, where the sources should be representative of the scenario that needs to be better understood. This brings us to the next requirement of data resources, namely, are they available?

One of the areas of greatest strategic interest over the past years, and one that will continue to be, is the concept of customer satisfaction. Organizations across industry sectors seek to maintain operations that make their customers happy. However, one of the trickiest variables to attain are metrics that actually measure customer satisfaction. Consider the request by a restaurant owner to better understand whether the operation is yielding customer satisfaction. Most descriptive driver variables are present (menu, ambiance, pricing, service), but the performance or target metric remains elusive. Unless market research tactics of asking patrons to fill out surveys are initiated, the variable may remain difficult to acquire. The important point to remember for this issue is that just because your proposed analysis makes sense, don't assume that even obvious variables are available, where strategic initiatives may be required to generate data for that variable.

Data can be relevant (e.g., contain those variables that are essential to describing processes and have the appropriate currency to the chosen business) and available, but data often contains errors or inaccuracies that can render it unusable in its current form. Errors from data input, whether it be human- or technology-based (column overwrites) or even mislabeled data, can be dangerous to any type of analysis, where seemingly sound results based off of inappropriate inputs will be misleading, to put it mildly.

Finally, the process of acquiring the most robust data source to produce the most informative mining results often includes incorporating variables from a variety of sources (e.g., flat files, web metrics, streaming feeds, legacy databases, central warehouses). Unfortunately, these data sources include recording standards that do not always provide a seamless pathway to conducting analytics. Today's data sources can often include minute, hourly, or daily data points (e.g., web metrics, sensor, electronic data feeds). Analytic models, on the other hand, may require data at the individual consumer level of detail or rolling monthly time series structure, or perhaps daily activities. Data mining methods require analysts to manage data resources into an apples-to-apples format before any true decision support analysis can be initiated.

With all this being said, let's provide a procedural framework for managing data resources so that they provide an accurate and relevant input into a decision support model that is produced by mining or even general analytics such as business intelligence applications.

## ESSENTIAL STEPS TO MANAGING DATA RESOURCES FOR MINING AND ANALYTICS

The process of managing data resources in order that they can become quality inputs to be mined for actionable information involves an organized and stepwise order of activities. As is required for any analytic-based project, the process begins with thinking first and analyzing later. More formally put, this step is the problem definition.

The *problem definition* involves in-depth deliberation over what the true focus of the analytic-based project is looking to better explain. When a decision maker of a banking institution says, "I want to know whether my Internet marketing initiatives are effective," some analysts would be quick to make assumptions in their interpretation of this problem and begin the analytic process. The problem definition stage, however, requires the analyst and business expert to incur a meeting of the minds to hash out a detailed project definition that addresses this business need. An illustration of the process would include the following set of clarifications of the problem.

- Define Internet marketing. (Is it a particular IM tactic, or overall IM initiatives?)
    Banner ad (particular banner types?)
    Mobile apps
    Paid search activities
- Clarify what is meant by the term *effective*. Does *effective* involve cost considerations or is it just consumer response based? Can *effective* be defined by a metric such as
    Click rate
    Conversion (interaction with bank or number of new e-banking accounts)
- Over what time frame is the problem defined? (Are we interested in effectiveness over the past month, quarter, year?) For Internet

marketing tactics, analytics may need to be conducted on an even shorter time frame to truly understand their effectiveness.

Day of week measures

Time of day (hourly measures)

These are just some factors that must be deliberated between the project initiator (usually upper management), business stakeholder, analyst, and data expert, where answers to corresponding questions should be designed in an analytic perspective. Answers to project-specific details should be formatted according to selected data elements and data variables. This forces the idea of qualifying whether the project is simply a query and report-based initiative or data mining project, or whether the endeavor is realistic at all, given existing data resources.

The problem definition stage plays an essential role in qualifying an analytic initiative. It requires existing stakeholders (e.g., analysts, decision makers, data personnel) to formally design a data structure that provides the explanatory value to the project objective. Data relevance, availability, accuracy, and format are key factors to consider during this process. The problem definition stage provides value by reducing wasted time in pursuing a suboptimal analytic endeavor and also enlightens the organization of potential data deficiency issues that can be addressed by pursuing a data collection initiative for variables that may be essential to an important business objective. To sum up the value of the problem definition process:

Identifies the type of analytic project to be undertaken:
- Online analytic processing (OLAP) or basic dashboard reporting
- Statistical/investigative analysis of data variables
- Multivariate data mining

Identifies data sufficiency issues:
- Does essential data exist at the required amounts and formats to provide a solution?

Remember, not all problems require data mining. Some can be answered through simple spreadsheet applications that create reports that illustrate relevant information. Analysts should not force a multivariate application at data that simply isn't minable. Table 5.1 illustrates a prime example that depicts interesting data describing paid search activity in the Internet marketing spectrum. Paid search refers to the internet marketing strategy of paying for keywords (pay per click) that are associated with a website.

**TABLE 5.1**

Paid Search Activity

| Time | Keyword | Impressions | Clicks | Conversions |
|------|---------|-------------|--------|-------------|
| 4/28/08–5/4/08 | Keyword (example 1) | 1918 | 457 | 0 |
| 5/5/08–5/11/08 | Keyword (example 2) | 239 | 55 | 4 |
| 5/5/08–5/11/08 | Keyword (example 3) | 285 | 32 | 1 |
| 5/5/08–5/11/08 | Keyword (example 4) | 668 | 67 | 2 |
| 5/12/08–5/18/08 | Keyword (example 5) | 60 | 2 | 0 |
| 5/12/08–5/18/08 | Keyword (example 6) | 544 | 77 | 2 |
| 5/26/08–6/1/08 | Keyword (example 7) | 463 | 54 | 0 |

The initial instinct of the analyst is to mine the data to identify how keywords, impressions, and clicks may drive conversions (where a conversion is defined as a customer interaction with the company through the website). The inherent problem with this data is that the keyword variable is a unique element that requires analytics at the individual keyword level of detail and renders this variable as a poor candidate as a driver for conversions in a multivariate mining endeavor. Impressions and clicks refer to the amount of times a search advertisement is displayed on a search page and the amount of times that the advertisement is clicked on, respectively. Incorporating either of these as explanatory variables, in the attempt to explain the variance of conversions, would always introduce the question: If more clicks drive more conversions, then what drives clicks, or if more impressions drive more clicks or more conversions, then what drives impressions? The multivariate analysis is useless. A more useful analysis would simply be to sort particular keywords to determine which keyword resulted in more clicks or conversions. Once again, conducting a thorough problem definition and then applying the following steps in the data management spectrum will avoid the process of forcing mining applications to inappropriate data sets.

The following steps provide structure to the problem definition process and will ultimately produce a robust data resource that will be mined to identify noteworthy patterns.

## IDENTIFY YOUR PERFORMANCE METRIC

A problem definition always requires a greater understanding of some activity of an organization.

- What drives product sales?
- What type of person is more likely to respond to our campaign?
- What call center attributes yield the highest customer satisfaction?

The business problem will be defined by a performance metric or target/dependent variable. This variable represents the core issue of what the decision maker is seeking to better understand. In some cases the process of selecting an appropriate target variable may be simple. The first example above, product sales, is self-explanatory. In the case of attempting to estimate probabilities or likelihoods of future behavior of consumers or events occurring, the classic (0/1) binary variable is the simple choice, where (1) refers to a historic event having occurred in the past (e.g., a consumer responding to a marketing initiative) and (0) represents no occurrence. However, when the problem definition involves a more complex metric, the selection of a target variable may require the creation or generation of a variable through the input of a number of variables.

For example, if the problem definition states that the model is to analyze why a bank is experiencing a depletion of deposits in existing accounts, the target variable may require extensive deliberation on a metric that adequately depicts the process of depletion of deposits. Items that must be considered include the following:

- How is the change in account balances measured (by outright dollar amount or percent change, etc.)?
- Over what time horizon will the change in account balances be selected (change from a given month's ending balance on a year-over-year basis?)?
- What types of accounts are to be included (checking, savings, money market, etc.)?

The answer to this type of situation requires a joint analytic approach that involves the business expert, or the bank expert in this case, and the analyst. Only the business expert can shed light on the subtleties of the business environment that must be incorporated in the creation of a viable performance or target variable. Cutting corners in this step by selecting a generic variable can yield critical problems as the mining process evolves. Once a viable and appropriate target variable has been selected, the mining endeavor can move to the next step.

## FORMATTING YOUR DATA TO MATCH YOUR ANALYTIC FOCUS

What this section really focuses on is avoiding that age-old adage "comparing apples to oranges." One of the essential factors to producing a useful model is to format your data resources in a consistent approach that addresses the focus of your project definition. Most individuals would think that once a target variable had been identified, the next step would be to identify your independent or explanatory variables. Logically, that would make sense; however, one must define the level of detail of the data to be analyzed that corresponds with the project focus. This level of detail or format structure could render seemingly useful variables unusable.

Formatting issues to consider include not only the process to be analyzed, but also the way the analysis is to be structured. Will the model be a cross-sectional or time series focus? In other words, will the analysis seek to process data that describes a process over a snapshot of time (cross-sectional), or take on an initiative that requires a process over a period of time (time series). Cross-sectional data often entails a binary (0/1) target value, measuring whether an event occurred or not (e.g., someone opened or closed an account), but can entail outright numeric variables as well. In the realm of big data, a term that has evolved is micro-marketing. This entails the inclusion of descriptive/demographic and behavioral data of consumers as explanatory variables and some performance metric as the target. The corresponding format of this type of analysis requires that all variables be at the individual consumer level of detail. A simple banking application is illustrated below.

The data in Table 5.2 is used to identify the type of consumer that is more likely to actively use e-banking.

Both demographic dependent variables (age, marital status) and descriptive/behavioral variables (ATM use, checks written, monthly balance) must be at a consistent individual/customer level of detail that corresponds to the binary target of whether the person actively uses e-banking or not. Conversely, if the analysis turned from an individual consumer focus to a bank performance focus, all data elements of corresponding variables would have to pertain to a given bank.

When leveraging a time focus in an analytic model, a number of issues must be addressed in order to preserve the integrity of the approach. One of the most underestimated variables existing in applications across

**TABLE 5.2**

E-Banking Activity

| Person | Age | ATM Monthly Transactions | Marital Status | Monthly Checks | Accounts | Average Month Balance (Checking) | E-Banking |
|--------|-----|--------------------------|----------------|----------------|----------|----------------------------------|-----------|
| KDG | 53 | 5 | Married | 5 | Checking | $5597 | 0 |
| WEF | 50 | 8 | Single | 12 | Checking | $1974 | 1 |
| SHT | 29 | 24 | Married | 4 | Checking | $9626 | 0 |
| HH | 21 | 11 | Married | 0 | Checking/MMkt. | $1156 | 0 |
| GGN | 36 | 23 | Married | 7 | Checking/MMkt. | $5134 | 0 |
| THT | 32 | 22 | Married | 3 | Checking/MMkt. | $2330 | 0 |
| TTW | 54 | 3 | Single | 8 | Checking | $4173 | 1 |
| AHY | 21 | 13 | Single | 3 | Checking/MMkt. | $3314 | 0 |
| FDO | 46 | 28 | Single | 15 | Checking | $303 | 1 |
| JMG | 41 | 27 | Single | 7 | Checking | $5643 | 1 |
| BJU | 32 | 29 | Single | 9 | Checking/MMkt. | $8549 | 0 |

processes is the time stamp of a particular data resource. Depending on the level of detail of how an event is recorded, time data can describe elements in minutes, hours, days, weeks, months, and years. The analyst must follow the problem definition and maintain a consistent format when modeling the data. For example, the effects of advertising dollars spent on product revenue usually follow a monthly time series approach, where other applications such as train ridership analyses may seek to estimate daily ridership patterns over an extended period of time (see Table 5.3). The data resource to be modeled/analyzed must adhere to a consistent formatting structure that matches the focus of the analysis.

The train ridership analysis may entail additional formatting issues, which involve the transformation of a time/date variable (e.g., 03/15/13) to a categorical variable (e.g., Friday) in order to determine its effects on a particular metric. Consider the initial date column to the left. This simple data element can be categorized into three explanatory variables to describe ridership that resembles a classic seasonality analysis (what time elements impact ridership). The data variable can incorporate day, month, and year, where day has been included in the table. The important issue to keep in mind is that if day of week is chosen as the focus of the analysis in a ridership model, then all corresponding variables must be at

**TABLE 5.3**

Time Elements of Train Ridership

| Date | Day | Origin/Destination | Train | | Riders |
|------|-----|--------------------|-------|--|--------|
| 03/15/13 | Friday | Summit/Penn | Peak | 7:00 a.m. | 8,800 |
| 03/18/13 | Monday | Summit/Penn | Peak | 7:00 a.m. | 11,350 |
| 03/19/13 | Tuesday | Summit/Penn | Peak | 7:00 a.m. | 13,210 |
| 03/20/13 | Wednesday | Summit/Penn | Peak | 7:00 a.m. | 13,000 |
| 03/21/13 | Thursday | Summit/Penn | Peak | 7:00 a.m. | 13,350 |
| 03/22/13 | Friday | Summit/Penn | Peak | 7:00 a.m. | 9,100 |

that level of detail. This last point provides a transition to the next step in conducting a mining analysis, which involves identifying possible driver or independent variables that provide descriptive information as to what is affecting your performance metric.

## SELECTING DRIVER VARIABLES THAT PROVIDE EXPLANATORY INFORMATION

Identifying driver or independent data in the mining process involves the selection of variables that can possibly impact a given target or performance metric. In other words, the analyst must identify those variables that impact the movement or variance of a target/performance metric. The era of big data has added great value and complexity to this process. As we mentioned previously, big data is not just volume of data, but also the emergence of new data variables that describe/underpin processes. The value comes in the idea that decision makers can achieve a greater understanding as to what drives metric variances given the introduction of new data variables.

Consider the process of determining car insurance premiums. Traditional variables that usually are incorporated in this include driver demographic information, driving history, geographic location of driver activity, and automobile type, to name a few. The big data era with GPS data sources can perhaps augment this process given available information regarding accident rates at particular geographic locations. Insurance providers could potentially better estimate the risk of drivers who may routinely travel in such areas. Simply put, the existence of new driver variables from the big data era can provide greater explanatory information for decision makers. Chapter 6 illustrates the evolution of modeling consumer activities with the introduction of such new data sources including weather and web-related searches on relevant topics to add explanatory power to the analysis. However, with the emergence of new data variables comes the complexity of identifying these new data sources and merging them with existing data resources. This last concept requires thorough consideration of the data formatting section just described.

When selecting driver variables a number of issues must be investigated where again, the era of big data adds complexity to the process. A major technical modeling issue that arises when selecting and adding driver variables to an analysis is the existence of strong relationships between driver variables and also the potential of selecting a driver that is a proxy variable of your performance metric. In mining applications, strong relationships between driver variables result in collinearity, which renders the identification of a particular driver variable's impact on a performance metric unstable and of little value to the final analysis. The second point, which involves the selection of a proxy variable, is equally as detrimental to the analysis, where the resulting model incorporating a proxy would simply depict a near-perfect statistic on explained variance of the performance metric (e.g., $R^2$ of 0.99), but no real descriptive value to the decision maker as to the reasoning for the movement in the performance metric. Table 5.4 illustrates this.

A model that seeks to analyze the potential drivers of ATM fees that would incorporate the number of out-of-network transactions (number of transactions) as a potential driver has a major flaw. The performance metric of revenue/fees is estimated as a dollar amount charged per out-of-network transactions. It is therefore a direct function of the number of transactions variable. The model could be useful in determining the impact of geographic locations of fees generated by an ATM (e.g., zip code)

**TABLE 5.4**

Proxy Variables in ATM Usage

| Zip Code | Location | Number of Transactions | Revenue/Fees |
|---|---|---|---|
| 06550 | Drive-thru | 2100 | $4,200 |
| 06450 | Mall | 3400 | $6,800 |
| 06771 | Retail outlet | 6700 | $13,400 |
| 06466 | In bank | 1000 | $2,000 |
| 06470 | Gas station | 1200 | $2,400 |
| 06450 | Mall | 2400 | $4,800 |
| 06771 | Grocery store | 850 | $1,700 |

and a more detailed location variable (e.g., mall); however, the variable number of transactions will negate the impacts of these former variables given its proxy status for fees.

Analysts can perform a quick check to help safeguard against including variables in an analysis that are too closely related. Most mining software applications enable analysts to conduct a correlation analysis between those, where variables with extremely high correlation coefficients should be scrutinized more closely as potential causes for instable model results.

In the driver variable selection process, the inclusion of process experts is imperative once again. Analysts need to correspond with subject matter experts when seeking to identify the most relevant drivers that affect or impact the performance metrics. These experts not only possess inherent insights as to the scope of variables that come into play that describe targets, but also may be aware of where many of the data variables exist. In fact, the deliberation between the analyst and process expert may result in the creation of new variables.

The healthcare industry is increasing its emphasis on better understanding what drives patient satisfaction. With adequate data resources, data mining methods could easily be incorporated to provide explanatory information on this topic. The term *adequate* is the key here. It is only when process experts and analysts deliberate over the inputs to a model does adequacy become defined. Robust models that depict the factors that impact a patient's satisfaction require the input of subject matter experts in a healthcare facility who know the subtleties of the processes that affect the patient experience. Deliberations between analysts, healthcare service experts, and data professionals are essential to identifying available/relevant data that comprises the model.

- Decide over what time frame you wish to analyze data (over the past month, quarter, year).
- The area of the hospital to be examined (ER, ICU, LND, cardio, etc.).
- Query data repositories for variables that address the question at hand, such as
  - Attending physician
  - Diagnostic category of patient
  - Staffing of nurses (particular attending nurses and amount staffed)
  - Length of stay for the patient
  - Room style

Often when defining the important variables for an analysis, reality illustrates a lack of important data resources. At this point, if a key driver is not available, it needs to be generated.

## ACQUIRE AND ANALYZE YOUR DATA SOURCE

Now that all these steps have been followed with input from the analyst, subject matter experts, and IT data people, it's time to put your data resource together with the intent to mine it. Before you get too excited about identifying patterns and creating models, there are still some data management issues that need to be addressed. Some major factors to keep in mind include the following:

- The amount of data that is available
- Potential errors in your data
- The existence of outliers

What these factors generally refer to are polishing techniques to ensure your data has solid integrity. Whether you gathered your data from a central mart or warehouse or from a number of repositories around an organization, the process of extraction according to variable formats and consolidating them to one source can introduce data issues that can adversely affect your analysis.

### Amounts of Data

Depending on the mining analysis you plan on conducting, you must ask yourself: Do you have enough data? Segmentation techniques or undirected techniques such as clustering often require voluminous records in order for the analysis to be valid. This data volume issue is essential in the directed approaches of neural networks or regression as well. Consider a time series analysis where you wish to determine advertising effectiveness on product sales on a monthly basis, where seasonality comes into play. As an analyst you need a minimum of two occurrences of a categorical variable in order to determine any reliable patterns (e.g., advertising effects on revenue for February need at least two data elements of February). Also,

**TABLE 5.5**

Categories That Are Drivers

| Name | Age | Contact | Gender | Response |
|------|-----|---------|--------|----------|
| JCP | 20 | Email | M | Yes |
| FRE | 27 | Email | F | No |
| MBT | 55 | Mobile app | F | No |
| AWE | 41 | Phone | M | No |
| MIL | 38 | Mobile app | M | Yes |
| JBR | 29 | Email | F | Yes |

keep in mind that when working with categorical variables, each category is actually an addition of another driver variable to a model.

In the simple data sample in Table 5.5 that depicts some demographic and operational variables (e.g., how a person was contacted with a marketing message), the analyst must keep mind that each category in the contact variable introduces an additional driver variable and requires multiple instances of that variable. If you don't have enough data, you need to begin collecting it or seek other variables that are a proxy for those variables that are needed that may be in greater abundance.

We are now in the era of big data, however, and this may imply the analyst simply has too much data to manage. Keep in mind a few factors that can alleviate this issue:

- A random sample can be taken as a subset of the data resource.
- Consider those technologies that can handle large volumes of data.
- Consider the first step in the analytic process (define the problem you want to solve).

If your platform cannot handle/process millions of records of data, the analysts can use a random sample generator to extract much less voluminous but representative sample data from original sources. For voluminous data resources, many prominent mining vendors (SAS, IBM, etc.) have the ability to process extremely large data sets.

Perhaps the most important concept to keep in mind is the initial step of your project definition. Many times the problem to be solved provides a filter to the massive data resource problem. If you are looking to analyze marketing effectiveness on product sales or demographic response estimation, many times this analysis has to consider only more local markets (e.g., tristate) rather than a national database. In conducting healthcare process analysis, your problem definition may stipulate analysis according to a particular diagnosis or physician specialty. The focus of the problem often reduces very large data sets to much smaller resources.

In mining applications requiring the processing of truly big data (e.g., Internet-related analysis involving fraud detection or real-time financial market activities), real-time mining (e.g., streaming mining techniques) can be applied. This concept is described in Chapters 2, 8, and 9.

## Cleansing Your Data from Errors

Data input, extraction, and consolidation activities for analysis can often produce errors. These can take the form of column overwrites and blanks, to name a few. As simple as these errors may be, they must be addressed before the mining process is undertaken. Cleansing your data from these errors often depends on the type of data you are using. A blank in a time series approach can be addressed in a few ways. Consider the data in Table 5.6 that depicts a time series approach to estimating the impact of monthly advertising on product revenue.

The analysts can use interpolation to input a reasonable data point for the blank in April 2010. This is done by simply adding the ad spend data from March and May and dividing by 2. The analyst can also take an average of all April data points in the data set. Finally, the data point can be left blank, and the mining algorithm will simply ignore the row of data. This can pose a problem when the data set being used is small (remember, each month needs multiple data elements in order for a comparison to be conducted). Most importantly, a 0 is not an acceptable value to be input in the blank. Mining algorithms will interpret the 0 as a real number, and in the given case, this would greatly skew the analysis.

**TABLE 5.6**

Missing Data in Time Series

| Date | Price | Ad Spend | Revenue |
|------|-------|----------|---------|
| 010110 | $45 | $2100 | $4200 |
| 020210 | $43 | $3400 | $5800 |
| 030110 | $43 | $4700 | $6340 |
| 040410 | $41 | | $5800 |
| 050210 | $39 | $2800 | $5100 |
| 060110 | $40 | $2500 | $4800 |
| 070110 | $38 | $2200 | $3900 |

When dealing with cross-sectional data or data that represents a snapshot in time rather than longitudinal (an analysis over time), errors must also be addressed; however, techniques such as interpolation or averaging are not valid. Depending on the volume of data you are looking to mine, blanks can simply be ignored, as algorithms will skip that row (this is more acceptable with large numbers of rows in relation to columns of data). One of the problems with errors in data is that they may be difficult to identify given large data files. Can you envision yourself scanning 500,000 rows of data to identify errors? One way around this is to use software to do to the work for you. Mining platforms are equipped with data diagnostic functions that often involve visual capabilities. An example is provided in Figure 5.1.

A simple visual of a categorical variable distribution shows that the file contains roughly 45% married and 49% single individuals. The visual also shows the analyst that two additional categories exist, with one data element in each. The first is MXX, and the second depicts a blank. This informs that analyst that the data source contains two elements that are erroneous. The process of analyzing data variable distributions can be done with each variable in the data file.

When dealing with continuous variables (e.g., income), analysts should view the data distribution to identify elements referred to as outliers. Outliers are data points that fall significantly outside the normal distribution of the range of the data elements. A simple chart/visual of the variable distribution (Figure 5.2) depicts an outlier.

The normal range of the income variable is from $20,000 to $100,000. The outlier is a data point that is $1,000,000. Outliers are not errors but

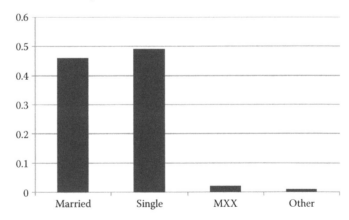

**FIGURE 5.1**
Charts depicting errors in data files.

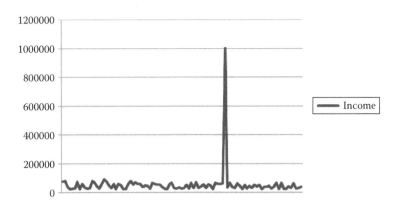

**FIGURE 5.2**
Visual depicting outliers.

anomalies in data. In other words, they are real and accurate data but don't belong in the sample you are looking to analyze. Consider them anomalistic entities that will skew your analysis.

## Transformation of Variables to Provide More Robust Analysis

At this point, your problem has been clearly defined, and variables identified, acquired, and screened for errors and anomalies. There is yet one more stage in the data management process that should be considered before mining the resource. This process involves transforming variables to possibly provide a more robust/descriptive analysis of the problem at hand. Transforming does not refer to reformatting a variable, but rather selecting a variable and transforming it to something else that may provide greater explanatory value to a model.

The classic example of this is depicted in the change from incorporating overall sales as a target variable to market share. Market share as a target often helps mitigate issues regarding seasonal variations in data (described later in this chapter). The transformation process is simply dividing the organization's revenue by the industry revenue to obtain a percent share of revenue or market share.

Another example of this is depicted in a product price variable, which may be used as a driver in a mining analysis. A company's product price often does not reflect initiatives undertaken by competitors. A more appropriate variable in some instances is the incorporation of relative price, or a company's product price relative to that of the average price of similar products in an industry. The transformation is simply individual product price, divided by the average price of similar products in an industry. The transformed variable now encapsulates competitive behavioral impact on an organization's revenue. An often overlooked variable in an employee performance or customer value analysis involves a start date variable of when an employee started a job or a customer first signed up for a service for your company. Although the variable in its crude form is difficult to use, a simple transformation that subtracts start date from some future date provides the variable "time at the job" or "duration as a customer," which can provide essential descriptive power to a model.

The transformation process usually comes after the near final data resource is to be mined. The analyst in conjunction with the business expert can brainstorm to create the data resource that will provide the most informative model for decision makers.

## IT'S TIME TO MINE

It seems as if the preceding activities were endless, but a point to be stressed at this juncture is that the integrity of any analysis is dependent on the quality of the data input that provides the building blocks to a model. A positive to consider at this point is that the better the prep, the easier the mining process, as the analyst can now unleash the power of selected techniques to uncover actionable information in the form of reliable patterns and relationships that may exist. The analyst must now use available statistical metrics to interpret the validity and output of the analysis.

When utilizing more traditional techniques such as regression, standard statistics to consider involve $R^2$ for overall explanatory power of the model and $t$- and $p$-statistics to measure individual variable significance within the multivariate endeavor. Other standard statistics include $F$-statistics and even Durban-Watson metrics. For machine learning approaches and segmentation and clustering methods, software platforms usually include some metrics that resemble the traditional statistics mentioned (e.g., goodness-of-fit metric), which are similar to an $R^2$. An important point to keep in mind is for the analyst to work with the results, rather than attempt to improve or change them by tweaking or massaging the data (which may introduce ethical breaches given the extent of such tweaking activities).

A more appropriate way of seeking to enhance a model's results is the addition of new data and remodeling the scenario.

## INTERPRETING THE RESULTS (AN INPUT FOR DECISION MAKING)

You've mined your data and results have been achieved, but if you think your work is done as an analyst, think again. Remember, mining data is done to provide actionable information for decision makers. This implies that mining results must be analyzed, interpreted, and perhaps remined to produce valued information for strategists. When interpreting the results of a model, the miner must keep in mind some essential issues:

- Do the model results produce reliable patterns/relationships applicable to the original project definition?
- Do the results make sense?

Just because data has been collected, cleansed, and processed with algorithms or mathematical equations, it doesn't mean that a coherent and meaningful result will be achieved. Data mining is not a crystal ball. The methods will only produce valuable results if patterns truly exist in the data. Once again, to achieve a sound interpretation of model results, the analyst needs to involve the input of a business/subject matter expert to help validate relationships and patterns identified. Even if mining results have uncovered some pattern not considered in the past, input from the business/process side needs to be consulted to qualify the meaning. When the mining process yields little value (e.g., patterns and statistics are suspect), the analyst needs to consider the following issues:

- Did you miss some important variables, or can existing variables be transformed to more accurately capture the process analyzed?
- Was there enough data describing the process (e.g., enough instances of data relative to variables used in the analysis)?
- Did you consider the correct mining approach in analyzing the business process (e.g., were lags considered for advertising effectiveness, or relative price for true price elasticity)?
- Did you miss outliers in the data resource?

The final section in this chapter provides some noteworthy insights to address to adjust your mining analysis in certain instances.

## COMMUNICATING THE RESULTS TO ACHIEVE TRUE DECISION SUPPORT

A common problem that exists in the realm of analytics and decision support is a potential disconnect in understanding between the analyst's perspective and that of the business/decision maker. Sophisticated miners are often entrenched in a data, statistics, and quantitative frame of mind, as they should be, but this can introduce an obstacle in the communication process in describing the value of resulting models. The decision maker is more focused on actionable information that can be utilized to enhance strategic initiatives, and not so much on the technical analytic methods with which it was generated. Delving into the realm of knowledge management, effective transfer of information is when the receiver of the resource fully comprehends its meaning. In other words, when presenting/communicating mining results, analysts must keep in mind the focus of the receiver of the information, which is the business or process expert. Involving too much technical jargon of how results were achieved can quickly inhibit the value to the audience. Some points to keep in mind when communicating analytic results are

- Know your stakeholders relative to the mining results (what their skill base is and what their interests are regarding strategy).
- Extract process-related, relevant information the mining model addresses when presenting the results to corresponding stakeholders to enhance the transfer effect to the ultimate user of the information.
- Involve a process expert that is well versed in analytic approaches to disseminate the model results to the business stakeholders.

Remember, a user base that has difficulty in understanding the value of a resource often chooses not to implement it, where the ultimate result is that it gets put on a shelf. Don't assume that the decision-making community will be awed by analytics.

## THE PROCESS IS NOT FINISHED YET (MONITOR THE RESULTS IN THE REAL WORLD)

Mining results can help enhance strategic initiatives on a number of fronts across functional areas of an organization. They can enhance response rates in marketing, better identify fraudulent activities, improve advertising effectiveness, increase site traffic, improve success rates of new store locations, etc. However, as was mentioned previously, data mining does not produce a crystal ball effect. Just because robust models were generated from high-quality data, their accuracy or performance in the marketplace can be subpar. Strategic initiatives based on analytics need to be monitored for their effectiveness in practice, where subpar results need to be investigated in order to identify the origin of the problems. Some of the problems may be mining related and some may not. Regardless of the source of the problem, decision makers must extract feedback from their strategic initiatives in order to learn from successes or failures. This feedback process is often connected to the problem definition stage.

Before embarking on the analytic endeavor, strategists sought to better understand a particular process by utilizing mining methods to uncover patterns. The process should have a performance metric that measures the process output. This provides a simple starting point to a feedback mechanism. If the marketing department sought to enhance email or direct mail responses through incorporating data mining, response rates following the marketing optimization process from data mining models need to be compared to rates prior to the endeavor. If the performance of the process has not been improved, consider the following points:

- Did the data resource that was mined reflect the characteristics in the market in which the results were deployed? In other words, did the analyst use out-of-date data that was not representative of the current market, or did the marketplace change from the state when the model was created? Macroeconomic factors play a significant role in this scenario. An abrupt change in the economy can quickly change consumer activity, which can affect process performance in any area.
- Did factors within a given organization change that may affect a given process performance (e.g., did outsourcing call centers result in consumer dissatisfaction that ultimately reduced product sales?)?

- Did competitor activity affect the performance of a strategic initiative? Aggressive price leadership moves, advertising campaigns, and new product introductions can render strategic performance anemic.
- Were poor modeling techniques utilized (e.g., missing important variables, not incorporating lags if required, including data elements outside the focus of the problem statement)?

## Business Intelligence to the Rescue

With the exception of the last factor (poor modeling), these issues largely encompass general strategy of an organization and are not particularly grounded in the results of data mining. An answer to identifying and addressing broad operational issues involves a well-informed employee base. Only a well-informed organization will be able to identify the source of problems, understand their roots, and take the appropriate action to address them. This introduces another form of analytics, mentioned earlier in Chapter 2, that involves the incorporation of a business intelligence (BI) platform. As we described, BI involves the effective management of data and ultimate creation and dissemination of actionable information. It begins with generating timely and accurate reports and making them accessible to those who require the content. The next stage is the creation of OLAP cubes that enable decision makers to navigate (slice and dice) through levels of details of descriptive variables according to relevant metrics over available time intervals. Finally, well-designed dashboards keep decision makers informed on an ongoing basis regarding operational key performance indicators (KPIs).

This pipeline of information needs to be accessible to those who require it to make informed decisions. The more traditional approaches involve the dissemination of information on organizational networks (web reports and cubes), where newer initiatives that enhance accessibility involve the incorporation of cloud technology. Cloud applications can streamline the information reporting process by providing accessibility to stakeholders wherever they may be.

The last factor listed that can yield suboptimal results in the marketplace involves the issue of poor modeling techniques. Effective mining requires not only that the analyst has as much pertinent data as possible to describe a particular process, but also that the modeler incorporates initiatives to most effectively describe the process. The following section provides some suggestions to keep in mind in the mining process in order to produce the most relevant results.

## ADDITIONAL METHODS TO ACHIEVE QUALITY MODELS

Just because data has been identified, gathered, and scrubbed for errors and outliers, there continue to be factors that must be kept in mind to achieve the best results from mining, where different processes introduce new factors to address. Consider the example of a vehicle manufacturer that wants to better understand radio and email advertising for its pickup truck category and is leveraging the data in Table 5.7. The data source that includes sales revenue for different regions around the country (state) may be problematic for a mining analysis. The analyst must realize that regions can vary in size and introduce differing consumer habits (some states are high purchasers of pickup trucks, while others are not). Therefore, effective radio and email advertising in one region may be offset by a naturally low-consuming region and provide little value to the endeavor.

Another modeling issue to consider is that certain states are larger and have greater populations, and truck purchases involve a naturally large sales volume. This could once again skew the impact of radio advertising. A method to consider alleviating this issue entails normalizing the data. This involves incorporating a performance measure such as per capita sales, which would account for the size of market differentials according to rows of data. Also, to address the potential of apples-to-oranges issue (including states around the nation in one data set), a more effective approach would be to analyze regions (e.g., northeast) that may represent a more homogenous consumer base toward the product. This would better illustrate the media/radio effect on sales.

**TABLE 5.7**

Adjusting Variables for Consistent Mining

| State | Dealers | Media | Average Air Time | Emails | Sales |
|-------|---------|-------|------------------|--------|-------|
| New Jersey | 60 | Radio | 35 min | 200,000 | $125,000 |
| California | 97 | Radio | 52 min | 350,000 | $86,000 |
| South Carolina | 55 | Radio | 45 min | 125,000 | $200,000 |
| Connecticut | 51 | Radio | 23 min | 195,000 | $145,000 |
| Nevada | 30 | Radio | 60 min | 85,000 | $67,000 |
| Florida | 69 | Radio | 75 min | 165,000 | $85,000 |
| Pennsylvania | 51 | Radio | 80 min | 175,000 | $220,000 |

## Advertising Effectiveness and Product Type

The area of advertising effectiveness introduces yet another modeling issue to consider, and this involves the measuring of advertising impact over time. Many advertising strategies are not meant to invoke immediate consumptive impulses, but rather build awareness for consumers to purchase over some time horizon. In seeking to measure true advertising effectiveness, the analyst should consider incorporating lags of the ad spend variable on sales.

Remember, in conducting a time series analysis, a minimum of two data points of each time interval is required for comparison purposes. In the data in Table 5.8, the modeler should consider mining the impact of January ad spend on January sales, January ad spend on February sales, and January ad spend on March sales. The amount of lagging usually is dependent on the type of advertising conducted (e.g., brand awareness) and the type of product. The impact of ad spend could have more immediate effects on more frequently consumed products (e.g., fast food), where there is little to no lag from the ad initiative. Once again, the input of business experts (advertising executive in this case) and analysts is essential to producing valuable results.

When seeking to analyze pricing initiatives, the modeler needs to consider seasonality patterns that could distort the true relationship between price and sales. A prime example is seen during the high-sales holiday season where despite no price discounts for products, actual sales may increase during November and December. The model relationship could potentially depict a scenario where price increases could be associated with sales increases. One way to mitigate this potential problem is to incorporate market share as a target variable rather than simply outright sales. If the sales of the entire industry rise during a high seasonal period,

**TABLE 5.8**

Implementing Lags in Modeling

| Date | TV Ad Spend | Radio Ad Spend | Relative Price | Revenue |
|---|---|---|---|---|
| 010110 | $10,150 | $2100 | 1.10 | $42,000 |
| 020210 | $24,000 | $3400 | 1.15 | $58,000 |
| 030110 | $30,000 | $3700 | 1.15 | $63,400 |
| 040410 | $15,000 | $3000 | 1.20 | $58,000 |
| 050210 | $18,000 | $2800 | 1.18 | $51,000 |
| 060110 | $13,000 | $2500 | 1.18 | $48,000 |

then market share for individual players should remain more consistent; therefore, the advertising effect would be more accountable for variations.

## Summing Up the Factors to Success (Not Just Analysts)

When conducting an analytic initiative of any particular process, it is highly recommended that a subject matter expert and data professional be involved. Collaboration between the analyst, process expert, and data expert is essential to uncover subtle issues that are critical to credible model development and analytics. Issues from the meaning of and availability of data variables and product and industry knowledge can add great value to the mining process, especially in the era of big data, where new variables have evolved and processes change (become faster and leverage new technologies). Just think of not involving the activities of mobile application marketing tactics on product revenue when seeking to truly explain marketing effectiveness, or perhaps not considering social media "product likes" on estimating the type of person that is more likely to buy a particular product. Chapter 6 depicts this concept as it illustrates the importance of considering search activity and weather data in developing models that help explain consumer behavior and sales.

## REFERENCE

Kudyba, S., and Hoptroff, R. *Data Mining and Business Intelligence: A Guide to Productivity.* Hershey, Pennsylvania: IDEA Group Publishing, 2001.

# 6

## The Internet: A Source of New Data for Mining in Marketing

*Robert Young*

### CONTENTS

## MARKETING LANDSCAPE AND INTERNET'S POSITION

Over the last decade (2003–2012) the Internet medium amassed critical consumer support, rapidly built shares of ad revenue, and now stands as the second most widely used marketing channel in North America.

## SHARE OF AD SPEND/SHARE OF TIME

The year 2000 is often identified as the benchmark start point when plotting the Internet's spectacular growth in ad revenue over the last decade. The chart below trends online and newspaper shares of ad revenue from the late 1990s to 2010–2011 in the United States, the UK, and Canada (share expressed against big six media).

In short, online up, newspaper down! Today, online ad revenue exceeds newspaper revenue in the United States and the UK. In Canada, online's ad revenue is expected to surpass newspaper levels in 2012.

**Share of Total Ad Revenue**
(of TV, Newspaper, Magazine, Radio, OOH, and Internet)

And so, over the past 10 years, the Internet medium has moved to firmly occupy the number 2 ad revenue position in North America and the UK. Many predictions abound suggesting that the TV medium will give up its number one revenue position to the Internet medium by 2015.

Online's ad revenue share advances on other media are more conciliatory than past intermedia share battles. The "legacy" or offline media have developed branded online revenue extensions, and therefore some small portion of online's ad revenue should be attributed back to the legacy media. However, the "creeping" online transformation of the TV medium has a unique dimension called connected TV.

Containing the elements of bidirectional interactivity, increased content offerings, and content schedules that respond to user profiles, connected

TV is now integrated into "smart TV sets" available in over 70 models on the market today. In this vision, TV commercials will be served, not scheduled. In the connected TV scenario, where online effectively takes over the body of TV, how does one categorize ad revenue: online or TV?

Today about 70% of the North American adult population uses the Internet weekly, up from a 50% weekly reach position in 2000. Each week 80 to 90% of younger adults are reached by online. Older 55+ adults exhibit lower levels of reach than younger adults—exhibiting in the 50% range weekly.

Another universal means of comparing consumer's usage of media is time spent per capita. Today all weekly adult 18+ time spent online, divided by the adult 18+ population, produces about 15 hours a week—2 hours per day. That compares with about 3 hours per day for radio and 3.5 hours per day for TV. In 2000, Internet's adult 18+ time spent per capita stood at only 5 hours a week—less than three-fourths of an hour daily.

The Internet medium appeared to reach a point of consumer usage critical mass in 2005, when weekly reach exceeded the daily newspaper medium and weekly time spent levels started to close in on the broadcast media. At this point in time, the Internet medium began an impressive run in ad revenue acquisition to present.

While online is treated as a singular medium for the purposes of calculating reach, time spent, and ad revenue shares, it is in fact a remarkably diverse medium consisting of multiple commercial platforms: search, social media, mobile. Unlike offline media, online represents an aggregation of reception senses: audio, audiovisual, and visual only. It is generally a medium of the one-on-one, and in this regard dramatically differs from the mass media one source/multiple simultaneous (or almost simultaneous) reception characteristic. Email and e-commerce are all highly interactive usages. There is nothing comparable in the pure offline media world.

## PAID, OWNED, EARNED, SHARED

Caused in large part by the emergence of the Internet medium, today's typical brand media mix is more complex than in the past, exhibiting smaller budgets per channel, resulting in increased challenges when attempting to determine cross-platform ad currency metrics and brand campaigns' return on investment (ROI).

With every new medium comes new typology. *Paid, owned, earned,* and *shared* are four words recently created to segment, in broad terms, digital media platforms. As the online medium grew and segmented thanks to broad consumer acceptance, these four marketing approach designations emerged. Originally considered specific to digital media, the terms can certainly encompass all offline platforms as well. The chart below provides definitions and examples of the four approaches in both new and old media.

**Media/Marketing Approaches New Terminology**

|  | Definition | Online | Offline |
|---|---|---|---|
| **Paid** | Brand pays for commercial/ad time/space. | Display Paid Search | 30" TV spot ½ page 4C ad |
| **Owned** | Channel is owned and operated by the brand. | Website Blog | In-house Magazine Direct Mail |
| **Earned** | The brand harnesses customer advocates. | Viral "Buzz" | Public Relations Word of Mouth |
| **Shared** | Social participation in the brand. | Facebook Twitter | Demonstration Sampling |

Getting complex? You bet!

Outside of new product launches, brand budgets have basically remained constant from year to year, but the number of paid, owned, earned, and shared platforms being deployed by marketers has grown significantly. Constant budgets plus more channels equal smaller budgets per channel, and so media marketers increasingly face difficulties comparing, measuring, and evaluating the vast array of new and old media channels at their disposal. Media modeling work performed by BrandScience (an Omnicom company) has determined that increases in paid media impressions result in increased traffic to owned channels, such as advertiser websites. Corporate websites tend to have low reach levels (less than 1% of broad segments of the population monthly). While the proportionate lift in traffic is significant, the absolute numbers tend to be small. Nevertheless, the lift is an additional benefit that accrues to the advertiser as a result of the paid media investment and is often overlooked and unmeasured.

The measurement labor cost increases as the expenditure (and often the derived revenue) per channel decreases. The media industry in North America has undertaken to address this challenge through an initiative called Making Measurement Make Sense. 3MS is a joint effort involving the Interactive Advertising Bureau (IAB), Association of National Advertisers (ANA), American Association of Advertising Agencies (4As), Newspaper Association of America (NAA), and Online Publishers Assocation (OPA).

Effort is being expended to develop audience metrics and ad currency standards required to ease the job of evaluating digital media and facilitating the crossing between online and offline media platform comparisons for brand advertising. If all goes well with this initiative, the industry will be able to measure digital media using offline metrics by mid-2014: target impressions, gross rating points, reach, and frequency. In addition, an industry-wide classification system for display ads, rich media, streamed video, and social activity will also be available.

Both off- and online media derive audience information from syndicated, sample-based surveys. For digital media, these new metrics represent "opportunity for ad exposure" language comparable to offline's media language. The common language will greatly simplify planning and negotiating activity that involves online and offline channels.

Nielsen and ComScore currently provide an online rating service in the UK, United States, and Canada that applies legacy media measurement concepts such as reach, frequency, and gross rating points (GRPs) to online ad campaigns.

There exists, of course, a measurement language that is uniquely digital, a language that has evolved and developed in lockstep with the evolution of the online medium, the language of clicks, ads served, words searched, tags, cookies, and web analytics. These are "machine metrics," actual binary transactions tracked, computer stored, dashboard displayed, referenced by online teams, and used to modify and upgrade digital campaigns on the go. They are derived from census and not survey.

Digital machine-based metrics provide an interactive "trace" between paid, owned, earned, and shared marketing activity and sales (or inquiry, application).

While the industry struggles to find an audience currency bridge between the old, offline media and the new, online media, the online world is moving down its own unique path of rapidly expanding machine-based metrics that drive the planning, execution, and maintenance of most online campaigns. There are many media practitioners who wonder if perhaps the online world's machine metrics and ROI-based measurement should be applied to legacy media rather than the other way around. As TV becomes "smarter" and as rates of cable "cutting" increase and as consumers receive their video fare via Internet to a greater and greater extent, this desire for ROI measurement of legacy TV could become a reality.

## RETURNS AND RATES

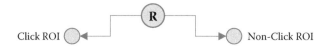

Machine metrics incorrectly apply sales to the last click in a progression of impressions generated by online and offline media, pressure which results in an unbalanced award of ROI to online media. Attribution modeling is designed to better understand the consumer's online history but doesn't address offline's hidden sale contribution. Only media modeling can unearth the sales contribution made by both online and offline channels in a campaign's media mix.

Imagine an offline (TV/newspaper), online display, paid search, website (with e-commerce capability) media mix in support of an electronics store retailer.

The offline TV and newspaper commercials/ads carry brand messaging, tagged with a message tag that encourages the prospect to attend to a website that features products on sale and an e-commerce facility.

The online portion of the media plan is designed to drive prospects directly to the website. Display ads are served, which when clicked direct the prospect to the website's package offer. Paid search words are linked to the website.

The chart on the following page lays out the online/offline dynamics when this mix of media is in play. The dotted lines in the schematic are traced by machine metrics. The solid lines in the chart reflect consumer interactions with the brand that are not measured with machine metrics.

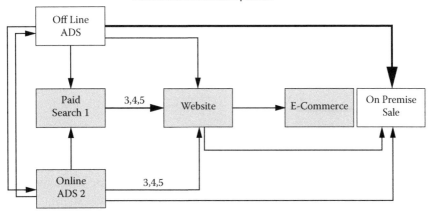

**The Media Mix Sales Dynamic**

**Machine-Metrics**
1. How often the search word is queried – Search Query Volume.
2. Number of ads served.
3. Click once exposure takes place.
4. Didn't click right away, but went to the site later.
5. Attribution modeling—the online history is recreated.

In this example, all measureable website connections will be assigned to either the display or search online activity. There is no digital trace if a prospect decides to visit the destination based upon exposure to the offline (TV/newspaper) activity. This website activity is called nonreferred traffic. There's no machine-based trace for those customers who go into the brick-and-mortar store following exposure to online display ads. All in-store sales (90% of total sales in the case of this retailer) are generated by the campaign outside of the digital trace. These sales cannot be assigned to a channel.

A prospect, moved by offline messages to access the retailer's website, is likely to do so by way of search (Google and therefore traced), but some might go directly to the website by way of entering the store's web address (not traced).

If a prospect, moved by the TV/newspaper messages, decides to click the online display ad, all benefit that accrues to the retailer from that click is assigned to the online display ad. The offline activity gets short shrift in the machine metric system.

There is irony illuminated by this example. Machine metrics, while providing the feel of infallibility, result in campaign returns by channel that are out of whack with reality, and because it's a machine-based data source, the results are usually unchallenged. Offline results outside of the field of machine counting are unassigned. Any benefits generated by "unclicked" exposure to online display ads are unassigned. Any increase in click rates caused by offline-generated awareness is unassigned.

## CLICK ROI

The media mix sales dynamic chart also identifies where five machine metric types kick in along with abbreviated descriptions. These five metrics allow for the calculation of click-based return on investment.

The first metric (1) is called search query volume. When a word or phrase ("flat screen TV") is entered into a search engine (Google), and if that word or phrase has been acquired, a paid ad message will appear that can be linked to the retailer's site. The engine provides an accounting of the query counts. ROI calculation is determined through simple division.

The second metric (2) is an ad served count that is provided by the company that has been hired to ensure that the display ads appear on the sites that have been utilized as part of the online display campaign. These served ad numbers are in the millions. Usually less than 3% of the served ads are clicked. The clicking of the search or display ad is captured as part of the website analytic, and this is the 3rd metric type.

Procrastinating clickers (4) may visit the retailer's website days after being exposed to the search or display ads. These consumers are tagged (at least their computers are) and identified. And so even if there is a delay in the click to a website, a metric can be created.

The 5th metric, called attribution modeling, is a relatively recent development and uses tags and algorithms to track a prospect's online history. This addresses the awarding of all sales to the last click in a line of online transactions, but only within the confines of online.

## NONCLICK ROI

The only way both offline and online channels in a marketing mix can be fairly evaluated for ROI is through media modeling. This is a nonclick approach to determining return on investment.

Media modeling (also called market mix modeling, sale impact modeling) applies statistical analysis to historical time series data and is designed to unearth the relationships or response functions between individual driver variables such as TV vs. online display activity and the target variable of concern, such as sales. The time series can span a couple of years and often uses weekly data. Driver variables can include weekly expenditures in a wide range of online and offline channels, as well as nonmarketing effects, such as weather, general economic activity, and extraneous consumer behavior. Other nonmarketing drivers can include on/off situations such as holidays.

Marketers perform media modeling in order to understand the patterns of effectiveness and efficiency exhibited by different marketing investments. By understanding these patterns or response functions, the marketer can optimize the marketing mix and squeeze out more sales revenue without increasing the marketing expenditure.

Media modeling projects also provide marketers with insights relating to base sales, the proportion of annual sales that exist when marketing activity is nonexistent. Marketers are often shocked to learn that only 10 to 15% of their company's annual sales are generated as a result of marketing efforts in the short term. Of course, long-running marketing voids erode brand equity, and the long-term base sales will weaken.

The ability of media modeling to include the examination of extraneous, nonmarketing variables is very important. The examination of a bank's credit card launch cannot be complete without the inclusion of a timeline of consumer confidence indexes. The success or failure of a restaurant's sales promotion needs to be considered in the context of outdoor temperatures and precipitation.

## MEDIA MODELING AND INTERNET'S NEW ROLE

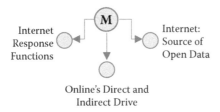

The Internet provides marketers with a highly responsive addition to the traditional offline channels, and in this respect the Internet has a new marketing role to play. But the Internet also provides marketers with a new, readily accessible open data source that can be used to quantify and populate time series databases for extraneous driver variables.

## INTERNET RESPONSE FUNCTIONS

Media modeling demonstrates over and over again that online's true ROI can exceed the ROI performance indicated by machine metrics alone, and that offline and online activity can work together to improve overall campaign ROI.

The chart below displays response functions for eight different media channels on a one sale/media expenditure scale. Channels that rise up on the far left-hand side of the chart (search) have higher (steeper) ROI rates than channels on the far right-hand side (newspaper). These patterns of response were derived from media modeling work that was performed at PHD Canada in 2012 for a client in the telecommunications business.

There are a couple of important findings contained in this chart that have been confirmed through media modeling work performed throughout the PHD global network. Note that online channels tend to be more efficient producers of ROI than offline channels. But also notice that the online channels have sharper diminishing return curve response function patterns than offline channels. In other words, online channels are great first choice channels in a media mix, but they become increasingly inefficient as weekly expenditures rise. In effect, online channels hit a sales ceiling sooner than offline channels, a function of the online medium's lower reach capacity compared to the more established offline media.

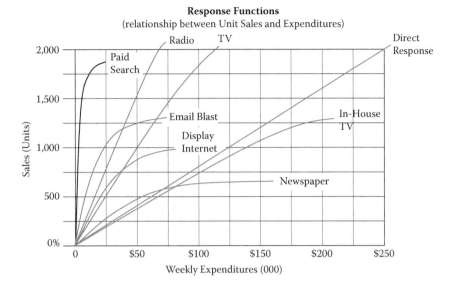

**Response Functions**
(relationship between Unit Sales and Expenditures)

The correlation between low-reach/sharply diminishing curves and high-reach/more gradually diminishing return curves is particularly noticeable when it comes to direct mail. In the telecommunications case (see chart) the direct response (DR) channel's response function is linear, suggesting that there is no diminishment in effectiveness with this medium as weekly expenditures increase. DR is a channel that is effectively capable of reaching 100% of a consumer population by virtue of its delivery system (home and newspaper delivery).

The TV response function curve (see chart) produced an ROI that, in this case, was not as beneficial to clients as the radio medium. Not surprisingly, both the radio and TV curves began to flatten at similar weekly spend levels. These two media have similar depths of consumer reach each week.

Newspaper was the least responsive channel in this particular media mix. In this case a "perfect storm" of characteristics existed; shallow sales impact coupled with high weekly cost. In this case a free transit daily paper was utilized. This ROI picture is not representative of most heavy daily newspaper executions.

The relationships plotted in the chart reflect each channel in isolation, as if the channel alone was being employed in the service of the marketer. Media modeling work also provides for examination of combinations of two, three, or more channels working in tandem. Sometimes simultaneous usage of multiple media creates synergistic impacts on target variables (sales). In other words, sometimes TV + Internet display create a positive impact on sales that is greater than the sum of TV and Internet display in isolation. The addition of the one channel improves the performance of the other channel. This dynamic is also called an assist, and it is critical that the software used for media modeling is capable of capturing this dynamic.

The synergistic effect or "lift" effect is often seen with combinations of TV and search. TV drives awareness, which drives exploration, which drives search and e-commerce transactions or store visits. In more general terms, lift is most pronounced when creative/message consistency exists between channels and when website identification is featured in the offline creative.

Of course the efficacy of the ROI insights derived from the response functions is only as reliable as the legitimacy of the media modeling work. And modeling legitimacy is driven to a large extent by the accuracy of the historical time-sensitive channel costing data that serves as the model's drivers. Modelers must build channel cost files over the campaign time period that properly reflect when the brand messaging was *consumed* modified by when the messaging was *digested*.

The need for correct representation of media channel cost by week (or other applicable time unit) applies to all channels utilized in a campaign, both online or offline channels.

Identifying the timing of brand messaging consumption is a straight-forward process. Channel cost must be allocated to the campaign time units (weeks) in proportion to the impressions generated by the channel of the campaign time period. If 10% of the campaign's online display impressions occurred in week 5, then 10% of the campaigns display cost must be allocated to week 5. The assignment of the right channel cost to the right week in the campaign is the first step in building an accurate time sensitive driver.

The second step in building accurate time patterns for channel costs requires adjustment to reflect how consumers *digest* brand messaging. Message *digestion* refers to recall and persuasiveness—properties that diminish over time. This diminishment is called *memory decay* (recall decays by 20% per week, for example). The reciprocal of memory decay is called *adstock* (if week one recall is indexed at 100, the week two adstock index is 80). *Adstock* is an industry term that describes the extent to which message impact deteriorates over time. An adstock value of 80 (a half-life of 80) reflects full impact week 1 (100), 80% of week one impact in week 2 (80), 80% of week 2 impact in week 3 (64), 80% of week 3 impact in week 4 (51), and so on, until impact virtually disappears.

Different media channels have different average adstock values. The pattern of brand message recall spreads over a longer period of time for the TV medium (80 on average) than for, say, the daily newspaper medium (0) where message recall tends to be exhausted within the medium's week of impressions. Radio adstock factors are low (20-60). Search adstock is nonexistent. Magazine adstock is in the 60 range, as long as costs reflect the very long average issue readership impression "tail" that exists among monthly magazine readers. Out-of-home is usually purchased in 4 week blocks. Therefore the 4 week unit cost must be assigned evenly over each of 4 weeks and then each week must be adstocked at a value ranging between 40 and 60.

Online display can exhibit a wide range of adstock values because the ad units employed by advertisers are varied; from high impact "rich" ad units, to lower impact static display units. Online video adstock resembles TV.

A channel's adstock value (or memory decay) is affected by factors other than the size and nature of the ad unit being used. High levels of brand "equity", built through consistent messaging and long term advertising support, produces larger adstock factors for the carrier channel. Hot competitive activity diminishes a channel's adstock value; low competitive heat increases a channel's adstock value.

Each channel's average adstock value serves as a starting point for the modeler. Optional adstock patterns should be prepared and tested within the model for each channel. The model fit will improve as each channel's adstock option approaches consumer reality. When the model fit can no longer be improved, the most relevant channel adstock patterns will have been achieved.

## INTERNET: SOURCE OF OPEN DATA

Extraneous drivers require a numeric time series, and this quantification can often be determined through creative use of Internet sources.

In 2008 a widespread listeriosis (a food-borne bacterial infection) outbreak in Canada occurred and was linked to cold cuts produced in a Maple Leaf Foods plant in Toronto, Ontario, leaving eight dead and many suffering. Sandwich quick service restaurants reported declines in sales over the summer of 2008 as consumers avoided all cold cuts from all sources. Media modeling that was undertaken in 2009 for a PHD QSR client addressed the question of sales decline caused by this consumer backlash.

The challenge that faced the media model undertaking was the creation of a time series that quantified, on a weekly basis, consumer's fears concerning listeriosis. A week-by-week survey measuring consumer's concerns on a scale of 1 to 10 over the measurement period (2008) would solve the problem, but that data didn't exist and obviously couldn't be created retroactively. What to do?

Google Insight (now called Google Trends) provided the historical picture. It was felt that the weekly volume of Internet searches for the word *listeriosis* could function as a surrogate for consumer's weekly awareness of and concern over the issue. Google Insight provides the capability to track search volume by week, anywhere, over any period of time. The weekly volume data is expressed as a weekly index, 100 being the peak volume week. Here's what that data looked like.

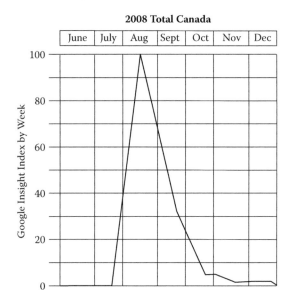

The listeriosis outbreak actually began mid-July 2008 but didn't reach peak awareness, according to Google search volume records, until mid-August. Awareness/concern tapered off quickly to late October and gradually petered out by the end of January 2009. The time series of Google Insight indexes were added to the database of driver variables that included weekly media promotion expenditures, weather, and holidays.

Here's an excerpt of the database, where columns are the driver variables used in the media modeling project, showing the listeriosis factor in combination with weekly media cost data and other drivers.

| | D4 | | | | $f_x$ | no | | | | | |
|---|---|---|---|---|---|---|---|---|---|---|---|
| | A | B | I | J | K | L | M | N | O | P | Q | R |
| 1 | Wk # | Weekly Sales | 3 Sand Total | CLI | List | AverMaxTemp | Percip | TV | TVAdSk | Digital | Digital Sk | Drop |
| 2 | 1 | 777.3 | 124.6 | 228.7 | 0.0 | 21.7 | 11.8 | 143.8 | 143.8 | 0.0 | 0.0 | 0 |
| 3 | 2 | 792.7 | 124.6 | 228.7 | 0.0 | 25.8 | 9.2 | 144.5 | 259.5 | 0.0 | 0.0 | 0 |
| 4 | 3 | 791.7 | 124.6 | 228.7 | 0.0 | 26.3 | 61.8 | 34.3 | 236.1 | 0.0 | 0.0 | 0 |
| 5 | 4 | 785.5 | 124.6 | 228.7 | 0.0 | 21.2 | 9.8 | 26.2 | 197.8 | 0.0 | 0.0 | 0 |
| 6 | 5 | 765.1 | 124.6 | 228.7 | 0.0 | 26.0 | 29.6 | 0.0 | 128.1 | 4.8 | 4.8 | 0 |
| 7 | 6 | 636.4 | 128.5 | 228.7 | 0.0 | 24.6 | 0.2 | 0.0 | 58.3 | 4.8 | 8.8 | 0 |
| 8 | 7 | 745.3 | 128.5 | 228.8 | 0.0 | 27.9 | 50.4 | 138.5 | 138.5 | 4.8 | 11.7 | 0 |
| 9 | 8 | 784.6 | 128.5 | 228.8 | 0.0 | 27.5 | 79.4 | 131.0 | 241.8 | 0.0 | 8.8 | 0 |
| 10 | 9 | 796.8 | 128.5 | 228.8 | 25.0 | 25.6 | 52.2 | 55.1 | 243.0 | 0.0 | 5.7 | 0 |
| 11 | 10 | 774.5 | 152.0 | 229.0 | 50.0 | 26.8 | 11 | 52.3 | 230.4 | 0.0 | 2.9 | 0 |
| 12 | 11 | 680.3 | 152.0 | 229.1 | 75.0 | 24.0 | 54.4 | 0.0 | 155.0 | 0.0 | 1.0 | 0 |
| 13 | 12 | 722.4 | 152.0 | 229.2 | 100.0 | 24.3 | 20.2 | 0.0 | 79.6 | 0.0 | 0.0 | 0 |
| 14 | 13 | 700.7 | 152.0 | 229.3 | 87.0 | 25.5 | 9.8 | 0.0 | 31.9 | 0.0 | 0.0 | 0 |
| 15 | 14 | 642.8 | 152.0 | 229.3 | 73.0 | 23.7 | 8.2 | 0.0 | 10.5 | 0.0 | 0.0 | 0 |
| 16 | 15 | 591.5 | 122.8 | 229.3 | 60.0 | 24.9 | 13.8 | 0.0 | 0.0 | 0.0 | 0.0 | 0 |
| 17 | 16 | 702.3 | 122.8 | 229.4 | 47.0 | 22.6 | 50.6 | 149.0 | 149.0 | 0.0 | 0.0 | 0 |
| 18 | 17 | 735.7 | 122.8 | 229.4 | 33.0 | 20.0 | 0 | 114.5 | 233.7 | 0.0 | 0.0 | 0 |
| 19 | 18 | 736.4 | 122.8 | 229.2 | 26.0 | 21.1 | 2.8 | 111.8 | 292.8 | 0.0 | 0.0 | 0 |
| 20 | 19 | 711.0 | 191.4 | 228.9 | 19.0 | 14.5 | 25 | 26.9 | 244.7 | 0.0 | 0.0 | 0 |
| 21 | 20 | 653.9 | 191.4 | 228.7 | 12.0 | 17.6 | 7.6 | 0.0 | 164.2 | 0.0 | 0.0 | 0 |
| 22 | 21 | | | | | | | | | | | |

The resulting media model isolated the listeriosis sales impact to be –8% at the point of peak awareness (week 12).

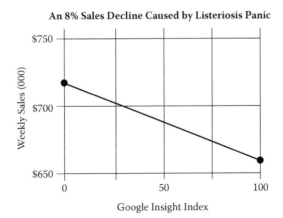

**An 8% Sales Decline Caused by Listeriosis Panic**

Google Insight opens new media modeling doors because weekly, quantifiable, historical, accurate data exists for any topic that has triggered search activity. The data exists as long as search volume can logically stand in as a surrogate for a consumer awareness-like driver variable.

For example, one of the driver variables for media modeling work done for an electronics retailer was in-store traffic triggered by consumers' awareness of and interest in Apple's iPhone (summer 2008) and the new Microsoft Windows 7 release (fall 2009). Weekly Google Insight search volume data was generated for iPhone and Windows 7 searches and entered into the model in the same way as the listeriosis case. A sales lift of +5% occurred in the peak week of iPhone mania. Windows 7 sales increased during its peak search period, but not to the same extent. The iPhone search volume (darker curve, below) was far greater and more prolonged than Windows 7's search volume (lighter curve, below).

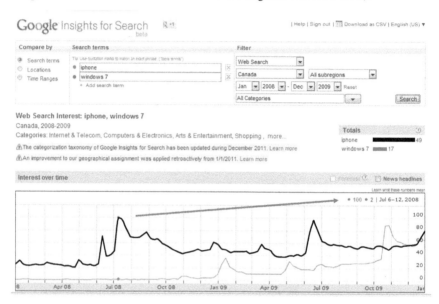

One obvious example of Internet-accessible data, that is, a key driver of retail sales, is historical weather data. Decent modeling fits for brick-and-mortar-based retail activity require the inclusion of a weather driver variable. Weekly mean temperature and average weekly precipitation can be accessed for all North American cities from a wide range of sites. For some countries the data is free; for others a small fee is required.

These are examples of how the Internet now provides access to data that allows marketers to expand the number and nature of driver variables that can be examined in the media modeling process. Data access via the Internet is helping media modeling become more reflective of the real marketing landscape.

The chart below provides a summary of four additional valuable Internet data sources that can be used, with some imagination and creativity, to help increase the utility of media modeling.

http://technorati.com/

Technorati is an Internet search engine that searches for, categorizes, and rates Blogs.

http://www.alexa.com/

Alexa provides traffic data, global rankings, and other information on thousands of websites.

Google
http://www.google.com/insights/search/
http://www.google.com/trends/

Google Insight provides search volume patterns over time as well as top related and rising searches.

http://thedatahub.org/

The Data Hub contains 3,865 datasets (as of July 2012) that can be browsed and downloaded.

http://getthedata.org/

Get The Data is a Q+A forum.

## ONLINE'S DIRECT AND INDIRECT DRIVE

We have traced the rise of consumer uptake and advertiser acceptance to the online medium in North America. Today the Internet is a medium that reaches more consumers than print media but still ranks below radio and TV media's weekly reach. Weekly time spent with the Internet is beginning to approach the 4 and 5 hours per week spent with broadcast media.

Diversity of platform, as well as impressive gains in consumer usage uptake, accounts for the strong number 2 ad revenue position currently held by the Internet media.

But online channels are oil to offline channel's water. The industry has had difficulty mixing the two media forms in the most effective and efficient ways. Those with online expertise are uncomfortable with offline media. Those with offline expertise are struggling to catch up to Internet's accelerating complexity.

Online ROI, as determined by machine metrics, are often accepted as gospel by online insiders but distort contribution among channels inside the online world and fail to allocate any ROI benefit to offline media. Additionally, machine metrics appear to underestimate the online medium's total sales contribution. Those exposed to online display ads, like those exposed to TV commercials, are impacted by brand messaging and take action in store—transactions beyond the purview of machine metrics. Online ad exposure produces nonclick sales.

Only through media modeling can the individual and collective returns of online and offline driver variables be gauged. Work done to date suggests there is a marketing time and place for media channels from both worlds.

The Internet also indirectly drives marketing decision making by providing an open source of data and analytics that helps improve the efficacy of media modeling. Consumer attitudes, fears, concerns, and actions can be examined through the surrogacy of search volume. This brings media modeling closer to the real world occupied by consumers, which in turn results in more realistic assessments of online and offline returns on media investment.

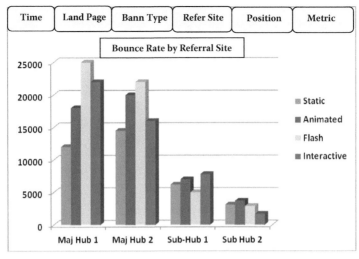

| | Maj Hub 1 | Maj Hub2 | Sub-Hub1 | Sub Hub2 | Total |
|---|---|---|---|---|---|
| Static | 12000 | 14500 | 6200 | 3100 | 35800 |
| Animated | 18000 | 20000 | 7000 | 3700 | 48700 |
| Flash | 25000 | 22000 | 5000 | 2900 | 54900 |
| Interactive | 22000 | 16000 | 7800 | 1700 | 47500 |
| Total | 77000 | 72500 | 2000 | 11400 | 186900 |

**FIGURE 2.2**

Banner performance multidimensional cube.

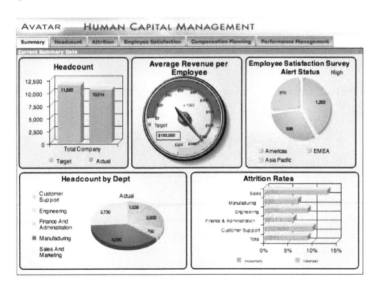

**FIGURE 2.3**

Clearly designed employee analytic dashboard. (From http://www.dashboards-for-business
.com/dashboards-templates/business-intelligence/business-intelligence-executive-
dashboard; Domo, Inc., http://www.domo.com.)

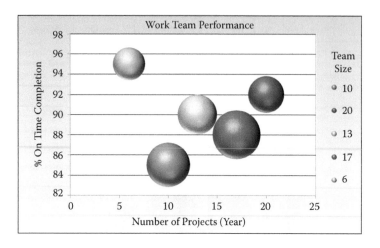

**FIGURE 2.11**
Bubble chart depicting workforce team performance.

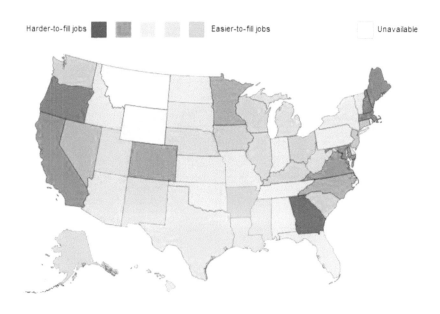

**FIGURE 2.12**
Heat map that illustrates areas of hard-to-fill job vacancies. (From Wanted Analytics, http://www.wantedanalytics.com.)

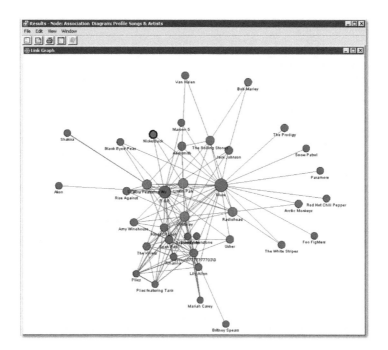

**FIGURE 4.3**
Network plot of artist listening rules derived from market basket analysis.

**FIGURE 7.1**
Heat map hot spot. (From http://provim.net/heat-maps.)

**FIGURE 7.2**

Website activity analytics. (From Google Analytics. Google and Google logo are registered trademarks of Google, Inc. Used with permission.)

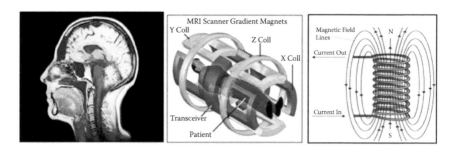

**FIGURE 12.6**

MRI scan, schematic of scanner gradient magnets, and magnetic fields generated. (From the Magnetic High Magnetic Field Magnetic Laboratory, University of Florida, http://www.magnet.fsu.edu/education/tutorials/magnetacademy/mri/fullarticle.html.)

# 7

# Mining and Analytics in E-Commerce

*Stephan Kudyba*

## CONTENTS

## THE EVOLVING WORLD OF E-COMMERCE

It seems that when anyone considers conducting analytics in e-commerce, whether it be reports, dashboards, or mining, the first thing they think of is website activities. However, given the evolution of the electronics products market, wireless communication, and social media applications, the term *e-commerce* has taken on a vastly new and complex meaning. Consider marketing initiatives in today's bold new e-commerce world. Only years ago, analysts focused on click rates and banner views and traditional email activities. Today the e-commerce marketing professional must be versed in such concepts and strategies as

- Deriving product likes on social media
- Developing apps to engage customers
- Maintaining active Facebook accounts
- Understanding what platforms people are using to engage their marketing tactics
- Sending text messages
- Better understanding email formats
- Managing consumer comments on blogs
- Engaging customers to acquire insightful market feedback
- Understanding consumer activity on websites

These are just some of the noteworthy activities to keep in mind when considering strategies to achieve success for an organization. One major advantage all these activities involve is the generation of data that measure corresponding activities that underpin many e-commerce-based initiatives, and of course with data comes analytics.

Chapter 2 provided essential basics to various analytic approaches that can be leveraged to help provide decision support for strategists. In all the concepts mentioned above, the analyst must make the decision as to what level of analytics is necessary for his or her operation. Many times simple graphic displays in the form of dashboards (with access to real-time data) may suffice in providing pertinent information. More dynamic multidimensional cubes may be required, or perhaps more complex mining applications to estimate likelihoods, associations, and predictive power may be the solution. The key to any of the analytic methodologies lies in their robustness in providing a well-rounded view of the process they are addressing. For example, consider the simple notion of understanding effectiveness of an organization's mobile app initiatives.

Assume that your organization has produced a well-functioning application that it wants to send to users in order to maintain an active engagement. One way to leverage analytics to better understand the success of that initiative is to include relevant data variables that provide information that fully describes that scenario. Merely sending apps to consumers and monitoring whether it is downloaded does not imply a successful endeavor. A better performance metric is utilization of the app. However, utilization must be clearly defined as to meaningful utilization (active and continuous engagement on a daily/weekly basis). Other variables that must be considered include:

- Type of technological platform the consumer uses (Android, iOS, etc.)
- Consumer's response to alerts/messages
- Type of consumers that are either active or nonactive engagers

These variables, if analyzed in the correct format over relevant time horizons, can provide strategists valuable information as to effectiveness of mobile app initiatives. Poor consumer activity/engagement of a down-loaded app can quickly give an organization a better understanding of whether the functionality of the app is relevant to the marketplace, or per-haps the wrong target market was chosen as a primary user base.

## BASIC EMAIL REPORTS

Sometimes more basic analytics are adequate for strategists to quickly extract knowledge of a particular initiative, where more routine activities simply require a timely and accurate report of basic metrics describing results from an initiative. Consider the highly utilized activity of text messaging or traditional email messaging of a consumer base. Perhaps an organization's focus is more on effective and timely sending of these com-munications to large segments of the marketplace. Here general metrics regarding responses are necessary. A simple report with core metrics to this routine activity with supportive graphics is all that an organization may require. Consider metrics within an email marketing initiative:

- Number of emails sent
- Emails delivered
- Number of emails bounced
- Number of emails opened
- Amount of clicks on links in email
- Conversions of clicks

The metrics above provide core information to consider regarding email marketing initiatives. A simplistic but noteworthy variable involves the number of emails delivered. A report that illustrates that if you send

100,000 messages, but only 90,000 are delivered, provides the strategist with basic but very actionable information. Simply because an email address has been acquired doesn't imply that it is still active. In the case above, 10,000 emails may need to be scrubbed from the active list. Bounce rate also provides a mechanism to filter or optimize future email endeavors. The rate of email opens provides another source of vital information. If only 5% of emails sent are being opened by recipients, perhaps the marketer needs to consider more enticing subject headings or email IDs that send the messages. Later in this chapter we will address these factors when describing mining applications in email marketing.

## ANALYZING WEB METRICS

Websites provide a host of trackable metrics that depict visitor activities that provide decision makers with information to optimize site layout, enhance marketing effectiveness, or simply enhance the communication effect of the organization with the marketplace regarding its products and services. Prominent metrics that often are leveraged in site analytics include the following:

- Page views
- Time spent on pages
- Navigation route with a website
- Click rates on banners or icons
- Bounce rate
- Conversion or interaction rates
- Source of traffic (geographic, referral sites, unique or repeat visitors)

All these metrics describe traffic during different times of the day that may be initiated by a host of marketing tactics. Initial page views may be a result of paid and generic search initiatives, email and text messaging, or even traditional advertising initiatives, such as radio, TV, or print. In order to fully understand basic metrics generated at the site level, we must consider a combined effort of ongoing strategic marketing tactics (e.g., e-commerce, TV, direct marketing). Remember, just because an organization has built a website doesn't imply that consumers will automatically access it; the marketplace usually needs a little incentive to visit it.

Regardless of the marketing push to the site, analysts can leverage available metrics to better understand their website effectiveness. In order to do this, insightful consideration of those metrics needs to implemented. For example:

> Bounce rate can be a powerful metric in describing a market's response to your organization. A high bounce rate can imply that either the site display is poorly designed, as viewers simply aren't interested in what they are seeing, or the marketing initiative that pulled a particular market segment to the site landing page was not appropriate for the organization's products or services (e.g., the message may have been misleading). However, the analyst must consider not just total bounces, but a bounce rate or number of bounces per views.
>
> A total bounce count of 10,000 may be high in a given day, but if a TV initiative drives 2 million visitors to a site, the bounce rate (bounces/views) may be in the realm of normal activity.

Of course one of the most popular areas of analytics for websites remains simple traffic patterns throughout a site layout. This includes analyzing how site visitors navigate around a site once they have engaged it. A common essential piece of information for decision makers involves such navigation elements as where traffic came from, hot spots in select pages, time spent on pages, and route of navigation, to name a few. These areas provide decision makers with actionable information on where to display advertisements or invoke interaction with visitors, optimize site content, and focus marketing tactics in attracting more traffic.

Time spent on particular pages could signify either a source of interesting content to visitors or a possible glitch in the site (poor information that is not understandable, or difficult options to navigate out of an area). Other metrics, such as back page, should be analyzed in such cases. More time spent on pages due to interesting or hot areas provides actionable information to leverage marketing tactics.

Analyzing sources of traffic, or where traffic originated before coming to a particular website, can provide a great source of strategic information. Geographic areas of traffic origin can provide decision makers with a better understanding of the target market of a company's products and services, and once again can help fine-tune marketing initiatives. A quick view of analytics can illustrate whether a target market is local, regional, or national, where paid search and banner display activities can be optimized accordingly. For example, strong traffic at the county level can provide insights for the following:

- Keyword selection
- Better selection of complementary, local sites to display banners
- Filter out IP addresses outside the target market

As we mentioned in Chapter 2, visuals can play a vital role to strategists when analyzing web metrics. Although pure numbers that depict metrics as described above are essential to conducting fine-tuned, detailed analytics in pursuing strategic initiatives, it is usually a well-designed visual that provides decision makers with a quick understanding of web-related activities. Hot spots in websites and traffic sources through heat map visuals quickly give analysts a robust view of what is happening. Hot spots in websites (see Figure 7.1) generally depict traffic activity in certain sections

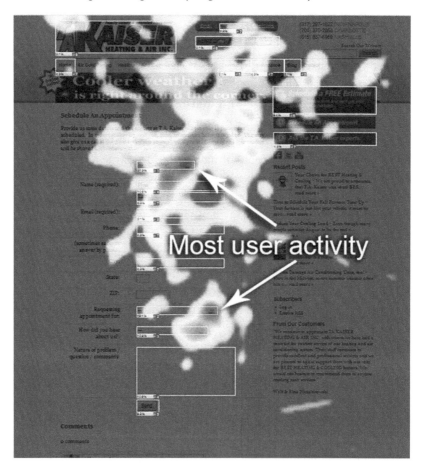

**FIGURE 7.1**
**(See color insert.)** Heat map hot spot. (From http://provim.net/heat-maps.)

of a page (e.g., upper left or middle right side of a particular page). Sifting through the core numbers that underpin this could be a more time-consuming process and provide less immediate knowledge impact to the analyst/strategist.

## REPORT GENERATION

Organizations with robust data capabilities can easily generate reports and visuals of the relevant areas of analytic interest in the spectrum of e-commerce, where simple business intelligence applications provide ample capability to display and leverage available data. Interactive cubes that display various variable dimensions numerically or graphically or real-time dashboards are essential components to information generation.

For organizations less equipped in data management and report/analytic generation, all hope is not lost. Service providers such as Google Analytics or even cloud facilitators provide a host of data-generated analytics to organizations. As we mentioned previously, the advantage to e-commerce-based marketing or strategic initiatives is that activities are all trackable. Sometimes outside vendor providers can provide timely, robust analytic capabilities and save organizations resource cost from developing these capabilities internally. Google Analytics provides robust analytic capabilities for many types of organizational e-commerce activities (Figure 7.2).

## FROM RETROSPECTIVE ANALYTICS TO MORE PROSPECTIVE ANALYTICS WITH DATA MINING

The previous section focused on developing analytics to quickly display activities that are ongoing for particular e-commerce-based activities. This gives analysts a solid understanding of what is happening to their organization and provides insights as to strategic initiatives relative to that information (e.g., hot spots and ad display or traffic origin and paid search optimization). The next step in analytics involves leveraging data resources to generate models that provide more mathematically and statistically based information on possible reasons why things are happening

**FIGURE 7.2**
**(See color insert.)** Website activity analytics. (From Google Analytics. Google and Google logo are registered trademarks of Google, Inc. Used with permission.)

and what is likely to happen by identifying patterns and associations between variables.

In Chapter 3, we included a host of data mining methods that can be deployed in order to identify noteworthy patterns, relationships, segments, and clusters in data resources. In this section we will refer to more directed data mining approaches in leveraging data in the e-commerce spectrum.

## Defining E-Commerce Models for Mining

E-commerce-based data models can take on a variety of forms. For many analysts, the term *mining an e-commerce initiative* refers to mining web-related data to determine optimal strategies for cross-selling products or simply displaying strategic information to visitors as they are navigating a website. However, the evolution of the electronic commerce and communication world has opened up new data sources that can provide strategic information that doesn't necessarily involve website-related activities. Elements such as traditional email marketing or market correspondence through social media or mobile applications provide a robust source of data to better understand target markets (who they are, what they like, and what they do).

## Better Understanding Email Tactics

Many email marketing campaigns focus on the acquisition and transmitting of emails to a population that hopefully includes a segment of a company's target market, where content involves an email subject head and a message that delivers a chunk of product or service information to the recipient. Given the low cost of this tactic, many marketers emphasize email volume (numbers of email transmissions) and frequency (repetitive transmissions) with the hope that something will stick, where *stick* refers to recipients that actually open, read, and respond to email. The ultimate metric that depicts campaign success usually involves a conversion by a recipient (e.g., someone who opened the email and clicked on a link asking for more information, or purchasing or subscribing to some offering).

Despite the seemingly low cost of this initiative, the process of acquiring relevant and authentic email addresses can be a time-consuming and resource-utilizing activity, so why not better understand what types of emails are more effective in generating conversions from recipients, rather than just make do with an expected 0.01% response rate and potentially be viewed as a spammer? A strategist must consider the components of a traditional email from both the creator and the receiver of the message. The electronic communication can be broken down into three main components: the sender ID, the subject heading, and the general content of the message. General strategic tactics are to focus on providing pertinent content in the general content area; however, this may be shortsighted given the possibility that many receivers don't ever open emails from unknown sources. Email marketers should consider format styles of sender ID and subject headings in optimizing email activities in junction with other relevant data (e.g., descriptive information of the recipient to focus on target market). These variables can be analyzed/mined to determine their effectiveness as measured by select performance or target metrics. These metrics can include whether an email was opened, and or if it resulted in an interaction by the recipient. An additional piece of information that can yield descriptive value to the model is to categorize the type of email content (e.g., types and number of links and pictures and general structure).

The modeler can utilize directed mining techniques such as logistic regression or neural networks to estimate the likelihood an email will be opened or the likelihood a message may result in an interaction (click on a link). Generally, the entity/organization that is conducting the email campaign has some information on the email recipient, through either previous interactions through web activities or product purchases. Descriptive information on the recipient in conjunction with email attributes provides the driver variables to corresponding performance metrics. Other operational type variables, such as the number of emails sent, could also be included in the model. Consider the data illustration in Table 7.1.

The 0/1 binary enables analysts to model the likelihood that emails with a particular type of recipient and frequency, sent along with a particular subject heading on the message, will be opened. This mining analysis provides significant value, as it can yield strategic information on the type of email subject heading that communicates to the market segment and invokes a response. However, marketing strategy should not incorporate deceptive tactics via email IDs and subject headings, where both variables should be relevant to the organization and the message to be communicated. Although the cost of emailing remains inexpensive on a relative basis to other marketing initiatives, the effectiveness of the tactic should not be taken lightly. The combination of basic data resources and appropriate analytic capabilities can quickly yield insights as to better understanding the marketplace.

**TABLE 7.1**

Email Modeling

| Email ID | Age | Gender | Number of Emails | Subject Heading | Opened |
|----------|-----|--------|------------------|-----------------|--------|
| Style1@email.org | 25 | Male | 1 | Heading 1 | 0 |
| Style1@email.org | 30 | Male | 3 | Heading 1 | 0 |
| Style2@email.org | 28 | Female | 2 | Heading 2 | 1 |
| Style3@email.org | 40 | Male | 3 | Heading 2 | 1 |
| Style3@email.org | 45 | Female | 2 | Heading 1 | 0 |
| Style2@email.org | 34 | Female | 1 | Heading 2 | 0 |

## Data Resources from Social Media

There has been significant excitement regarding the potential data resources that social media platforms can provide to analysts to better understand consumer behaviors toward products, services, or entities in general. Facebook pages include a host of data, including comments, images, network connections, and metrics such as likes, friends, etc. Much of this data is in unstructured form, for which analytic applications such as text mining are required, and some of it is structured as well. Despite the excitement regarding the potential of extracting significant insights from the social media space, the jury is still out regarding actual returns or strategic value that has been achieved. Most benefits have been in the form of marketing initiatives (offering coupons for likes and leveraging friend networks).

One particular metric may provide value to analysts regarding the identification of individuals who comprise a target market for products and services. Product, service, or company "likes" provide structured data resources that depict a consumer's perception. Without having to extract product purchase information (which sometimes does not depict a true like of a product), organizations can better understand who comprises their consumer base. A simplistic data illustration is provided in Table 7.2.

The key to leveraging a social media platform to better understand consumer interests and behavior is through creating structured data from unstructured elements through text mining applications and combining this with structured sources. In the preceding illustration the hobby variable can contain types of movies, clubs, travel, etc., that all need to be structured and categorized to be analyzed with data mining methods. The resulting information provides strategists with a much more well-rounded understanding of the type of consumers that have a positive outlook on their products and services. The term *well-rounded* refers to the idea of not

**TABLE 7.2**

Social Media Data

| Product | Gender | Age | Hobbies | Friends | Like |
|---|---|---|---|---|---|
| Sport equipment | Female | 35 | Movie | 100 | 1 |
| Sport equipment | Male | 30 | Travel | 180 | 0 |
| Sport apparel | Female | 28 | Clubs | 250 | 1 |
| Sport apparel | Male | 42 | Clubs | 50 | 0 |
| Sport apparel | Female | 27 | Groups | 350 | 1 |
| Sport fantasy | Male | 22 | Games | 290 | 1 |

only the type of person as indicated by age or gender, but also behavioral aspects. Better understanding a variable such as hobby provides strategists with actionable information in augmenting existing products or services (e.g., launching products corresponding to different hobby categories) to achieve greater customer cohesiveness. Strategists can also enhance marketing initiatives by leveraging avenues that appeal to hobby categories.

## Mobile Apps: An Organization's Dream for Customer Relationships

Perhaps one of the most overlooked innovations in the current evolution in the world of wireless and electronic communication is the development of mini-applications that perform a wide variety of functionalities, from games to search to visual experiences that are offered to consumers either for free or for a fee. Once consumers download apps to smartphones or tablets, etc., there is a direct line of potential ongoing communication and connection between that organization and the consumer. Applications can raise the awareness of the particular organization with the user and can also facilitate regular communication. Unfortunately, this phenomenon has been discovered, and the number of apps on the market is increasing almost exponentially. The answer to this increased competition for app providers is to develop apps that consumers find valuable and want to use. This can be a daunting task, however, given the vast array of consumer tastes, electronic platforms used, and app functionality. Once again, one analytic technique that can help organizations better understand their app success is mining.

As we've mentioned a few times throughout this book, one of the main advantages of the electronic, wireless world is the ability to record data of various activities that transpire, whether it be consumer or purely operationally based, where one of the by-products is big data. The mobile app world also has the advantage in this data experience and can tap into one of the most vital data resources, descriptions of its users. Mining applications can leverage demographic and behavioral/utilization activity to help organizations better understand consumer preferences in the app world. With this information decision makers can then apply resources to the development of those applications that will be valued by downloaders, and thus increase consumer cohesiveness (e.g., increased brand awareness and maintaining ongoing communication).

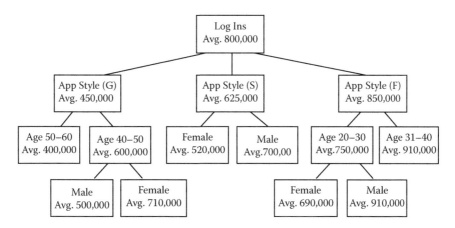

**FIGURE 7.3**
Segmentation decision tree.

Given the wide variety of apps, data issues that miners should address involve a categorization of existing apps. If source apps are so voluminous, categorization applications could be implemented to create the driver variable of type of app. Once application functionality has been categorized, then miners can begin to investigate performance metrics such as usage rates of apps. Consumer demographics factors need to be added to the mix to determine the type of individuals that find value in types of apps. Segmentation mining techniques can be deployed to provide a decision tree visual of the breakdown of usage rate by type of app by type of person. See Figure 7.3.

This type of mining method can be applied in a message response analysis in a mobile app or even smartphone environment, where directed mining techniques can estimate likelihoods of individuals who respond to messages. In a big data environment these initiatives can be used to leverages GPS feeds. Individuals more likely to respond to different message styles can be sent communications while they are visiting or approaching retail outlets. The benefit of contacting individuals likely to interact reduces the spam effect of messaging total populations.

## Movie Genre, Now an Online Endeavor?

In the old days of analog telephones and dial-up Internet, the movie viewing experience was dominated by Blockbuster rentals or going to a theater. However, we've all seen how this has changed dramatically with the evolution of firms such as Netflix and cable providers offering various forms of visual content on different platforms. The home TV is not so much a TV anymore, but an active part of the Internet where an increasing amount of movie viewing is through online selections among a variety of genres. Once again, the electronic world, with the advantage of data capture, can now facilitate a better customer experience by better understanding movie genre by household or even individual consumer. Following similar procedures previously described, organizations providing movie or visual content can optimize the consumer experience by matching visual types with consumer interests. So now when top picks are displayed, it's not so much by population sentiment but can be customized to the user watching. The big data electronic era will most likely drive the concept of improving the customer experience forward by adjusting information offerings more toward the user at the moment. This provides a perfect transition to the world of websites.

## Factors to Consider in Web Mining

Try to remember all the random pop-up ads that were displayed throughout web pages just a few years ago, where users were feverishly seeking to find the *x* function to quickly delete them. Now consider the magical presentations of complementary offerings to products you recently searched in your most recent site navigation. Although the world of optimally designed web offerings is not here yet, progress is being made, where ongoing mining initiatives attempt to better understand various attributes of web visitors and discovering what they like.

Before we embark on the mining activities essential to enhancing site functionality for the customer experience, it's important to note an often overlooked issue in web marketing. Despite the electronic/digital platform of the Internet, sound marketing concepts that underpin marketing tactics in a brick-and-mortar environment should be adhered to. Think of what a website really is: a platform for organizations to communicate what they do and offer consumers, which also provides a means to interact with them. A website is almost like a billboard; in other words, its real focus is a marketing platform. So before turning up the heat on analytics for banner displays or cross-sell initiatives, organizations need to establish a well-functioning site that provides an easy-to-navigate experience that clearly communicates its products and services to visitors. Your site may have the best cross-selling offerings or quick promotional coupons at checkout, but if the visitor is irritated by not being able to find things he or she is interested in or your shipping policies are unattractive, your mining initiatives could be largely wasted.

## Beginning the Mining Process

In other marketing-related analytic initiatives, applications quickly call for demographic inputs to be added to the projects to quickly understand consumer behavior and to micro-market. However, one limitation of web activities is that unless organizations are proactive to gather demographics, automated trackable metrics for this information won't be available. But not to worry; detailed visitor information may not be a dire requisite for marketing on the web. Remember, what much of analytics is looking to indentify is repeatable patterns that lead to interactions from visitors on the web. Pages viewed and links clicked on provide a type of visitor profile as to what commonly precedes a click on a banner, coupon, or even a purchase. So as nice as demographic information may be to add to the equation, understanding site behavior can be an entity labeled as "visitor activity patterns," where these patterns are captured by models. In general, mining activities for web marketing look to leverage data from different sources. These sources could include

- Historical navigation activities from visitors
- Information acquired from customer interactions and log files
- Current navigation activities

Historical activities refer to what visitors have done on previous web visits (e.g., pages they viewed and links or icons clicked on) that is connected to computer IP addresses. Information from customer interactions includes demographic and general visitor information as provided in emails, forms to fill out to receive items, create accounts, etc. Finally, current navigation activities refer to what visitors are doing on a real-time basis. These data sources can be mined with different methodologies (e.g., segmentation and machine learning, etc.) to identify patterns. Analytic techniques such as market basket analysis, item affinity, or collaborative filtering are leveraged to identify likelihoods of one event happening given the occurrence of another. In other words, if a visitor who purchased hiking boots clicked on a link for an outdoor life brochure, what's the likelihood that he or she will purchase camping equipment or respond to a coupon offer for products in that spectrum?

Algorithms process the available data described above to understand what's likely to happen on a historical basis:

> If visitor A shows that he or she spent 10 minutes on page 1 of a site and then clicked on a link navigating to page 3 and then clicked on product A link

for information, then the next time he or she visits, show complementary product or products to A.

Or on a real-time basis:

If visitor A has viewed the home page and clicked on product category Z and then on link C2, then display a banner b coupon for a product or display complementary products at checkout.

Finally, if customer descriptive information is available, the scenario may be as follows:

If the visitor is male and age 25 and navigates to page 3 and clicks on information link R, then display banner style E on side of page 1.

Mining methods simply process available data sources to identify navigation types, so when additional or new visitors navigate a site, the models identify the type of activity pool they may fall into and then provide likelihoods of what these visitors may react to (Engage, 2001; Macromedia, 2001).

## Evolution in Web Marketing

Mining methods provide insights as to identifying what visitors are likely to click on or interact with in a given web session. But marketers must apply evolving technology and expertise to take this a step further. Years ago, banner styles were somewhat limited in format; however, with the progression of amount of memory and processing speed, new visuals that may be more appealing to visitors are becoming more commonplace. Banners that move, crawl, provide game platforms, change images of people that talk, etc., must all be considered in the mix of what consumers may react to. This doesn't stop at the consideration of slick banners or pop-ups, but the content of offerings. Coupons are a key driver of consumer draw to sites and interactions. Marketers must apply effective marketing concepts to drive the value of their initiatives to conversions. For example, coupons with time dimensions (offers expire at some date) may be more effective at getting visitors from merely clicking to converting through sales.

## The Customer Experience

Mining analytics are essential to attempting to provide a customized experience for visitors, a process that has progressed in the past decade and will most likely progress more quickly in the future. With the introduction of integrated consumer platforms (tablets, smartphones, TV with Internet, PCs, etc.), providers are acquiring massive big data on individuals' activities. With this information, the application of sophisticated mining techniques will more and more connect individual consumers with things they are more likely to find value in (products, services, general informational resources). The future should probably entail platforms (websites, TV, smartphones, radio stations) that more and more know their users and provide them with things they are interested in.

## REFERENCES

Engage, Inc. Turning Your Brick and Mortar into a Click and Mortar. In *Data Mining and Business Intelligence: A Guide to Productivity*. Hershey, Pennsylvania, IGI Publishing, 2001.

Macromedia, Inc. Improving the Web Experience through Real-Time Analysis (A Market Basket Approach). In D*ata Mining and Business Intelligence: A Guide to Productivity*. Hershey, Pennsylvania, IGI Publishing, 2001.

# 8

## *Streaming Data in the Age of Big Data*

*Billie Anderson and J. Michael Hardin*

### CONTENTS

### INTRODUCTION

Data collection occurs at a rate never before encountered, via cellular phones, the Internet, and social media. Modern businesses must make real-time decisions as data is received. The capacity to make decisions with immediacy is key to the operation of the most successful companies. One successful company that owes its success to using data in real time is Amazon.

Amazon has dominated the retail book market due to the fact that the company can use online data to understand a customer far beyond the ability of a brick-and-mortar bookstore. For example, when book buying went online, Amazon could track other books customers looked at by how they navigated the site, how much they were influenced by online advertising, and what books they did not like. Amazon then developed real-time algorithms that could provide suggestions to customers as they were shopping in real time. These algorithms and the utilization of real-time data gave Amazon a massive advantage over traditional bookstores in customer analysis, which has made Amazon a mighty force in the retail book market.[1]

Retail businesses are not the only industry making use of streaming big data. Beyond business applications, streaming data analysis can be helpful if one needs to be warned or alerted to a security breach, disease outbreak, service warning, or detect credit fraud. But to comprehend streaming data, one must understand it as a part of big data analytics.

Big data is a database so large and complex that traditional database management tools cannot process and analyze the data. Usually, big data databases contain in the realm of multiple petabytes. A petabyte is a unit of information equal to 1 quadrillion bytes. Big data databases contain complex and diverse types of data that are collected from multiple sources.

Big data usually contains the following types of data:

- Traditional data types, such as customer and transactional information
- Computer-generated data, such as weblogs and website navigation
- Machine-generated data corresponding to text data from call center applications, supply chain systems, stock trade information, and equipment logs
- Social media data that includes blogging sites such as Twitter and Facebook platforms
- Multimedia data such as audio, video, images, and graphic objects

Many of the data types described above cannot be stored and analyzed in a traditional data warehouse constrained by fields and limitations, due to the amount and type of data collected. For example, in a streaming data application, a wide variety of data types are being collected, such as call logs, financial tickers, real-time name recognition, sensor networks, social media, email, photographs, video streams, or weblogs. An analyst needs to be able to process and explore these types of raw, unstructured massive databases and make decisions in a timely manner.

This book chapter will define streaming data and discuss why streaming data cannot be stored and analyzed in traditional databases. An example of how researchers are developing streaming data applications will be given. Two case studies from the fields of healthcare and marketing advertising are reviewed. The chapter will conclude with an examination of potential streaming data applications on the horizon.

---

## STREAMING DATA

Situations in which data are streaming, arriving in real time from their sources, are becoming increasingly prevalent. The demand to analyze the data as it is received and make decisions quickly is growing as well. This demand comes not only from the search for a competitive advantage (as in the Amazon example), but also from a desire to improve lives. For example, healthcare equipment is designed to continuously create data. The ability to analyze healthcare data in real time provides benefits unique to the medical field. In one project, the University of Ontario Institute of Technology is helping Toronto hospitals be "smarter" by designing a system that allows doctors and other healthcare providers to analyze data in real time. The real-time system allows the healthcare providers to receive more than 1000 pieces of unique medical diagnostic information per second. This real-time analysis platform is being used as an early warning system, allowing doctors to detect life-threatening infections up to 24 hours sooner than in the past.[2]

The age of streaming data initiated dramatic changes in how analysts collect and analyze data. Previously, in a traditional data analysis situation, the data would be collected and stored in an enterprise data warehouse (EDW). EDWs played a critical role in academic research and business development throughout the 1990s. A data warehouse serves as a large repository of historical and current transactional data of an organization. An EDW is a centralized data warehouse that is accessible to the entire organization. When it was time to perform an analysis, the historical data would be pulled from the EDW; then several statistical analyses were performed, and a report was generated and given to the decision maker in the organization.

The problem with a traditional EDW is that given the volume and velocity of data available to organizations today, traditional approaches to decision making are no longer appropriate. By the time the decision maker has the information needed to take action, updated data and information are available, making the initial decision outdated. For example, social media capture fast-breaking trends on customer sentiments about products and brands. Although companies might be interested in whether a rapid change in online sentiment correlates with changes in sales, by the time a traditional analysis was completed, a host of new data would be available. Therefore, in big data environments, it is important to analyze, decide, and act quickly and often.[3]

In a streaming data application, data are generated in real time, taking the form of an unbounded sequence of text, video, or values. Since traditional database structures are not applicable in a streaming data environment, new database technology is being developed to store streaming data types. One such system is a data stream management system (DSMS).[4] A DSMS is a set of computer hardware that maintains and queries streaming data.

The main difference between a DSMS and an EDW data architecture is the data stream. A DSMS differs from a traditional EDW in that new data are generated continually and the arrival rates may differ dramatically, ranging from millions of items per second (e.g., clickstreams of a consumer on a retail website) to several items per hour (e.g., weather station monitoring such as temperature and humidity readings). A traditional EDW queries static data to generate statistics and reports, but a DSMS constantly queries streaming data in an effort to give the end user the most up-to-date real-time information possible.

Another key difference between a DSMS and an EDW is the way in which data is stored. In a DSMS the data is stored in memory for as long as processing the data is needed. An EDW uses disk space to store the data. The EDW data architecture is more expensive since hardware has to be purchased to store the massive amounts of data that is being generated. Figures 8.1 and 8.2 show a schematic difference between the EDW and DSMS data architectures.

In order to develop and implement streaming data algorithms for any environment, scalable storage is essential to the strategy for streaming data in a flexible computing environment, leading to a streaming algorithm for the data environment that is effective. The algorithm will go through much iteration, but should culminate in an efficient method for the end user to analyze the data stream effectively and make a decision in a timely manner. This sequential development will require a statistician, a domain expert, and computer engineers who will develop the system. One methodology of developing a real-time analysis system is profiled in the following paragraphs.

A group of researchers from the Los Alamos National Laboratory recently detailed their efforts to develop a streaming data algorithm in which radio astronomy is the motivating example.[5] They sought the mitigation of noise,

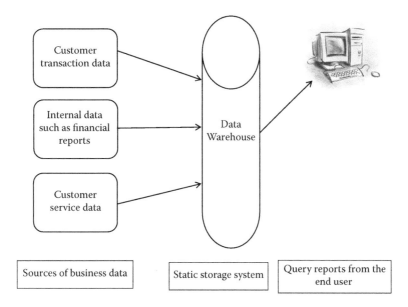

**FIGURE 8.1**
Enterprise data warehouse architecture.

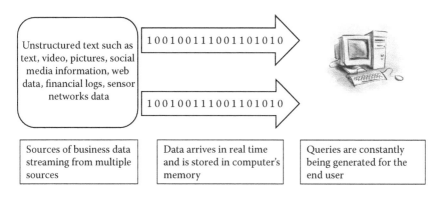

**FIGURE 8.2**
Data stream management system architecture.

or radio frequency interference (RFI), to enable the real-time identification of radio transients or transient astronomical events that emit electromagnetic energy in the radio frequency domain. RFI, that is, man-made radio signals, can hinder the identification of astronomical signals of interest. Real-time identification of radio transients is crucial because it would permit the telescope observing an interesting radio event to redirect other assets to collect additional data pertaining to that event. Further, systems may collect so much data that it is prohibitively expensive or impossible to save all of it for later analysis. In this case, the data of interest must be identified quickly so that they may be saved for future study.

The authors of the Los Alamos study note that when developing a real-time framework for analysis, the computational details are only one part of the overall system. Network bandwidth and storage are key components of the real-time structure for analysis. Network bandwidth is the rate at which data can be received over a network connection or interface. In the author's study, network bandwidth was exposed as a limiting factor. Scalable storage systems are needed for sustaining high data streaming rates.

## STREAMING DATA CASE STUDIES

Researchers from various fields have developed intriguing real-world applications using streaming data for different application areas. This section outlines those applications, which come from the medical and marketing fields.

### Healthcare Streaming Data Case Study

Influenza is a respiratory disease known to be a global health concern due to the disease's ability to cause serious illness or death.[6,7] Much work has been done in developing and implementing surveillance systems for influenza. A multitude of ways exist to develop an influenza surveillance tracking method. A traditional influenza surveillance system would begin with a patient admitted to a hospital; the patient would be monitored while in the hospital.[8] A more contemporary approach links Google researchers to healthcare officials from the Centers for Disease Control, using Internet searches to monitor what part of the population has influenza.[9] The purpose of these surveillance systems is to alert healthcare workers to a potential influenza outbreak so that medical practitioners can intervene before the outbreak reaches a pandemic level.

One group of researchers has recently developed a digital dashboard allowing it to monitor influenza outbreaks using data from multiple sources in Hong Kong.[10] A dashboard is a visual user interface that summarizes pertinent information in a way that is easy to read. The use of dashboards was initially part of business applications that help managers and high-level executives make decisions. With a healthcare focus, the researchers in Hong Kong used the dashboard system that would update with real-time data sources such as

- Weekly consultation rate of influenza-like illness reported by general outpatient clinics in Hong Kong
- Weekly consultation rate of influenza-like illness reported by general practitioners
- Weekly influenza virus isolation rate
- Weekly overall school absenteeism rate
- Weekly hospital admission rate of children aged 4 and under with principal diagnosis of influenza

These metrics were tracked in real time, and if the researchers noted a spike in any of the dashboard graphics, they could alert local healthcare officials.

## Marketing Streaming Data Case Study

Online advertising plays an important role in advertising market strategies with the growth of the Internet. Currently, one of most widely used revenue models for online advertising involves charging for each click based on the popularity of keywords and the number of competing advertisers. In this pay-per-click (PPC) model, the advertiser pays only if its advertisement is clicked. The PPC model leaves room for individuals or rival companies to generate false clicks (that is, click fraud), which poses serious problems to the development of a reliable online advertising market.

PPC is a relatively new advertising model; it emerged onto the Internet in 1998. Originally introduced by Goto.com, the idea was that sponsored versions of the search term would be auctioned off to the highest bidder. Beginning in 2000, Goto.com began selling its services to many of the largest search engines of the time. Goto.com changed its name to Overture in 2001 and controlled nearly the entire PPC search market. Yahoo purchased Overture in 2003. There was one exception to Overture's dominance: Google also had a PPC model that it developed internally.[11]

In 2002, Google altered its model and began offering the Google paid search results on other search engines (Overture made a similar move the year before). Google's new model was known as Adwords. Adwords was an adoption of Overture's model in which advertisers bid on how much they would pay per click. This model allows advertisers to buy their way to the top of a search posting; that is, the highest bid gets the most exposure.

Google strategists realized there was a problem with this approach: if an advertiser bid its way to the top of the ranking with an irrelevant ad, and no one clicked on it, then no one made any money from the advertising. Google introduced click-through rate, as a measure of the ad's relevance, into the ranking algorithm. If an ad with a lower bid per click got clicked more often, it would rank higher. The rest is history; the click-through rate approach is what has turned Google into the billion dollar company it is today.[12]

With such intense competition, one can see why detecting click fraud is a major concern. Researchers in the Department of Electrical and Computer Engineering of Iowa State University have proposed a method of detecting click fraud in the PPC model using streaming data.[13] Possible sources of click fraud come from

- Search engines or online ad publishers
- Ad subdistributors
- Competitors
- Web page crawlers

When assessing which clicks are valid or invalid in a clickstream, duplicate clicks are a major consideration. The authors from Iowa consider two scenarios for the duplicate click issue.

*Scenario 1*: A normal client visited an advertiser's website by clicking the ad link of a publisher. One week later, the client visited the same website again by clicking on the same ad link.
*Scenario 2*: The competitors or even the publishers control thousands of computers, each of which initiates many clicks to the ad links every day.

Obviously the first scenario is not fraud, but the second scenario is click fraud. The authors used a time-based jumping window as the basis of their analysis. In this scenario, a time dimension has to be specified. For example, one should examine clicks over a unit of time—second, minute, hour, day, etc. Then the window of time that is specified is broken down into subwindows. The information and statistics gathered on the clickstream over the entire time window is based on the combination from the smaller subwindows. The statistics that are calculated to detect if the click is fraudulent or not are based on a theoretical algorithm known as the Bloom filter. In summary, the Bloom filter detects if the click is a duplicate over a jumping window. If the click is determined to be a duplicate, it is marked fraudulent. When new clicks are added to the stream (or another subwindow), the oldest clickstream data is deleted. Clickstream data is constantly being fed into the algorithm to determine if clicks are fraudulent or not.

The main advantage of the author's approach is that high-speed clickstreams can be processed in a way that uses less computer memory, thus speeding up processing time in determining if the click is fraudulent or not.

## Credit Card Fraud Detection Case Study

Credit cards are responsible for $25 trillion in transactions a year at more than 24 million locations in 200 countries. It is estimated that there are 10,000 payment transactions every second around the world.[15] Credit card fraud costs the United States $8.6 billion annually.[16] Since there is a global economic impact for credit card fraud, researchers around the world in the data mining community are actively developing methods to thwart this problem. One statistical method that is being used to detect credit card fraud is clustering. Sorin (2012) provides a comprehensive overview of the contemporary statistical clustering techniques that are being used to detect financial fraud.[17] One of the techniques he describes in his publication is a clustering method that combines streaming data to detect credit card fraud.[17]

Clustering is an unsupervised data mining technique. An unsupervised technique is one in which there is no outcome or target variable that is modeled using predictor variables. Clustering isolates transactions into homogenous groups. The clustering algorithm can work on multidimensional data and aims to minimize the distance within clusters while maximizing the distance between clusters. With an arbitrary starting point of $k$ centers, the algorithm proceeds iteratively by assigning each point to its nearest center based on Euclidean distance, then recomputing the central points of each cluster. This continues until convergence, where every cluster assignment has stabilized.

Often the purpose of clustering is descriptive. For example, segmenting existing transactions into groups and associating a distinct profile with each group will help determine what transactions need to be looked at more closely.

Traditional clustering methods cannot analyze streaming data since one of the underlying assumptions for clustering analysis is that the data is in a traditional static database. Tasoulis et al. (2008) have developed a cluster algorithm that will generate clusters on streaming data.[18] The main idea of the algorithm is to cluster transactions in moving time windows. The data in the time windows are recentered to the mean of the data points they include at each time point in a manner that depends on each transaction's time stamp. Every time a new transaction (data streaming point) arrives, the clusters are updated. The algorithm has a "forgetting factor" that deletes the data points when they are no longer informative in building the clusters.

Creating a clustering technique for streaming data for a credit card application has the potential to uncover hidden fraudulent transactions in massive streaming credit card data. As new transactions occur, finding out how clusters evolve can prove crucial in identifying what factors make the transaction fraudulent. Several issues that are important in streaming data credit card detection are

- Detecting the fraudulent transaction as soon as it occurs
- Detecting equally well both types of changes, abrupt and gradual
- Distinguishing between real evolution of the clusters and noise

If the transaction is found to be fraudulent, the analyst must do the following:

- Make sure the transaction is not out of date (the importance of using moving time windows)
- Archive some of the old clusters and examples

The second point is to create a data stream analysis technique that is efficient. Streaming data is like a river: data flows in and data flows out. The analyst only gets to see the data one time, so it is important that the algorithm is efficient and has been trained properly to detect fraudulent transactions. The algorithm needs to "remember" what a fraudulent transaction looks like.

---

## VENDOR PRODUCTS FOR STREAMING BIG DATA

Many streaming data types are unstructured, such as text logs, Twitter feeds, transactional flows, and clickstreams. Massive unstructured databases are too voluminous to be handled by a traditional database structure. Two software industry giants, SAS and IBM, have recently developed architectures and software to analyze unstructured data in real time and to allow analysts to understand what is happening in real time and take action to improve outcomes.

## SAS

SAS is a statistical software company that has strength in offering end-to-end business solutions in over 15 specific industries, such as casinos, education, healthcare, hotels, insurance, life sciences, manufacturing, retail, and utilities. In December 2012, the SAS DataFlux Event Stream Processing Engine became available. The product incorporates relational, procedural, and pattern-matching analysis of structured and unstructured data. This product is ideal for customers who want to analyze high-velocity big data in real time. SAS is targeting the new product to customers in the financial field. Global banks and capital market firms must analyze big data for risk and compliance to meet Basel III, Dodd-Frank, and other regulations. The SAS DataFlux Event Stream Processing Engine merges large data sets for risk analysis with continuous data integration of internal and external streams. These data sets include market data feeds from Bloomberg, Thomson Reuters, NYSE Technologies, and International Data Corp.

## IBM

IBM is a hardware and software giant, with one of the largest software offerings of any of its competitors in the market. IBM is currently on its third version of a streaming data platform. InfoSphere Streams radically extends the state of the art in big data processing; it is a high-performance computing platform that allows users to develop and reuse applications to rapidly consume and analyze information as it arrives from thousands of real-time sources. Users are able to

- Continuously analyze massive volumes of data at rates up to petabytes per day
- Perform complex analytics of heterogeneous data types, including text, images, audio, voice, video, web traffic, email, GPS data, financial transaction data, satellite data, and sensors
- Leverage submillisecond latencies to react to events and trends as they are unfolding, while it is still possible to improve business outcomes
- Adapt to rapidly changing data forms and types

- Easily visualize data with the ability to route all streaming records into a single operator and display them in a variety of ways on an html dashboard

---

## CONCLUSION

Data mining of big data is well suited to spot patterns in large static data sets. Traditional approaches to data mining of big data lags in being able to react quickly to observed changes in behavior or spending patterns. As use of the Internet, cellular phones, social media, cyber technology, and satellite technology continues to grow, the need for analyzing these types of unstructured data will increase as well. There are two points of concern that still require much work in the streaming data field:

1. Scalable storage solutions are needed to sustain high data streaming rates.
2. Security of streaming data.

Continuous data streaming workloads present a number of challenges for storage system designers. The storage system should be optimized for both latency and throughput since scalable data stream processing systems must both handle heavy stream traffic and produce results to queries within given time bounds, typically tens to a few hundreds of milliseconds.[14]

Data security has long been a concern, but streaming big data adds a new component to data security. The sheer size of a streaming data database is enough to give pause; certainly a data breach of streaming big data could trump other past security breaches. The number of individuals with access to streaming data is another security concern. Traditionally, when a report was to be generated for a manager, the analyst and a select few members of an information technology (IT) department were the only ones who could access the data. With the complexity of streaming data, there can be analysts, subject matter experts, statisticians, and computer and software engineers who are all accessing the data. As the number of individuals who access the data increases, so will the likelihood of a data breach.

Settings that require real-time analysis of streaming data will continue to grow, making this a rich area for ongoing research. This chapter has defined streaming data and placed the concept of streaming data in the context of big data. Real-world case studies have been given to illustrate the wide-reaching and diverse aspects of streaming data applications.

## REFERENCES

1. McAfee, A., and Brynjolfsson, E. 2012. Big data: The management revolution. *Harvard Business Review*, October, pp. 60–69.
2. Zikopoulos, P., Eaton, C., deRoos, D., Deutsch, T., and Lapis, G. 2012. *Understanding big data: Analytics for enterprise class Hadoop and streaming data.* New York: McGraw-Hill.
3. Davenport, T., Barth, P., and Bean, R. 2012. How 'big data' is different. *MIT Sloan Management Review* 54(1).
4. Ozsu, M.T., and Valduriez, P. 2011. Current issues: Streaming data and database systems. In *Principles of distributed database systems*, 723–763. 3rd ed. New York: Springer.
5. Michalak, S., DuBois, A., DuBois, D., Wiel, S.V., and Hogden, J. 2012. Developing systems for real-time streaming analysis. *Journal of Computational and Graphical Statistics* 21(3):561–580.
6. Glezen, P. 1982. Serious morbidity and mortality associated with influenza epidemics. *Epidemiologic Review* 4(1):25–44.
7. Thompson, W.W., Shay, D.K., Weintraub, E., Brammer, L., Cox, N., Anderson, L.J., and Fukuda, K. 2003. Mortality associated with influenza and respiratory syncytial virus in the United States. *Journal of the American Medical Association* 289(2):179–186.
8. Weingarten, S., Friedlander, M., Rascon, D., Ault, M., Morgan, M., and Meyer, M.D. 1988. Influenza surveillance in an acute-care hospital. *Journal of the American Medical Association* 148(1):113–116.
9. Ginsberg, J., Mohebbi, M., Patel, R.S., Brammer, L., Smolinski, M.S., and Brilliant, L. 2009. Detecting influenza epidemics using search engine query data. *Nature*, February, pp. 1012–1014.
10. Cheng, C.K.Y., Ip, D.K.M., Cowling, B.J., Ho, L.M., Leung, G.M., and Lau, E.H.Y. 2011. Digital dashboard design using multiple data streams for disease surveillance with influenza surveillance as an example. *Journal of Medical Internet Research* 13(4):e85.
11. Douzet, A. An investigation of pay per click search engine advertising: Modeling the PPC paradigm to lower cost per action. Retrieved from http://cdn.theladders.net/static/doc/douzet_modeling_ppc_paradigm.pdf.
12. Karp, S. 2008. *Google Adwords: A brief history of online advertising innovation.* Retrieved January 1, 2013, from Publishing 2.0: http://publishing2.com/2008/05/27/google-adwords-a-brief-history-of-online-advertising-innovation/.
13. Zhang, L., and Guan, Y. 2008. Detecting click fraud in pay-per-click streams of online advertising networks. In *Proceedings of the IEEE 28th International Conference on Distributed Computing System*, Beijing, China, pp. 77–84.
14. Botan, I., Alonso, G., Fischer, P.M., Kossman, D., and Tatbul, N. 2009. Flexible and scalable storage management for data-intensive stream processing. Presented at 12th International Conference on Extending Database Technology, Saint Petersburg, Russian Federation.

15. Woolsey, B., and Shulz, M. Credit card statistics, industry facts, debt statistics. Retrieved January 31, 2013, from creditcards.com: http://www.creditcards.com/credit-card-news/credit-card-industry-facts-personal-debt-statistics-1276.php#Circulation-issuer.
16. Aite Group. 2010. Payment card fraud costs $8.6 billion per year. Retrieved from http://searchfinancialsecurity.techtarget.com/news/1378913/Payment-card-fraud-costs-86-billion-per-year-Aite-Group-says.
17. Sorin, A. 2012. Survey of clustering based financial fraud detection research. *Informatica Economica* 16(1):110–122.
18. Tasoulis, D.K., Adams, N.M., Weston, D.J., and Hand, D.J. 2008. Mining information from plastic card transaction streams. Presented at Proceedings in Computational Statistics: 18th Symposium, Porto, Portugal.

# 9

---

# *Using CEP for Real-Time Data Mining*

*Steven Barber*

## CONTENTS

## INTRODUCTION

Complex event processing (CEP) is a relatively new category of software whose purpose is to process streams of events, perform a set of computations on them, and then publish new streams of events based on the result of these computations.

On the surface, this discipline sounds like every other kind of computer programming since Lovelace (input, compute, and output), and of course, that is true. What makes CEP interesting is its narrow focus on input events that arrive in streams, and on computations that generally seek to take in very large numbers of relatively raw events and, by operating on them, produce streams of output events that have more meaning to the enterprise—that represent events at a higher level of abstraction or value than the events that went in. With CEP, what we're interested in, primarily, are the events that are arriving right now. The CEP system receives an event, acts on it immediately, and then there's another event arriving to take care of. There's no attempt to hold all the previous events in memory for a long time—the CEP process squeezes what's interesting out of the event as it arrives and discards what's not interesting. This focus on real-time (as it arrives) push as opposed to pull is at the core of what CEP is.

All this is not to say that CEP can't be used to look at stored or historical data—it often is, especially when application testing is going on. However, the usual case is for the CEP system to play back stored historical data as if it represented events that are arriving in streams, and not to scan over large historical stores of now-static data.

CEP, being a streaming data-oriented technology, is not often used for pattern discovery in the same way a data warehouse is. CEP is very often used to match already known patterns against arriving data, and then, once the match occurs, to take some action based on the recognition of that pattern. For example, if a securities trader believes that three upticks followed by two downticks in the same second means something, then a CEP application can be easily made to look for that pattern and generate an output event whenever that pattern occurs. Another common use of CEP is for creating caches of information that can be used with interactive discovery-oriented tools so that new patterns or conditions can be discovered more or less live, and then acted upon manually before it is too late to act, or to explore the data visually in order to perceive interesting patterns in the first place, which then, once identified and validated against longer-term trends, can be the basis for future automation by another CEP application.

## QUANTITATIVE APPROACHES TO STREAMING DATA ANALYSIS

CEP systems provide the ability to operate on, or transform, input events into output events in a number of ways. The model for CEP processing tends to be declarative rather than imperative, data flow-oriented rather than control flow-oriented, and push-oriented rather than pull-oriented. Events arrive or happen, and then the events are presented to the first operation in the application, which operates on the event and in turn emits zero or more events in response to the next operation in the stream of operators, which processes the event(s) generated by the upstream operations, and so on until no events are emitted or an output is reached. It is the arrival of the event that triggers the CEP processing—the CEP processor does not periodically scan for events, but rather reacts to events immediately when they arrive. This property makes CEP systems very responsive, with minimal processing latency.

Once this event-oriented model is grasped, the kinds of operations that may be performed in a CEP application are somewhat different than in traditional imperative languages. Rather than if/then/else and for and while loops, there are event- and stream-oriented operators, like Aggregate, Filter, Map, and Split. Rather than keeping state in variables, generally state is kept in relational tables and retrieved via streaming joins of arriving events with the contents of the tables. Streams are partitioned into windows over which operations are performed. The effect of this model is that operations are performed at a higher level of abstraction than in traditional programming languages—closer to the concerns of application domains, and without developers having to pay attention to tracking lots of lower-level housekeeping details.

## EVENT STREAM PROCESSING EVOLUTION IN RECENT HISTORY

### There Is Always More Data, and It Isn't Getting Any Simpler

The need for event processing systems arises from the observation that with modern communication and information technology, there is always going to be more data than humans can contend with directly, and that every year there is more data: more in volume and more types. Further, the relationships between arriving data are arbitrarily complex. Making sense of the data at our fingertips is not easy. Being able to recognize which events are interesting, or which match some pattern we are interested in, is something that simply must be automated. Events may be arriving thousands or even millions of time per second, and often it is valuable to respond to them as quickly as we can, perhaps within microseconds. For example, these days most of the securities trading in the major equities and currency markets occurs within a few hundred microseconds of an order's placement in a trading venue. The ability to respond that fast to an order tends to encourage the placement of yet more orders, more quickly, in order to gain tiny advantages in trading.

## Processing Model Evolution

### *The Orthodox History of CEP: Long-Needed Switch from RDBMS-Based Real-Time Processing to Event Stream Processing*

In the social history of technology, CEP seems to have grown out of the relational database world. (To the extent that attempts to standardize CEP languages have been made, the resulting languages tend to look like Structured Query Language (SQL).)

### *RDBMS: Store, Then Analyze*

In an off-the-shelf relational database management system (RDBMS), data is stored in relational tables, usually kept on disk or some other relatively slow persistent storage medium. Increasing the relative slowness of RDBMSs, not only is the base data stored on disk, but also the indexes in the tables, as well as transaction logs. Once the data is written to the table, subsequent read queries reextract the data for analysis—reading data usually involves scanning indexes and then reading the data back off the disk. In the early days of creating event-oriented systems, RDBMSs were pretty much what was available for structured storage, and the default was to put stuff there. Unfortunately, as data arrival rates and volumes began to rise, traditionally structured RDBMSs were unable to keep up. For example, when doing automated securities transaction processing with, say, the usual North American equities trade and quote messages, RDBMSs are happy to process maybe a few thousand transactions per second, if well tuned. However, the equities markets now generate hundreds of thousands of messages per second, and the cost of an RDBMS that can handle that amount of traffic is astronomical, if not infinite. This style of processing is sometimes called an outbound processing model (Figure 9.1).

CEP proceeds from this fairly simple high-level observation: not every event need be stored by every process that receives it. If we need to store every event for later, it might be better to do that separate and in parallel to the analysis of the event, and perhaps we don't need to have our event persister operate with the Atomicity, Consistency, Isolation, Durability (ACID) transactionality of a traditional relational: a simple file appender might be just fine and will give us a couple orders of magnitude of additional performance on the same hardware—from thousands of events per second to hundreds of thousands per second. The CEP engine receives the events in parallel with the persister, and indeed, since it is operating against memory instead of disk, could easily process millions of messages

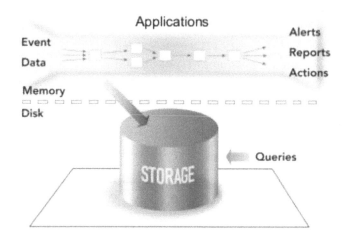

**FIGURE 9.1**
CEP: Analyze, then store, or analyze while storing.

per second if persistence were not required. This change is head-slappingly obvious in retrospect, but easy to miss if the organization is used to reasoning in a database-y way (and the work and time involved in reorienting an organization that has multiple competing priorities should not be underestimated). This style of processing is sometimes called an inbound processing model.

*Turning the Database on Its Side*

Another way to think about the relationship between database and CEP systems is this way: in a relational database, generally speaking, data is stored persistently in a set of tables, and queries against the tables occur transiently. In CEP, the queries against a set of streams run persistently, and the data flowing through the streams is what's transient.

### Another View: CEP Is a Message Transformation Engine That's a Service Attached to a Distributed Messaging Bus

Despite CEP's database-oriented conceptual heritage, in practice it is often useful to imagine a CEP application as if it were a stream-oriented asynchronous computation service attached to a distributed messaging bus. Events go in, get operated upon, events go out. CEP's push-based processing model is directly analogous to a receive message callback in a typical messaging application programming interface (API), for example. Viewing the

CEP application as a distributed service usually leads to the right answers when reasoning about the system architecture, especially in terms of how to characterize and establish particular qualities of service at the interfaces and designing for scalability and recovery. Further, distributed messaging is largely a solved problem: there are numerous off-the-shelf message buses that work just fine. There is no need to reinvent them just for CEP; we only need to make relatively simple bus adapters in order to leverage them fully.

### The Wheel Turns Again: Big Data, Web Applications, and Log File Analysis

What we are seeing in the current big data revolution, at least in the part of it where the data in question is generated from the operation of web applications with many millions of users, is an entire subindustry built with interactive transaction processing in mind, but not with much orientation to needs of eventual downstream analytics processing. At least in the database world, the data is in a predefined and consistent format as data. In the web application world, much transaction data tends to be serialized into log files, often locally on boxes that are then gathered centrally for subsequent analysis after the fact. Creating the log file is pretty slow: stringifying all that data and then writing it to disk is computationally expensive, tends to be relatively verbose, and perhaps the log file formats were not designed with after-the-fact data mining activity as a top priority.

#### Store (in Log Files), Then Analyze (with, for Example, Hadoop)

As a result, big data tools such as Hadoop and Flume tend to be oriented toward scraping data out of log files. This is also a computationally expensive process, since parsing nonuniform log message formats can require a bit of smarts. Thus, the famous Hadoop MapReduce paradigm exists to distribute this work over many nodes and forward correlation and aggregation work to other processors, perhaps more central. This log file orientation is changing, though, and newer systems targeted at real-time big data analytics such as Twitter Storm and Apache Kafka are starting to look more like CEP.

### Rise of Inexpensive Multicore Processors and GPU-Based Processing

Beyond the focus on high-performance processing typically near the core of the CEP value proposition, CEP came of age around the same time that multiprocessor-based hardware became widely available and inexpensive. In the mid-2000s, when CEP first became commercially available, two- and four-core servers were starting to become common in enterprise settings. Now, 32- or 64-core servers are easy to find and fit within most IT shop budgets easily. In addition, massively parallel graphics processing units (GPUs) began to appear and could be put in a common desktop workstation for several hundred dollars. With rising data volumes and tighter latency requirements, being able to take advantage of readily available cheap CPU cycles has great appeal. Most existing programming systems don't automatically take advantage of this power, but CEP languages generally do, at least for some important classes of data-driven application partitioning.

## ADVANTAGES OF CEP

### Visual Programming for Communicating with Stakeholders

Most commercial CEP authoring tools provide ways to visualize CEP programs as flow diagrams. For some CEP languages, the visual representation is a view that generates text-based code, and for others the language itself is natively visual: not just visual representation, but visual programming.

The visual representation emphasize that events come in streams, are processed by passing through multiple stages of transformation or aggregation, and may be routed through various internal streams before being published to external systems as event streams via adapters.

There are two primary benefits to visual representations of programs. The first is for the developer: the visual primitives allow the developer to plot out the flow of each event and keep the flow between components visible. Dependencies are easy to see as well.

The second benefit is that the meaning of a visual flow-based presentation is often quite clear to other stakeholders in the development process, such as the business people who commissioned the system. With the flow visible, communication between various human groups is easier.

An experienced CEP developer can design the application so that the program reflects what ordinarily would be drawn into a Visio-style block diagram of the system, with each top-level block able to be drilled down into to reveal more detailed logic at lower levels of abstraction.

The flip side of visual programming is the potential of the creation of very confusing flow diagrams. Developers sometimes speak of "spaghetti code" even with text-based languages when the code is disorganized and hard to follow; a visual language, improperly used, can make code that literally looks like tangled pasta strands. It takes a fair amount of discipline and a willingness to rework the application architecture once hidden dependencies are discovered in order to keep the flow diagrams clean. This is usually worth the effort, as confusing programs tend to be expensive to maintain and tend only to get more confusing over time. Further, identifying interdependencies and minimizing them tends to be good for performance, especially performance improvements that can result from parallelization. Visual programming doesn't cause spaghetti, but it does tend to make it more obvious. Not all developers appreciate having to keep their designs clean, even though there's great payoff in doing so over the life of the application.

## CEP EXAMPLE: A SIMPLE APPLICATION USING STREAMBASE

Below is a simple StreamBase application called MarketFeedMonitor. sbapp. It listens to a stream of securities market data, calculates throughput statistics and publishes them to a statistics stream, and also detects drastic falloffs in tick volume and sends a message representing an alert about the volume drop-off. These statistics and alerts aren't necessarily valuable for all possible applications of the market data, but they are very interesting to a subset of the market data recipients: very interesting to the market data operations group, for whom volumes and falloff can be an indication of the physical health of the market data infrastructure itself, and secondarily to traders—human or automated—as inputs to trading decisions. For example, some trading strategies are only valid when the frequency of ticks is high, and very often an automated trading strategy should simply stop trading or get out of the market entirely if traffic falls off, either due to technical glitches or because something sudden and unusual is happening in the market itself. The output events are an example of the kind of higher-level value that can be mined in real time from the stream of ticks as they rush past.

In this application, the market data is the "simple" event data, relatively raw and voluminous, and the output is the "complex" data—orders of magnitude fewer events, aggregated and summarized, and suitable for particular targeted applications with value to certain parts of a business. The output is a higher-level abstraction, derived from the input, from a particular perspective.

The application is expressed using a language called EventFlow, which is the visual programming language used by almost all StreamBase developers. EventFlow is a truly visual language in that there is no other representation of the program in some other form like text; the icons and arrows themselves are renderings of the semantic units directly executed by the StreamBase runtime. When authoring an EventFlow application, the developer drags and drops icons that represent executable EventFlow components directly onto an application canvas, fills out sheets of properties to customize each component to the needs of that particular application, and then connects the components together with arcs (arrows) that represent the possible paths of the flow of events through the application (Figure 9.2).

## EventFlow Concepts and Terminology

An sbapp is a StreamBase application (and not coincidentally the extension of the names of files that contain individual sbapps). The word *application* in this context has a specific meaning: it's a unit of EventFlow logic that could be executed as a stand-alone unit. A single .sbapp file is also said to be a *module*.

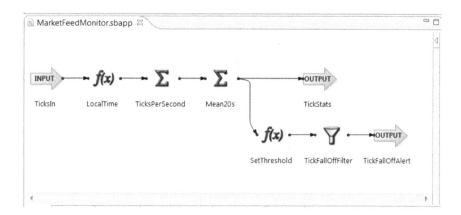

**FIGURE 9.2**

MarketFeedMonitor EventFlow application. (From © Copyright TIBCO Software, Inc. All rights reserved. Used with permission.)

In StreamBase, a module is the fundamental unit of functional composition and reuse: a module can refer to another module and direct streams of tuples through the reference into another module, and back out again.

What is an event? Conceptually the existence of an event is a discrete representation that something happened. The contents of the event represent information about that event. In StreamBase, events are represented by a *data type* called a *tuple*. Individual tuples are instances of a subtype of tuple determined associated with a specific *schema*. A tuple contains a single value for each *field* in its schema.

A schema, in turn, has a name and a set of schema fields. A schema field consists of a name and data type. Note that there are two subtly different meanings of the word *field* here: to recap, a field in a schema is a pair of a name and data type. For example, there might be a field called quantity whose data type is int (meaning a 32-bit integer). A tuple of that schema would then be said to have a field called quantity that has a value specific to that tuple instance, for example, 100.

A single EventFlow application file, or module, contains a set of EventFlow *components* and *arcs*. Each component is represented by an icon on the application canvas. There are several types of components in this application: input streams, output streams, and operators.

Operators are components that perform a specific type of runtime action on the tuples streaming through them. Each operator instance is configurable using settings in the Properties view for each operator instance. Some properties require expressions in which the values of fields of incoming tuples can be referenced. An operator may have input ports and an output port to which a connection arc may be attached. Tuples flow into an operator from input ports, and flow out through output ports. The relationship of input tuples to output tuples is defined by processing rules of the type of the operator. As we step through the example application, we'll describe how the operators in the application work.

A *stream* is a potentially infinite sequence of tuples. The term *sequence* is intended to imply a strict ordering of events in the stream, based on the order of the events' arrival into the stream. In StreamBase, though not in every CEP system, all the tuples in a stream must have the same schema.

In StreamBase, there are a number of different kinds of streams. We'll consider three of them in this introductory exposition: input streams, output streams, and arcs.

*Input streams* define an entry point into a StreamBase application, and declare the schema of tuples that traverse the stream. Applications may have as many input streams as they need.

*Output streams* define an exit point for tuples from a StreamBase application. The schema of an output stream must match the schema of the connection arc attached to the output stream's input port.

*Arcs* (or more specifically, the type of arcs shown in the example application, which are known as connection arcs) are the lines that connect components on the EventFlow Editor canvas. Connection arcs indicate that the output tuples of one component flow to the input port of the next downstream component, and thus indicate the flow of tuples between operators in an application.

## Step-by-Step through the MarketFeedMonitor App

Let's look at the individual components in this application the way an EventFlow developer would. We'll work from left to right, from the input through to the output.

TicksIn

The leftmost component, represented by a purple arrow, is an input stream named TicksIn. The Edit Schema tab of the Properties view for

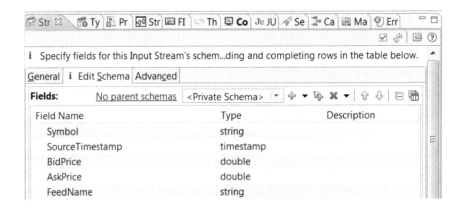

**FIGURE 9.3**

Schema for the TicksIn input stream. (From © Copyright TIBCO Software, Inc. All rights reserved. Used with permission.)

TicksIn specifies the schema of the tuples that will arrive on this stream, and is a simplified representation of a typical securities quote (Figure 9.3).

Tuples that arrive at an input stream are processed by sending them out the output port of the input stream to the next component downstream, as carried by the connection arc attached to the output port. Arriving tuples are processed one at a time, fully to completion, before the next arriving tuple is processed. *To completion* here means "as far as it can be," until there is nothing left to do with that tuple. We'll see how far that means as we go through the rest of the operators.

LocalTime

The LocalTime component is an instance of a Map operator. With a Map operator, as its $f(x)$ symbol suggests, the output tuples are the result of applying simple functions to the values of the fields of its input tuples. A Map operator has exactly one input port and exactly one output port, and outputs exactly one tuple every time it processes an input tuple. In general, the schema of operator output ports are independent of the schema of the input ports; in practice, there are conventions for copying input schemas to output schemas, so that we often say tuples are "passed through" an operator—logically, though, output tuples are different tuple instances than input tuples.

In the case of the LocalTime map, the Output Settings tab of the Properties view is configured as shown in Figure 9.4.

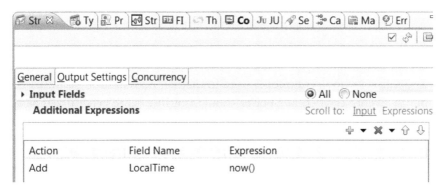

**FIGURE 9.4**

Output Settings tab for LocalTime map operator. (From © Copyright TIBCO Software, Inc. All rights reserved. Used with permission.)

The Input Fields choice here is All, which means that all the fields of each input tuple appear in each output tuple, and the values of the output field with the same name as the input field are copied directly from the value of the corresponding field in the input tuple. The Additional Expressions grid allows the EventFlow developer to add, replace, or remove fields in the output tuple relative to the input tuple. For the LocalTime map, we add one field called LocalTime to the output schema. The value of the LocalTime field for a given output tuple will be the result of the evaluation of the built-in function now(), which returns the date and time that it now is on the system where the function is executed, down to millisecond resolution.

The LocalTime field is going to be used as a time series basis for the aggregations that happen downstream. In particular, the values of the LocalTime field have the property that they monotonically increase with each arriving tuple, a property that the series of arriving SourceTimestamp values in the input schema may or may not possess. We'll elaborate on why that's important when we discuss the Aggregate operator.

(As an aside, and to forestall objections, it is a far from optimal software engineering practice to reference the system clock inside the business logic of an application—the source of time values should be considered to be external to the application's logic in order to create a repeatable (and auto-matable) set of functional regression tests for the application. Designing applications for testability is a much larger topic for a different book, and here we add the time stamp from now() inside this simple example app. In practice we would have that in a separate module, if at all, that could be connected to either live or test sources of market data as we choose.)

TicksPerSecond

TicksPerSecond is an instance of an Aggregate operator, represented by a sigma symbol, commonly used in mathematics to mean summation, but in EventFlow perhaps better thought of in a more generalized sense of summarization. We could spend a long time discussing the complete semantics, capabilities, and details of the Aggregate operator—and in our documentation and EventFlow classes we do—but for the purposes of this brief overview we will stick to the basics.

Aggregate, like Map, has one input port and one output port. Unlike Map, Aggregate typically does not emit a tuple from its output port every time an input tuple arrives. Aggregate typically emits many few tuples than it consumes; the results emitted by Aggregate are due to applying aggregation functions to windows of tuples in a stream.

The Aggregate operator creates conceptually treats a stream as if it were a series of (possibly overlapping) segments called *windows*. Windows open, close, and emit tuples based on events, and in TicksPerSecond these activities are based on the values of the LocalTime field in the arriving tuples. (When a window is controlled by arriving field values, we call the bases of the aggregation a *field dimension*.) TicksPerSecond has a single dimension called TicksPerSecondDim, and in the configuration dialog shown in Figure 9.5, we can see that TicksPerSecond will open a window, close a window, and (implicitly and by default) emit a tuple for every second of time represented by the values of the LocalTime field. These windows are nonoverlapping; that is, every tuple in the stream appears in one and only one window.

In StreamBase, a window almost never actually contains all the tuples that are assigned to it by dimension processing. Rather, the window contains the incremental state of its eventual result, which is usually very compact relative to the size of the set of its input tuples. Thus, each field in the

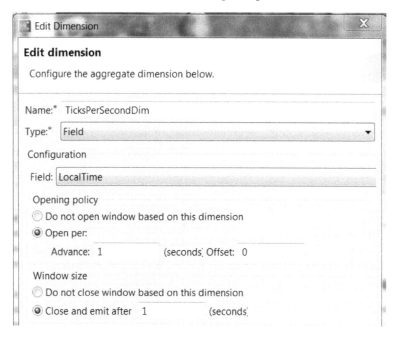

**FIGURE 9.5**

TicksPerSecondDim Aggregate dimension configuration dialog. (From © Copyright TIBCO Software, Inc. All rights reserved. Used with permission.)

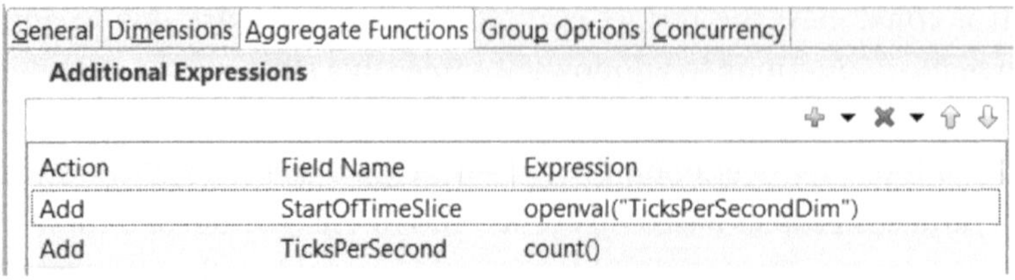

| General | Dimensions | Aggregate Functions | Group Options | Concurrency |

**Additional Expressions**

✛ ▾ ✖ ▾ ⬆ ⬇

| Action | Field Name | Expression |
|--------|------------|------------|
| Add | StartOfTimeSlice | openval("TicksPerSecondDim") |
| Add | TicksPerSecond | count() |

**FIGURE 9.6**

TicksPerSecond Aggregate operator Aggregate Functions tab. (From © Copyright TIBCO Software, Inc. All rights reserved. Used with permission.)

output tuple is specified in the Aggregate Functions tab to be the result of applying an aggregate expression to the set of input tuples that make up the window. Each time a tuple arrives, the TicksPerSecond operator evaluates each aggregate expression in the Aggregate Functions tab, and updates the incremental result in the window, conceptually in a field in the window with the field name specified. When it is time to emit a tuple (and in this case, TicksPerSecond will emit a tuple each time a window closes), the final result of each aggregate expression is calculated, and then creates an output tuple that contains the result of the aggregate calculation (Figure 9.6).

TicksPerSecond has two aggregation expressions, each a direct invocation of a built-in aggregate function. For each window, the StartOfTimeSlice field will contain openval("TicksPerSecondDim")—the openval() of a window is the lowest value of that field that could possibly be in the window, and in the case of a time stamp value, that will be the beginning of second of time. The TicksPerSecond field contains a count of the tuples in the window—the count() aggregate function is a very simple function that increments its value with each input tuple, and returns that count when the result tuple is created.

The final piece of configuration for the TicksPerSecond operator is to specify a Group By field. When Aggregate is grouping, that means that a separate window is created for each unique value of the set of group by fields configured for that operator instance, for each range of tuples that would be in a window as otherwise controlled by the windowing dimensions. Effectively, grouping creates a logical partition of a stream into parallel substreams for each group value, at least while being processed by the Aggregate operator.

While the value of a Group By field may be the result of evaluating any expression, here the FeedName grouping field is just the value of the input field called FeedName. Group By fields appear in result tuples along with the fields specified in the Aggregate Functions tab. The FeedName in this

| i Specify group bys by adding and completing rows in the table below. | |
| --- | --- |
| General Dimensions Aggregate Functions i Group Options Concurrency | |
| ☐ Omit Group By fields in output | |
| **Group By:** | ✢ ▼ ✖ ▼ ⇧ ⇩ |
| Output Field Name | Expression |
| FeedName | FeedName |

**FIGURE 9.7**
TicksPerSecond Aggregate operator Group Options tab. (From © Copyright TIBCO Software, Inc. All rights reserved. Used with permission.)

example application is intended to identify the source of the market data tuples—typically that will be a trading venue such as NYSE or NASDAQ in the case of direct exchange feed or a market data consolidator such as Thomson Reuters or IDC. Market data feeds typically have their own connection infrastructure; thus, keeping statistics based on feed can be useful for identifying issues related to the infrastructure or the feed source itself (Figure 9.7).

So, the output of TicksPerSecond will be a stream of tuples that contains one tuple every second, for each feed's market data that is carried in the input stream. The output tuples will contain the time each second began, the name of the feed, and the number of tuples that arrived during the second.

Mean20s

The next operator is an Aggregate called Mean20s. Mean20s has a single field dimension based on the StartOfTimeSlice field output by TicksPerSecond. This dimension causes a new window to open every second and close and emit every 20 seconds. The windows overlap in terms of the time ranges they cover. This means that every arriving tuple can potentially cause the aggregate functions in 20 separate windows to update their calculations. Mean20s is also grouped by FeedName. The aggregate functions in Mean20s are shown in Figure 9.8.

The StartOfTimeSlice field will again be the lowest possible time value in the window.

AvgTicksPerSecond is the average of the incoming TicksPerSecond values over the length of the window; this creates, effectively, a 20-second moving average for each feed.

| General | Dimensions | Aggregate Functions | Group Options | Concurrency | | |
|---|---|---|---|---|---|---|
| **Additional Expressions** | | | | | | |
| | | | | | ✛ ▾ ✖ ▾ ⇧ ⇩ | |
| Action | | Field Name | | Expression | | |
| Add | | StartOfTimeSlice | | openval("Mean20sDim") | | |
| Add | | AvgTicksPerSecond | | avg(TicksPerSecond) | | |
| Add | | StdevTicksPerSeco... | | stdev(TicksPerSecond) | | |
| Add | | LastTicksPerSecond | | lastval(TicksPerSecond) | | |

**FIGURE 9.8**

Mean20s Aggregate operator Aggregate Functions tab. (From © Copyright TIBCO Software, Inc. All rights reserved. Used with permission.)

StdevTicksPerSecond is the standard deviation of the tuples in the window.

LastTicksPerSecond is the value of the last tuple to arrive in the window before it closed, the count of tuples that arrived during the 20th second of the window.

TickStats

Downstream of Mean20s there are two paths. One leads to the TickStats output stream, which provides a stream of tick statistics that others may listen to.

SetThreshold

The second path leads to the SetThreshold Map, which adds a falloff threshold value to the stream of 0.75, or 75%, in a field called AlertThreshold. Essentially this is a constant value to be used later.

TickFallOffFilter

The TickFallOffFilter operator is an instance of a Filter operator. This Filter will output a tuple that is the same as its input tuple on the only output port whenever the predicate for that output port evaluates to true. In this case the LastTicksPerSecond < AvgTicksPerSecond · AlertThreshold predicate expression will be true whenever the number of ticks in the most

| General | i | Predicate Settings | Concurrency | | | | | |
|---|---|---|---|---|---|---|---|---|

☐ Create output port for non-matching tuples

**Predicates:**    ✛ ▾ ✖ ▾ ⇧ ⇩

| Output Port | Predicate |
|---|---|
| 1 | LastTicksPerSecond < AvgTicksPerSecond * AlertThreshold |

**FIGURE 9.9**
TickFallOffFilter operator's Predicate Settings tab. (From © Copyright TIBCO Software, Inc. All rights reserved. Used with permission.)

recent second is less than 75% of the average number of ticks per second over the last 20 seconds (for each feed), which is not really a very substantial sudden drop-off in traffic, but rather a fairly high threshold set so that a simulated feed sends out alerts relatively frequently. (A more realistic threshold would be perhaps two standard deviations less than the 20-second mean—a very substantial drop-off) (Figure 9.9).

TickFallOffAlert

Finally, the generated falloff alert tuples are output on the TickFallOffAlert output stream. At this point, we have reduced hundreds of thousands of input events per second to perhaps a few each day—only those that meet the criteria we've specified in this application, and only those that have significance for this particular business function.

Figure 9.10 shows a view of the MarketFeedMonitor application running within the StreamBase Studio IDE.

This view shows one of the TickFallOffAlert tuples—you can see that LastTicksPerSecond < AvgTicksPerSecond · AlertThreshold would be 1.0 < 1.75 · 0.75, or 1.0 < 1.3125, which is true in this case.

## USES OF CEP IN INDUSTRY AND APPLICATIONS

### Automated Securities Trading

CEP is a natural fit in securities trading. To generalize very broadly, securities trading involves listening to market data and order and execution flow, and then placing orders in response, and keeping track of one's orders

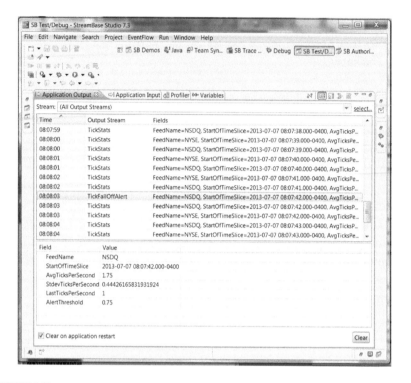

**FIGURE 9.10**

Application output view of a run of the MarketFeedMonitor application. (From © Copyright TIBCO Software, Inc. All rights reserved. Used with permission.)

and the executions against them. All of these things can easily be modeled as events. In automated trading, especially in the North American equities or equities options markets, it's not unusual to receive hundreds of thousands of events per second, and to publish perhaps thousands of events per second back to the markets.

There are numerous subapplications within the securities trading flow where CEP has been advantageously deployed. Most of the applications tend to be what are referred to as front office applications (actual trading), with a slow rise yet steady adoption in middle office (risk analysis, risk management, and regulatory compliance). CEP is not yet prevalent in the back office (for example, settlement and reconciliation).

Within the front office, some categories and patterns predominate:

- Market data management
- Signal generation/alpha-seeking algorithms
- Automated order management

- Execution algorithms
- Real-time profit and loss
- Transaction cost analysis

### Market Data Management

Trading firms pay significant sums of money for market data. The more up to the moment it is, the more it costs. Also, the more up to the moment it is, the more of it there tends to be and the less filtered and processed it is. Trading firms also tend to want to trade on multiple trading venues, which present similar kinds of data in widely varying formats.

There are other software product categories and indeed entire subindustries that are specifically focused on receiving and massaging raw market data into forms more convenient for internal processing. Market data consolidators such as Thomson Reuters and IDC, market data infrastructure and normalization vendors such as NYSE Advanced Technologies (Wombat), and tick store vendors such as OneTick make up the dominant subcategories. These are fine products and many in the industry use them. However, CEP engines are often used to perform processing either faster or in more specialized ways than come out of the box with the solution-focused products. Customized data cleansing, normalization, aggregation, consolidation, and statistic generation can be performed. Relative latency measurement between sources is also a popular application. Market data provider and infrastructure health monitoring and alerting functions are straightforward to develop with CEP engines. Sometimes, a firm will have a need only for a few venues, and therefore the cost to buy and maintain a more general market data infrastructure isn't justified—a CEP engine and a few venue adapters can do the job nicely.

### Signal Generation/Alpha-Seeking Algorithms

Algorithmic trading has been perhaps the marquee application for CEP engines over the past few years. While it is possible to develop very fast algo trading systems using lower-level programming technologies, the focus on high performance as well as easily changeable declarative code makes it relatively easy to adapt algorithms to rapidly evolving market conditions.

Signal generation algos listen to market data as well as order and execution flow in order to generate trading signals to downstream-automated trading systems. CEP engines can be used to build algo engines that manage strategy life cycles, positions, P&L, and interfaces to order management systems, and then each quant or technical trader can contribute its own "secret sauce" algorithm to the system.

There are numerous kinds of other algorithmic trading systems besides signal generators. Auto-hedging and market making are often referred to as different kinds of automated trading systems, but technically the only thing that varies between them are the algorithms used to trade or not to trade.

### Execution Algorithms

Once a trader, human or machine, determines that it's a good idea to place an order, there's a lot to be done with how and where to place the orders in various trading venues. For example, it might be desirable to split up a very large order over time to minimize impact on the market or to get a better average execution price. Or it might be that sending different parts of an order to different trading venues might result in a better or faster execution. The generalized term for this kind of application is execution algorithms, though there are a number of variants that represent different business opportunities or particular stages of the trade flow—the technology and software architectures for these variants are quite similar, even if the shape of the business opportunity and how it is sold is very different.

Execution algorithm engines are fairly straightforward to implement with a CEP engine, and the processing speeds are very good. It is common to provide for pluggable execution algorithms so that various methods are available to users of the system, or so that users may provide their own algorithms and take advantage of the provided infrastructure, which may be co-located with the trading venues or be on premises with the trading institution.

The most important subcomponents of an automated execution algorithm system are the execution algorithm manager, the order manager, the risk and compliance manager, the audit system, and the connections to upstream and downstream order sources and trading venues.

### Smart Order Routing

Smart order routing (SOR) is a widely implemented CEP application. Firms can use CEP to build SOR systems that automate the selection of execution venue and methodology in order to obtain best execution, systematize the selection process, and reduce execution costs. Smart order routing systems are implemented with a variety of levels of automation, from complete automation of retail flow trading to manual management and allocation of block trades. SOR systems can be deployed to augment an existing trade flow system, or form the basis for next-generation trading architectures. The most common asset routed is equities, though SOR systems can improve quality and cost of execution in any asset class. SOR systems often leverage other CEP applications as subcomponents: market data managers, execution algorithms, and transaction cost analyzers, to name just a few.

There are many inputs to an order routing decision. The goal of any system is to make the best decision for the firm and the client. To be *smart*, an order routing system must take into account more than just the parameters of the trade. It must also analyze real-time market conditions, and combine that with historical reference data about the security being traded, venue performance, and execution options.

### Market Data Analysis and Liquidity Detection

An SOR system constantly monitors the real-time conditions of the market. By analyzing behavior of market participants, volume curves can be adjusted, volatility can be estimated, and risk metrics can be calculated. Market data also enables the calculation of benchmarks, so that execution quality can be measured and monitored. Combined with execution history, benchmarks can be used to estimate transaction cost, demonstrate best execution, and verify the correctness of routing decisions. In addition to basic market data analysis, real-time data from multiple venues can be used to detect and predict available liquidity. SOR systems can also go beyond market data to predict liquidity, combining information from other asset classes or even unstructured news data to estimate market depth. Historical executions also enable prediction of the efficacy of execution methods.

### Real-Time Profit and Loss

As trading automation continues to grow pervasively throughout the capital markets, an increasingly important aspect of optimizing trading strategy is monitoring profit and loss in real time. With automated strategies typically trading at high frequencies, it is possible for profits and losses to accumulate rapidly. While many organizations may compute this at end of day in batch mode, with today's volatile markets, it has become highly desirable to move to a system of real-time calculation. By enabling the profit and loss of a strategy to be monitored in real time, and also allowing the strategy to use these calculations to adjust its own behavior, trading profits can be maximized while risks are minimized.

For example, a strategy may take an approach where the more profit made, the more resources are available with which to trade. It is important to separate the overall performance of the system (the organization's true profit and loss) from that of each strategy. By maintaining real-time potential profit and loss (P&L) calculations for each strategy in conjunction with the risk manager, it becomes possible to identify those strategies or instruments that did not achieve their potential due to overall system constraints and those that are underperforming. This enables the balance between the strategies to be adjusted more accurately.

A real-time P&L manager is an application that monitors live trade flow and calculates and reports the dynamic profit or loss along various axes, such as client, account, desk, instrument, and venue. An real-time P&L application may be a subcomponent of an alpha-generation algorithm system as described above, or it may be a stand-alone application that is connected to one or more trading systems to present a consolidated view of trading activity.

### Transaction Cost Analysis

Financial markets are inherently volatile, characterized by shifting values, risks, and opportunities. The prices of individual securities are frequently changing for numerous reasons, including shifts in perceived value, localized supply-demand imbalances, and price changes in other sector investments or the market as a whole. Reduced liquidity adds price volatility and market risk to any contemplated transaction, and in the face of this volatility, transaction cost analysis (TCA) has become increasingly important to help firms measure how effectively both perceived and actual portfolio orders are completed.

Conceptually, TCA represents the difference between two amounts, and a CEP platform can play an active role in computing TCA in real time. The first amount represents the amount if the transaction was instantaneously executed at the price prevailing when the portfolio manager made the decision, without any additional costs. The second amount represents what would have been or actually was realized. This second amount includes direct costs, such as commissions, settlement costs, and taxes, as well as indirect costs from timing delays, market impact, and missed opportunities. The difference between these two amounts is often referred to as transaction *slippage*.

Increased slippage amounts directly reduce investor returns and hurt relative performance vs. the performance of competing investment managers. In an environment of increased regulatory scrutiny and fierce competition, TCA has become a staple at buy-side firms to analyze the efficiency of their entire investment processes.

## CEP IN OTHER INDUSTRIES

### Intelligence and Security

Data gathering systems used for intelligence, security, and defense must be able to "sense and respond" to patterns of events that indicate pending threats. Traditional data management and analysis software architectures cannot keep pace with the volume and velocity of the data streaming into many of today's modern intelligence systems. CEP provides government agencies and systems integrators with the ability to quickly solve real-time data processing and analytics challenges that previously have been time-consuming and often intractable.

CEP's powerful real-time processing architecture enables users to consolidate data across multiple sources and formats, and monitor complex conditions to identify patterns of events that indicate a need for action. CEP is ideal for real-time message/text analysis, combat theatre surveillance and battalion monitoring, real-time surveillance and alerting, and network monitoring.

Here are some further details on how the government and military sectors are leveraging CEP:

Intelligence and surveillance: A key challenge in providing watertight security is to effectively capture, filter, analyze, and act on flows of data from disparate sources in real time. Federal, state, and local law agencies are constantly generating related information from monitoring of networks, emails, financial transactions, watch lists, and other sources. As a result, it is increasingly difficult to aggregate this real-time data into a holistic view that can help identify imminent or potential threats. With CEP, these organizations are able to easily organize, filter, and interpret streams of high-volume information in real time.

Intrusion detection and network monitoring: Military and civilian agencies rely on their information systems and networks to execute their missions. These systems need to be protected from malicious attacks by hackers and terrorists. CEP is an invaluable tool in creating applications to detect and shut down such attacks. By capturing and analyzing network traffic in real time—at data rates of tens to hundreds of thousands of messages/second—CEP is well suited to fully protect critical information infrastructure.

Battlefield command and control: Modern warfare has become a "digital battlespace." Information about the locations and status of force components can be transmitted between all personnel, providing streamlined coordination and shared knowledge. With CEP, information streams of sensor data containing locations and status of battlefield resources can be captured, analyzed, and acted upon instantaneously. There's now more accurate information available more quickly, empowering better decisions to be transmitted faster and with the highest precision.

## Multiplayer Online Gaming

To maintain leading-edge game experiences as well as profitability, game developers must continually meet the demand for increased functionality and generate innovative pricing models. This dynamic environment strains the systems and applications that power these new services—especially the networking, operational support, and business support systems that monitor and manage player actions and help developers plan, develop, and implement game upgrades. "Pwning" can be a real threat, and can lead to functional lag times, insufficient capacity as player numbers increase, and less than desired monitoring of player behavior.

Game developers continually work to improve content, functionality, and context to personalize and optimize the player experience. CEP empowers developers and publishers to process and analyze high-volume, real-time data. With CEP, developers can build and deploy real-time applications for centralized interest management, in-game metrics, policy enforcement, real money transfer (RMT), and more.

Here are some of the applications that leading game developers have built with CEP:

Interest management: In order to provide a premiere game experience, each player's actions must be unique and self-selecting. What they do, who they interact with, what they accomplish, when, and in what order, must be their choice at as fine a granularity as possible. Systems must be able to keep up with the myriad details and crushing data deluge whether there are 50 or 50,000 simultaneous players. CEP can assist with load leveling to manage these wide variations from launch throughout the life span of the game.

Real-time metrics: Monitor and manage game metrics in real time. Track each player's movements and actions, and their interactions with others and the game environment. CEP can monitor for unexpected outcomes, manage or eliminate undesirable behaviors—ensuring that players always have the premium experience they expect—and can help developers understand behavior patterns and plan future enhancements.

Managing user-generated content: In-game communications, avatars, and other user-generated content are a highlight of many games. But user-generated content must be closely monitored to maintain game quality. CEP can react rapidly to these events, sending alerts or triggering an automatic response per developer preference.

Website monitoring: With clickstream and transaction rates soaring, a growing number of high-traffic games are seeking to monitor and react instantaneously to game-generated, real-time events. CEP enables gaming companies to analyze and react to clickstreams in real time. With CEP, gaming companies can customize ad promotions and in-game transactions in real time.

## Retail and E-Commerce Transaction Analysis

Whether you need real-time systems to generate in-store promotions to mobile devices as customers walk through your stores or to improve returns from e-commerce sites, CEP can offer solutions to enable real-time interaction, upselling, and cross-selling, maximizing your revenues.

CEP software can reduce the time to market for building custom real-time data systems. Applications built with CEP are able to aggregate live and historical data from multiple systems, process according to multiple business rules, and send out alerts, such as upsell and cross-sell promotions, live while consumers are in your stores or on your website.

Some of the challenges being addressed through CEP include

In-store promotion: Once you have people in or near your retail locations you need to tailor offers to their needs, based on social media, past purchases, store visits, and other background data to maximize revenue. CEP allows you to aggregate data from multiple references points, watch trends, and take actions on a store level or at a consumer level.

Website monitoring: With clickstream and transaction rates soaring, a growing number of high-traffic e-businesses are seeking to monitor and react instantaneously to website-generated real-time events. CEP enables e-businesses to analyze and react to clickstreams in real time, which in turn enables the immediate delivery of personalized cross-sell or upsell offers, or online product merchandising customized to the real-time activity of site visitors. By analyzing current web activity data and correlating this with stored customer history data, personalized offers can be generated that match the web customer's current interests and activity.

Fraud detection: Fraud detection and prevention applications are all moving toward real time. Traditionally, fraud detection has relied on querying stored transactional data for patterns of illicit activity; however, this approach simply detects the fraudulent activity after it has occurred. CEP enables firms to quickly build applications that capture and back-test up to years of transactional data to detect patterns indicative of fraud—and also easily run these applications on live event data to prevent fraud the moment it is attempted. In addition, CEP integrates with popular visualization software, enabling users to easily monitor operations and detect potential fraud via customized charts and interactive dashboards. By leveraging CEP's real-time processing and analytic capabilities, businesses can highlight and halt suspicious traffic that may be fraudulent in real time and avoid damaging financial losses.

## Network and Software Systems Monitoring

Critical information systems must be continuously monitored and protected from malicious attacks by hackers. But, existing systems are often not equipped to track and respond in real time to the massive amount of network access data generated every second. CEP applications can monitor and correlate network log data in real time at rates of up to hundreds of thousands of messages/second. CEP can also detect signature patterns of suspicious activity and shut down such attacks before they negatively impact your operations. Additionally, to protect mission-critical information infrastructures, CEP can serve as the foundation for a network monitoring solution. This can then ensure compliance with internal security guidelines or external regulations, such as Sarbanes-Oxley.

## Bandwidth and Quality of Service Monitoring

Adherence to service level agreements (SLAs) is an issue that requires real-time monitoring of service management data and generation of detailed quality of service (QoS) reports. CEP engines provide a high-performance platform for capturing, monitoring, and analyzing customer traffic data. By offering a global view of customer traffic volumes and potential service quality issues, CEP can help drive real-time intervention or rerouting of traffic to address problems as they occur.

# EFFECTS OF CEP

## Decision Making

### *Proactive Rather Than Reactive, Shorter Event Time Frames, Immediate Feedback*

Even though many systems are constantly processing messages in near real-time, much transaction data is captured first and analyzed later, sometimes much later, such as overnight or at the end of the week or the end of the month. Trends and rare events are noticed, but sometimes not in time to really capitalize on them. Some of the reason for delayed analysis is simply organizational habit from times when transaction volumes were much lower and the pace of business was slower, and some of the delay is due to applying outdated technology architectures to the problem that simply can't keep up with the pace.

The key is to be able to search through the data as it arrives, and also to present it to human and automated users in a form that allows both exploration and action.

## Strategy

### *From Observing and Discovering Patterns to Automating Actions Based on Pattern*

CEP can be used for data observation and pattern discovery, essentially by using data visualization user interface applications such as Datawatch's Panopticon that lets users slice and dice and drill down on data that is streaming in real time. Streaming output from CEP applications can also be cached in any in-memory database and browsed with more standard front-end tools.

One of the crossover points between big data/big analytics approaches and CEP is that batch-oriented big data processing can be used to discover patterns in the data.

Once a repeating pattern of interest is discovered, a CEP developer can then modify a CEP application to recognize the new pattern and take appropriate action when the pattern is seen. These actions can range from just sending an alert message to a console to entering an order for a securities trade to changing the terms of an online offering and so on.

## Operational Processes

### *Reduced Time to Market Due to Productivity Increases*

The overall software development cycle is shortened with CEP because of efficiencies in communicating requirements between business stakeholders and developers using a visual paradigm, because the design follows the pictures, and because coding itself is taking place at a relatively high level of abstraction.

### *Shortened Development Means Ability to Try Out More New Ideas*

Because development is faster, more new ideas can be tried out in the same amount of time. This is appropriate when, for example, a given trading strategy can become ineffective in a matter of days or weeks.

## SUMMARY

CEP provides real-time analytics for streaming data. CEP engine products feature not only high performance but also ease of development to address rapidly changing market opportunities. CEP architectures typically do not keep vast data sets all in memory at once, but rather aggregate and correlate incoming data according to long-standing continuous queries against the streams, issuing results to downstream systems. CEP has been around for almost a decade, but its use has been concentrated in capital market front office applications. With the newfound appreciation for big data, data science, and big analytics now reaching the mainstream, CEP is poised to apply its value to real-time processing in the same way that big data tools have been applied to more static data set processing.

StreamBase is a trademark or registered trademark of TIBCO Software, Inc. or its subsidiaries in the United States and other countries. Other product and company names mentioned herein may be the trademarks of their respective owners.

# 10

## Transforming Unstructured Data into Useful Information

*Meta S. Brown*

## CONTENTS

## INTRODUCTION: WHAT'S HOT IN DATA ANALYSIS TODAY? UNSTRUCTURED DATA!

The increase in media attention to analytics in recent years has many people thinking that the data analysis methods used in industry today are new. For the most part, that is not the case. The statistical theory that underlies most data analysis techniques currently in use was known well over a century ago. Statistical applications were widespread in advertising by the 1920s, when advertisers tracked the effects of small variations in ads, such as differing headlines or copy, primarily through counting the returns of coupons. Every modern introductory statistics course covers the Student's *t*-test for comparing means, which is nearly a century old and based on theories first published by William Gossett, then an employee of Guinness Breweries. By the 1940s, manufacturers were making extensive use of statistical process control methods, to ensure consistent results in manufacturing processes. Quality engineers still learn and use the concepts and techniques developed by Walter Shewart of Western Electric in the 1920s, which moved the profession beyond inspection of finished items toward an understanding of causes and prevention of quality problems. Yet there are also areas where the data analysis techniques, and the markets, are still young and developing.

The hottest challenge in data analysis now lies in data that isn't data in the traditional sense. When the information you need is held within an audio recording, a still or video image, or in text, perhaps text written in a language that you do not understand, what you have is unstructured data. It's something of a misnomer to call any of these things unstructured. Written languages have structure, as your English teacher surely taught you. Audio files would not function if they did not have a defined structure for encoding and decoding sound. When we say that data is unstructured, we mean only that it isn't structured like the simpler forms of data that yield readily to mathematical data analysis techniques.

In some respects, it is not new to seek mathematical structure in things that naturally have no such structure. Researchers studying medical treatments or farming methods understand that neither human beings nor soybeans can be input directly into a mathematical model. Instead, they describe their subjects in ways that make analysis possible. The person's physical bulk is described by measuring and recording weight and height using accepted methods. Blood pressure, blood counts, and other measures describe more details of the person's condition. It's the same with the soybeans—measures of weight and dimensions, as well as laboratory assays of composition, reduce nature's creations to numbers and categories—raw material for mathematical analysis. Yet we never refer to a human being, a plant, or anything that is entirely natural as data.

The dividing line between nature and data is the computer. Speech is not data, but a recording of speech, in an electronic file, is data. A tree is not data, but a digital photograph of a tree is data. We call these things data because they are stored and accessed in the same way as conventional data such as numbers. When the data is unstructured, we must first discover the structure within it before we can subject it to conventional data analysis.

It is no simple matter to isolate the meaningful and useful structure within unstructured data sources. Human beings, despite our sophisticated abilities to interpret language, often do not agree on the interpretation of any given bit of text. In fact, even a single human being may make different interpretations of the same text on different occasions. Yet, while the interpretation of words, images, and other unstructured data is, by nature, both challenging and imperfect, it can still be valuable. And, as the world's stock of unstructured data grows, so does the opportunity to profit by extracting information from that data and putting it to good use.

## TEXT ANALYTICS IN A BIG DATA CULTURE

The volume of unstructured data is growing; there is no dispute over that. More people have access to data capture devices such as computers, digital and video cameras, and scanners than ever before. People are producing more documents, image files, and other types of electronic data each year. What's more, the size of individual files is increasing. Not so many years ago, a digital image of 1 megabyte was considered quite large, yet today cameras in telephones produce images several times that size.

Solution vendors, business media, and even popular media have made much of the expanding volume of electronic data. Big data is widely equated with big value. Pitches for text analytics solutions often open with statistics about the volume of unstructured data, with the underlying implication that "lots of data equates to lots of money, so buy now or be left out of the coming gold rush." These messages should be approached with caution and a touch of cynicism.

If you are considering analysis of unstructured data, you are most likely focusing on text. This may be a matter of necessity—perhaps you have an internal text data source, such as comments from warranty claims, but lack resources to read and interpret all of it, or you may feel outside pressure to investigate text data sources that you have not used before, such as social media posts. This type of pressure is often driven by vendor marketing efforts. That's not to say that you should disregard it, but rather that it is up to you to seriously consider your specific business needs and evaluate solutions in that context.

Many of the "statistics" quoted about unstructured data are meaningless. Like rumors repeated many times, the sources are not identified, the context lost, and the methods unexplained. Even the best statistics need context to be fully understood. Take this example from IDC, a leading market intelligence firm:

> IDC estimates that in 2006, just the email traffic from one person to another—i.e., excluding spam—accounted for 6 exabytes (or 3%) of the digital universe.[1]

That's certainly a lot of email! A most impressive statistic, and the source is clearly identified. But what is the significance of this statistic to your business? First, does that number include attachments? A single video attachment may be as large as the text content of a thousand emails. Are the attachments of any use to you? How about text content of email? Do you have access to it? Are you free to use it for analysis? If so, are there secondary implications—what are the security and privacy concerns? Assuming you are free to analyze the text content of certain email messages, what reason would you have to expect that the information has value to you? What business problem can you reasonably expect to address with the information?

It's true that there is a lot of unstructured data today, but what really matters is only the data that is available to you and its relevance to your own business needs.

## Driving Forces for Text Analytics

The business community has made substantial investments in developing a massive body of user-generated text, and in the storage and management of that text. In many cases, the investment has been made by founders, venture capitalists, or existing businesses without any immediate payback. Often, that's the plan—build traffic now, monetize later. Other times, it just works out that way. Now, these investors are looking for hard returns.

A 2011 market study reported that the majority of those who have acquired text analytics technology are not yet achieving positive returns.[2] This should not be taken to imply that text analytics cannot pay, or that only a few stand to benefit. Rather, it is a matter of poor planning. Consider that the benefit most often promoted by vendors in this space is insight, that is, information that enables marketers to better understand their current or prospective customers. If that description seems vague, it is for good reason. Broad descriptive information without clear ties to customer behavior provides weak guidance for decision making, at best.

So, how can this content produce returns for investors? As always, there are just two broad categories of financial returns: revenue increases and cost decreases. Perhaps the simplest examples lie on the side of decreasing costs. Automation of any activity that is otherwise done manually is a good opportunity for reducing costs, particularly when the activity is done often.

It's a common practice in survey research, for example, to include open-ended questions, where respondents may give any reply they wish, without restrictions such as a checklist of options. A typical example might read, "What could we do to improve the quality of your dining experience?" Replies to open-ended questions are typically categorized by subject according to rules developed by the market research firm. The process involves sending the responses to a third-party "coding house" where the actual categorization is done manually, often by fairly transient staff such as college students working part-time. The service is costly, the turnaround slow, and the quality of work inconsistent. Coding of open-ended response subjects is an excellent application for text analytics. Elimination of third-party fees for coding yields clearly defined savings to offset investment. This alone may be sufficient to achieve positive return on investment (ROI). In addition, greater consistency and reduced turnaround provide better support for decision making, which should lead to revenue increases. Although such revenue increases may be more challenging to attribute to text analytics (since many factors go into management decisions), the value derived from them is nonetheless real.

## Difficulties in Conducting Valuable Text Analytics

Critics of text analytics nearly always point out the same issue—the results are not perfect. This criticism is legitimate.

Human language is vague, and open to differing interpretations. Take the example, "I bought a new car yesterday." Is this a positive statement? Is it negative? Taken by itself, it's reasonable to say that it is neither. There are no words in the sentence that indicate either positive or negative sentiment; it's a straightforward statement describing what happened, and no more. Yet, what if we knew that the speaker had been driving an old and undependable car for a long time? That information might lead us to interpret the statement as positive. Then again, what if the speaker could ill-afford a new car, and had hoped to keep the old one going for another year or two? Perhaps then, we'd interpret the same statement as negative.

Deriving meaning from language is no simple task, and often depends on information that is not contained in the words themselves. Different individuals often interpret the same passage of text in different ways, and in fact, the same individual may interpret a single bit of text in a different way on one occasion than another. Machines have the advantages of speed and consistency, but they lack the background knowledge and sophisticated language competency of humans. Text analytics is difficult and will never be perfect. Make peace with that, and build value by seeking applications where speed and consistency are primary concerns.

## THE GOAL OF TEXT ANALYSIS: DERIVING STRUCTURE FROM UNSTRUCTURED DATA

Author John Harney credits Hurwitz and Associates for this definition of text analytics: "the process of analyzing unstructured text, extracting relevant information and then transforming that information into structured information that can be leveraged in different ways."[3] But this is only one of many definitions currently circulating. TechTarget's SearchBusinessAnalytics.com says it this way: "Text mining is the analysis of data contained in natural language text. The application of text mining techniques to solve business problems is called text analytics." Gartner's IT glossary (http://www.gartner.com/it-glossary/text-analytics/) definition for *text analytics* opens with "the process of deriving information from text sources" and goes on to list several common application areas. Some definitions, while reasonable, cover a very wide range of activity, much of which is not unique to analysis of text.

For this discussion, let's define *text analytics* narrowly as the conversion of unstructured text into structured data. The starting point is language as it is written naturally, stored in electronic form, and the endpoint might be a subject matter category or a relevance score. What happens beyond that point is no longer unique to text. Once the text is converted to conventional data, subsequent steps are nothing more than conventional data analysis.

So, the goal of text analytics is to derive meaningful structured data from unstructured text. Broadly speaking, the derived data must be suitable for some business application. Many of the sought-after applications involve predictive analytics, where the derived data is used as an input to a predictive model. However, there are other possible uses, including exploratory data analysis, where the object, as the name implies, is to explore the data and seek out descriptive patterns of interest, with no specific intent to model or make predictions.

## The Transformation Process—In Concept

There are two major classes of text analytics methods: statistical, which are grounded in mathematics, and linguistic, which use the rules of specific languages. Each type has unique limitations and capabilities. Mathematics offers little to cope with complex grammar and subtleties of meaning, but some mathematical techniques can be applied even to data where there is no specific information about the language of the data. Linguistic methods incorporate substantial information about language structure and meaning, but may stall when confronted with new cases, for which no specific rules are available, or in some cases of ambiguity. In practice, many text analytics applications combine both linguistic and statistical methods to yield more robust results.

The process used varies to fit the requirements of a particular analysis. For example, one common text analytics task is entity extraction, which is identification of specific types of language structures, such as names or addresses, within the text. With no special knowledge of linguistics, this might be done by scanning the data for certain types of "regular expressions" (a programming term for a string of text characters, some of which may have symbolic meaning), perhaps a number followed by a capitalized word or two, but the results might leave much to be desired. In fact, this author recently heard a programmer describe just such an application, developed at considerable expense, yet leaving users with the possibility that "1994 Chevy Malibu" might be identified as an address. An application that uses linguistic information can better separate actual addresses from other similar structures through examination of context and use of known grammar and vocabulary. Statistical methods can supplement linguistics to make the best choices in cases that remain ambiguous.

## What Can Go Wrong?

The greatest risk in text analytics is that an investment will be made and fail to yield useful results. In fact, this is a common experience. A less obvious, yet still common, risk is that useful results will be obtained, but at considerably greater cost than necessary. Failure to achieve positive return on investment is disturbingly common in text analytics, yet in most cases the problem is obvious—the investment was made without any plan for a way to increase revenue or decrease costs by using the information obtained from the analysis. The moral: do not invest in text analytics unless you have a specific business problem to address, a clear understanding of the costs associated with that problem, and reasonable means to put the new information into action.

There is also the possibility that a text analytics application will fail to function or provide misleading output. Analysis of written language is a very complex task, and no such application will ever provide perfect results. If, for example, you could never tolerate the possibility that the statement "That movie was wicked good!" might be classified as a negative statement, you probably shouldn't get into text analytics at all. But you can limit your exposure to sheer malfunction and lack of quality assurance by taking advantage of tools built by language and statistical experts, with professional quality assurance teams to support them. Do not reinvent the wheel. Define what you need to fulfill your individual business requirements, but do not presume that your unique requirements call for building tools or processes from scratch. Seek out good quality tools or components that can be assembled to meet your needs.

There are a number of text analytic methodologies. The following section provides a high-level overview of the prominent techniques.

### *Entity Extraction*

Entity extraction is the identification and labeling (often called tagging, marking up, or flagging) of specific structures, such as names, places, or dates, within a document. Important elements of information within a document can be used in a variety of ways—to organize documents by the subjects mentioned within them, to facilitate easier (human) reading by emphasizing key topics in the display (for example, by highlighting names), as a precursor to further analysis, or to easily retrieve documents that mention specific topics.

Entity extraction applications may use a mix of simple comparison of strings (sequences of characters) to define patterns, linguistic rules to identify the function of specific segments of text, and comparison to exhaustive lists of known entities. For example, an entity extraction process for place names might first simply identify capitalized terms, then use linguistic logic to determine whether the term is a noun, and finally compare the term to a list of known places. It could even be further refined with statistical methods to estimate a likelihood that an unknown term might be a place name.

Consider, for example, this brief news article:

June 14, 2015
06:10 PM ET

**DISGRACED POLITICIAN MAKES COMEBACK BID**

*By Alice Wu, Special to WXY*

(WXY)—Former U.S. Representative Fred Hancock, who resigned from his post in 2010 in the face of allegations of questionable relationships with as many as four staff members, is attempting a comeback. At a diner in his hometown of Portland, Alabama, Congressman Hancock announced his intention to regain his former office.

Campaign manager Guy Marsh confidently declared Hancock to be the best-known and most liked representative in the history of the district. He also claimed that the recent remapping of congressional districts would play in Hancock's favor.

The same article, when used as data, would likely be formatted in xml—a customizable code that is used for this purpose (and many other purposes, as well). This is how the xml-encoded article might look:

```
<xml>
<article id = 109877>
<date>
June 14, 2015
</date>
<time>
06:10 PM ET
</time>
<headline>
Disgraced politician makes comeback bid
</headline>
<byline>
```

```
By <reporter>Alice Wu</reporter>, Special to
<newsagency>WXY</newsagency>
<p type = lead>
(WXY)—Former U.S. Representative Fred Hancock, who
resigned from his post in 2010 in the face of allegations
of questionable relationships with as many as four staff
members, is attempting a comeback. At a diner in his
hometown of Portland, Alabama, Congressman Hancock
announced his intention to regain his former office.
</p>
<p>
Campaign manager Guy Marsh confidently declared Hancock
to be the best-known and most liked representative in the
history of the district. He also claimed that the recent
remapping of congressional districts would play in
Hancock's favor.
</p>
</article>
```

The information within brackets is a code, known as a tag, that specifies the function of various parts of the text. The tags <p> and </p> indicate the start and endpoints of paragraphs, <article> and </article> indicate the start and endpoints of an article, with id = 109877 providing a unique identifier for one specific article. A single file of data might contain thousands, or millions, of such tagged articles.

In this example, the tag <reporter> tells us that the name is that of the reporter, the person who wrote the article. If the information is properly collected when it is first entered into a computer, then this kind of functional role can be clearly defined. Yet, in many cases, the information that is useful for analysis is not specifically tagged from the start. For example, you might have an interest in the names and places mentioned within the article, which are not tagged. Text analysis techniques might be used to find and tag those parts of the data. So one possible output of the text analysis application might be data, in a form much like the original, but with additional tags, like this:

```
<xml>
<article id = 109877>
<date>
June 14, 2015
</date>
<time>
06:10 PM ET
</time>
<headline>
Disgraced politician makes comeback bid
</headline>
```

```
<byline>
By <reporter>Alice Wu</reporter>, Special to
<newsagency>WXY</newsagency>
<p type = lead>
(WXY)—Former U.S. Representative <name>Fred
Hancock<name>, who resigned from his post in 2010 in the
face of allegations of questionable relationships with as
many as four staff members, is attempting a comeback. At
a diner in his hometown of <location>Portland, Alabama</
location>, Congressman <name>Hancock</name> announced his
intention to regain his former office.
</p>
<p>
Campaign manager <name>Guy Marsh</name> confidently
declared Hancock to be the best-known and most liked
representative in the history of the district. He also
claimed that the recent remapping of congressional
districts would play in <name>Hancock's</name> favor.
</p>
</article>
```

In this example, new tags have been added to indicate the parts of the text that represent names and places. Notice that the <name> tags enclose names only, not titles such as "U.S. Representative" or "campaign manager." This is only a choice, and a different application, or a different researcher, might make a different choice. Perhaps only the names and places are needed. If so, it might be better for the output to have a format like this:

```
<xml>
<article id = 109877>
<name>Fred Hancock<name>
<location>Portland, Alabama</location>
<name>Hancock</name>

<name>Guy Marsh</name>
<name>Hancock's</name>
```

## Autoclassification

Autoclassification is a mechanized process of organizing documents into categories, by subject matter or other characteristics. The primary use of autoclassification is to facilitate identification and retrieval of documents meeting specific characteristics. It is also important as a precursor to analysis using statistical or data mining methods. When the term *text analytics* is used, some form of autoclassification is nearly always involved.

One major approach to autoclassification involves the use of an organized hierarchy of topics, known as a taxonomy, which defines how the body of documents (corpus) is to be organized. Linguistic logic (rules) may be used to identify the subject matter and assign documents to appropriate roles within that hierarchy. Alternative approaches may create document groupings automatically, or groupings may be defined by humans with sample documents assigned to each, with subsequent documents assigned to categories automatically, based on similarities to the sample documents.

Consider these example customer service requests that might be received through a web form:

> Date: 2013 06 17
> From: Robert W. Jones
> Account: 134254
> Message: My service has been going off and on for the past three days. I need this fixed today or I'm going to cancel my service and go with another company.

> Date: 2013 06 17
> From: Margaret Washington
> Account: 189807
> Message: I need to add another line. I want it before my son's graduation on June 24.

> Date: 2013 06 17
> From: Albert Zajac
> Account: 201432
> Message: How do I set up my voicemail? I've tried the Help files, but the instructions don't work for me.

> Date: 2013 06 17
> From: Jennifer O'Brien
> Account: 203112
> Message: I haven't had service for over a week. Your people promised this would be fixed days ago. I've really had it.

Messages like these, entering a queue of service requests, each need to be directed to the proper channel for service. The options vary with the organization. For example, both Robert W. Jones and Jennifer O'Brien have service problems and need help from a tech support or repair team. But there are differences in their two situations. Robert's service is intermittent, while Jennifer has no service at all. Robert is threatening to cancel his service, while Jennifer is expressing frustration, but making no specific threats. Margaret's request represents new business, and she has a deadline. Albert has a relatively minor problem, but it's likely he will need to speak directly with a support person in order to correct it.

If a text analytics application were designed to organize inquiries like these into categories, what would be the desired results? Perhaps each message would be directed to a queue for one specific type of assistance. There could be categories for customers with no service at all, for those with intermittent service, for those whose service is functioning, but who are having some difficulty with normal use, and so on. Ideally, the messages would also be prioritized, perhaps with those threatening to cancel service or those who have made several attempts to correct a problem getting higher priority.

In practice, text analytics applications such as these are still fairly new and primitive. They may classify items into the preferred categories much less than half the time. But even when humans perform the same task, the results are often poor. Potential cost savings and improved turnaround times may make even imperfect autoclassification applications valuable.

### Sentiment Analysis

Sentiment analysis is a specific type of autoclassification in which the categories reflect varying attitudes regarding the subject matter. Sentiment analysis is popular for assessment of public opinion, particularly in regard to brands and issues. It is widely used in connection with social media posts.

Despite its popularity, sentiment analysis is a particularly difficult and inexact practice, even compared to other forms of text analytics. Typical sentiment analysis methods use linguistic logic to find and assign weights to terminology within the text that reflects attitudes of the individual. These weights are usually summarized as a single positive or negative or positive/neutral/negative classification for the document. A single document may contain several subjects, and some applications will provide separate classifications for each subject. There are also examples where more than just two or three sentiment categories are given, or where sentiment is expressed as a score.

Sentiment analysis is frequently applied to social media. The market wants to know not just how many people mentioned a brand, but what message is conveyed. If the messages are not to be read individually, the alternative is to identify just the attitude expressed—did they love us or hate us? Most often, each mention is assigned a simple positive, negative, or neutral category, and the results summarized into pie charts. Some applications also identify the sentiment category assigned to individual comments, for those who are interested and have the patience to read them. Those who do review individual items are often frustrated, because sentiment analysis is inexact, and many comments will be misclassified.

### Search

Search is an automated process for on-demand retrieval of documents that are relevant to topics of interest. Search is the most widely used of text analytics functions today, and it has become so commonplace that many do not think of it as text analytics, but a separate category altogether.

Automated document search enables people to find documents containing useful information quickly when they are needed.

Speed is imperative when using search, and the key to rapid results in search is doing most of the work before the search takes place. New documents are indexed as they become available. That is, they are scanned and records of the documents' contents are organized into databases. These databases, in turn, are organized to allow for fast retrieval of lists—descriptions of documents relevant to any given topic.

## INTEGRATING UNSTRUCTURED DATA INTO PREDICTIVE ANALYTICS

The term *predictive analytics*, coined and popularized in the late 1990s, is a relatively new way of describing the relatively old practice of using statistical analysis and other mathematical techniques to predict behavior. Consider the field of direct marketing, where marketing vehicles such as catalogs and mailers have always been rather costly to produce and distribute in quantity. How have businesses dependent on these techniques been able to make a profit? The best direct marketers have developed a sophisticated understanding of which prospects are likely to buy, what products they prefer, and what types of copy, images and offers they find appealing. This understanding is based on aggressive programs of testing and statistical analysis. As online commerce has evolved, the largest and most successful online marketers have followed suit.

How does text fit into the predictive analytics scheme? It's an input, one more class of information that may have value for predicting behavior. But it does not easily lend itself to use in statistical analysis, data mining, or other mathematical methods. Preparation of any type of data for analytics is fussy, time-consuming work, but ordinary data preparation methods are of little relevance for text. The process that begins with text as it is written naturally and ends with a relevant and properly structured set of inputs for predictive modeling requires significant thought, planning, and attention to detail; this is the nature of text analytics.

Often, the object of text analytics is to derive from written text the same type of information that a sharp observer would glean from a personal conversation or observation of a subject's behavior. Consider a common type of goal for predictive analytics projects: identification of likely purchasers for a particular product. How would a sales professional assess a prospect's likelihood to buy that product in a personal interaction? She might make some visual observations—has the prospect done anything to show interest? Perhaps he stopped and looked at it, or picked up the product and tried it out. Or perhaps he asked about it. There may be other, subtler clues—he didn't notice or ask about that item specifically, but showed interest in similar things. Or perhaps there is something else about his behavior, his likes or dislikes, which mark him as a strong or weak prospect.

What kind of clues can be extracted from text? Most obviously, written language contains references to many topics; certainly these reflect the interests of the writer (some of them, at least). Much more than mere subject matter is revealed in the way that people write. Text also contains indicators of attitude toward those subjects, usually referred to as sentiment in the text analytics vernacular. Written language also contains indicators of the situation—formal or informal—and the writer's mood, personality, and education. Mentions of dates, places, names, use of profanity, or other specific usages may be relevant.

Once the project goals have been defined, work backwards and define a work plan, that is, a series of steps toward your goal. For example, if the goal is to predict likely buyers, you'll be developing a predictive model that makes the most of any conventional data you have about a particular prospect (such as purchase history and demographics), and aims to improve the model's performance by adding additional information derived from text. What text data sources might be available to you? Perhaps you have records of previous interactions with the customer—text entered directly by the customer through email or web forms, or indirect records, such as those entered by customer service personnel.

What is the nature of the text available to you? What language or languages are represented? Is it well-structured formal writing, or informal? Is it long or short? What information could a person gain by reading that text? How much of that information is actually written in the text, and how much is ascertained by reading between the lines? Machines are quick and accurate at manipulating the text itself, and not very good at more subtle tasks, so be realistic about this when assessing the potential value of your data sources. Look for valuable information that can be extracted directly from the text. If a person mentions your product, or a competing product, for example, you may be quite certain that you have a meaningful bit of information that may be useful. If you insist on assessing the writer's sentiment (I know she mentioned the product, but does she love it or hate it?), you may end up much less confident about what you have, with good reason.

Consider what data structures you can use. For predictive modeling, that means you will need to develop either a categorical variable or a continuous one, like a score. (There may also be occasions when you have some use for short strings drawn directly from the text that can be used without transformation.)

Only when you have gotten at least a rough idea of what type of text you will be using and what information you expect to obtain from it should you investigate tools. When you have a clear understanding of what you want to get out of your text, and what you require as output from a text analytics tool, it's likely that you will be able to eliminate most of the vast sea of offerings from consideration and concentrate on careful evaluation of just a few likely candidates.

## ASSESSING THE VALUE OF NEW INFORMATION

Recall that text analytics is the conversion of unstructured text into structured data. Once the useful bits of information have been extracted from the original text sources and used as the basis for creating new, structured data, what then?

The new variables, whether categorical, continuous, or a mix of the two, are structurally no different from conventional inputs used in predictive models, so they can be used in the same ways as any other potentially predictive variables in statistical analysis, data mining, or similar analytic methods. The beauty in this is twofold:

1. Text analytics provides analysts with new variables for use in modeling.
2. The only new techniques required are those used to transform text into conventional data structures. All subsequent analysis can be performed by using methods already known to the analysts.

So, how can an analyst assess the value of the new variables provided through text analytics? These variables can be used, and their predictive value evaluated, in exactly the same way as conventional variables. In the data exploration, modeling, and deployment phases, no new methods or resources are required.

## Using Information to Direct Action

No matter how fine an analysis may be, the information means nothing if it is not used. Returns are realized only when the information obtained through analysis is put into action. This requires management support and appropriate infrastructure. One person may develop some very remarkable analytics, with or without text, but analytics applications that are successful, meaning that they are used and yield concrete returns for the organization, always require a team.

If you are a manager, it is up to you to communicate clearly with analysts about which problems are significant to you, and for what reasons. If you do not let IT and other business areas know that supporting the analytic team is a high priority, they are likely to assume just the opposite. If you are an analyst, it is your responsibility to establish realistic expectations for what can be done with analytics, to be honest about what cannot be done, and clear about the resources required to do your own work and integrate the results into everyday operations. And everyone has the responsibility to question others, to speak honestly and openly about their concerns, and to do so early and often.

The person who invests in text analytics technology first and looks for ways to integrate the results into the business later is planning for failure. Profitable text analytics programs and projects begin with a clear business case and well-defined, reasonable goals. Since the same is true for any type of business investment, this should come as no surprise, yet somehow many organizations have managed to sign on the dotted line without having a realistic plan in place.

There's no need to go out looking for opportunities to use text analytics in your business. Instead, when you are confronted with everyday business problems, take a moment to consider whether there might be relevant text available, and what value it might provide in addressing your business problem.

The following examples may help you to be more aware of profitable opportunities to use text analytics in your own workplace:

### Application—Recommendation Engines

Recommendation engines are automated processes for suggesting products or services of interest to a current or prospective customer. Examples include product suggestions offered after completing an online purchase, movie suggestions provided by a streaming video service, and even possible mates selected for clients by a dating service.

Good recommendations result in increased revenues through add-on sales and greater customer retention. Historically, recommendation engines have two types of data available as inputs: past transactions, such as previous purchase history, and demographic or other information that may be shared by the customer or purchased from data brokers. Such data may provide limited information of predictive value for recommendations. Text data sources, such as the customer's social media posts, may reveal broader information regarding the customer's interests and tastes.

How does an analytics-driven recommendation fit into the flow of a transaction? The customer should be unaware of the process, so the data-driven recommendations should be displayed through conventional means. If you have made purchases online, you have likely noticed that when you add an item to the cart, you are immediately offered additional products to consider for purchase. This is the online analogy to the shoe salesperson who looks at a customer who has just selected a pair of shoes and points out the store's excellent selection of socks. Personalized recommendations also appear in email offers, customized home pages, and personalized banner advertising.

### Application—Churn Modeling

Churn modeling is the use of predictive modeling techniques to identify current customers at high risk of defecting to competitors. It is generally less costly to retain a customer than acquire a new one, making the savings potential, and hence the return on investment, for churn modeling attractive to many businesses.

Unhappy clients often give advance warning before their departure. If this warning takes the form of text, perhaps through email, a web form, or even a social media post, you have an opportunity to take note and address the problem. While the limits of sentiment analysis have been much discussed here, keep in mind that these messages are often less than subtle. Rather than struggle with the interpretation of each and every remark made by your clients, it might be most effective to begin by simply seeking out the obvious cases, such as the customer who states directly, "I am going to close my account."

### Application—Chat Monitoring

Chat monitoring is the surveillance of online communications for profanity or inappropriate activity, such as soliciting personal information from, or interaction with, children. Chat monitoring prevents losses associated with litigation and negative publicity. It also may promote customer retention, as with services offered to children whose parents have concerns regarding safety.

Without text, there would be nothing at all to monitor. The alternative to text analytics is the use of live human monitors, an unrealistic option for many large-scale web applications. In many cases, an adequate supply of attentive live monitors with the required language skills would not even be available, let alone affordable.

## SUMMARY

Text analytics methods stand out from most of the analyst's toolkit. In contrast to well-established techniques such as statistical analysis, operations research, and even data mining, text analytics is a relatively young and imperfect field. Yet the rapidly expanding body of electronic text, the pressure to derive value from this text and to do so rapidly, drives rising levels of interest and activity in text analytics. Text analytics is arguably today's hottest area of development in analytics, and will remain active for decades to come.

## REFERENCES

1. Gantz, J. F., Reinsel, D., Chute, C. et al. *The Expanding Digital Universe: Information Growth through 2010*. IDC, Framingham, MA, 2007. Available at http://www.emc.com/collateral/analyst-reprts/expanding-digital-idc-white-paper.pdf.
2. Grimes, S. *Text/Content Analytics 2011: User Perspectives on Solutions and Providers*. AltaPlana Corporation, Takoma Park, MD, 2011. Available at http://altaplana.net/TextAnalyticsPerspectives2011.pdf.
3. Harney, J. Text Analytics—Improving the Use Case for Unstructured Text. *KMWorld*, Camden, ME, February 2009. Available at http://www.kmworld.com/Articles/Editorial/Features/Text-analytics-improving-the-use-case-for-unstructured-text-52383.aspx.

# 11

## Mining Big Textual Data

*Ioannis Korkontzelos*

### CONTENTS

## INTRODUCTION

In the 21st century, human activity is more and more associated with data. Being so widespread globally, the Internet provides access to vast amounts of information. Concurrently, advances in electronics and computer systems allow recording, storing, and sharing the traces of many forms of activity. The decrease of cost per unit of data for recording, processing, and storing enables easy access to powerful well-connected equipment. As a result, nowadays, there is an enormous and rapidly growing amount of data available in a wide variety of forms and formats. Apart from data concerning new activity, more and more previously inaccessible resources in electronic format, such as publications, music, and graphic arts, are digitized.

The availability of vast amounts of data aggregated from diverse sources caused an evident increase of interest in methods for making sense of large data quantities and extracting useful conclusions. The common bottleneck among all big data analysis methods is structuring. Apart from the actual data content, analysis typically requires extra information about the data of various levels and complexities, also known as metadata. For example, consider a newspaper article. The data content consists of the title, the text, and any images or tables associated with it. Simple metadata would contain the name of the author, the date that the article was published, the newspaper page in which the article was printed, and the name of the column that hosted the article. Other metadata could concern statistics, such as the number of pages that this article covers and the number of paragraphs and words in it; indexing information, such as the unique identification number of this article in the newspaper's storage database; or semantics, such as the names of countries, people, and organizations that are discussed in this article or are relevant. In addition, semantic metadata might contain more complex types of information, such as the subtopics that are discussed in the article, the paragraphs in which each subtopic is addressed, and the sentences that report facts vs. sentences that express the opinion of the author [14].

In the above example, it is evident that the metadata corresponding to this kind of data only, i.e., newspaper articles, can be of many diverse types, some of which are not known a priori, but are specific to the type of further processing and applications that use this data. Considering the diversity of available data types, one can imagine the diversity of metadata types that could be associated with it. Most of the data available are not ready for direct processing, because they are associated with limited or no metadata. Usually extra preprocessing for adding structure to unstructured data is required before it is usable for any further purpose.

The remainder of this chapter discusses a number of data sources, focusing on textual ones. Then, an overview of the methods for structuring unstructured data by means of extracting information from the content is presented. In addition, moving toward a more practical view of data structuring, we discuss a multitude of examples of applications where data structuring is useful.

## SOURCES OF UNSTRUCTURED TEXTUAL DATA

One of the major means of human communication is text. Consequently, text is one of the major formats of available data, among others, such as recorded speech, sound, images, and video. Textual data sources can be classified in a variety of different aspects, such as domain, language, and style.

The domain of a text represents the degree that specialized and technical vocabulary is used in it. This is a very important attribute of text, because the senses of some words, especially technical terms, depend on it. For example, the meaning of the word *lemma* is different in the domain of mathematics and the domain of linguistics. In mathematics, lemma is a proven statement used as a prerequisite toward the proof of another statement, while in linguistics lemma is the canonical form of a word. A piece of text can belong to a specialized technical or scientific domain, or to the general domain, in the absence of a specialized one. Arguably, the general domain is not entirely unified. Even when discussing everyday concepts a certain level of technical vocabulary is being used. For example, consider an everyday discussion about means of transport or cooking. The former might contain terms such as *train, platform, ticket, bus,* and *sedan,* while the latter might contain terms such as *pot, pan, stove, whip, mix, bake,* and *boil.* The union of general words plus widely known and used technical terms comprise general domain.

Language is an important feature of text for a variety of reasons. Mainly, it is one of the very few hard classification general features of text, and it affects radically the methods of text analysis and information mining. Hard classification features are properties of text that can be used to partition a collection of items into nonoverlapping item sets.

Language is a hard classification feature in a collection of monolingual documents; i.e., each document can be assigned to a single language only. Moreover, the language of a text or textual collection dictates the methods that can be applied to analyze it, since for some languages there exist adequate resources for many domains, while others are much less or not exploited at all. It should also be noted that a document collection can possibly be multilingual; i.e., some of its parts may be in a different language than others. Multilingual collections usually consist of parallel documents; i.e., each document is accompanied with one or more translations of its contents in other languages. Another kind of multilingual collections is comparable documents, where each document corresponds to one or more documents in other languages that are not necessarily precise translations of it, but just similar.

Another equally important property of text is style, ranging from formal and scientific to colloquial and abbreviative. Text in different styles often uses different vocabularies and follows syntax and grammar rules more or less strictly. For example, the style of text in a scientific article is usually formal and syntactically and grammatically complete. In contrast, transcribed speech might be elliptical and probably missing some subjects or objects. In recent years, due to the proliferation of social networking websites, a new style of elliptical, very condensed text style has emerged.

Text domain, language, and style are properties orthogonal to each other. In other words, there exists text characterized by any combination of values for these properties. This large space of possible combinations is indicative of the variety of unstructured text available. Below, a number of textual sources are introduced and briefly discussed.

## Patents

Patents are agreements between a government and the creator of an invention granting him or her exclusive rights to reproduce, use, and sell the invention for a set time period. The documents associated with these agreements, also called patents, describe how the invention works, what is it useful for, what it is made of, and how it is made. From a text analysis point of view, patents are challenging documents. First, although there are several patent collections and search applications available, most of the documents are available as raw, unstructured text. Identifying parts of the documents that refer to different aspects of a patent, such as the purpose, impact, potential uses, and construction details, would consist of a basic structure step, which would in turn be essential for further processing toward building applications and extracting meaningful conclusions. Second, since a patent document addresses various aspects of an invention, the entire text is not of a single domain. Third, patent documents usually contain tables and figures, which should be recognized and separated from the textual body before any automatic processing.

## Publications

Books, journal articles, and conference proceeding contributions comprise the source of text that has been exploited via automatic text analysis methods the most. There are several reasons for this. Due to the diversity of scientific and technical publications available, this type of textual data is easy to match with any domain of application. Moreover, publications offer a natural level of universal structuring: title, abstract, and sections, which most of the time contain a method, a results, and a conclusion section. Some of the available publications offer some extra structuring within the abstract section into further subsections. In addition, many publications come with author-specified keywords, which can be used for indexing and search. In scientific publications, new research outcomes are introduced and discussed. As a result, publications are an excellent source for mining neologisms, i.e., new terms and entities.

## Corporate Webpages

Corporate webpages are a much less exploited source of textual data, due to the difficulties in accessing and analyzing text. Webpages currently online may combine different development technologies and also may follow any structuring format. This variation restricts the ability to develop a universal mechanism for extracting clean text from webpages, and dictates building a customized reader for each corporate website or each group of similar websites. Similarly, tables and figures can be represented in a variety of formats; thus, separate readers are necessary to extract their exact content.

Despite these difficulties, companies are much interested to track the activity of other companies active in the same or similar business areas. The results of analyzing webpages of competitors can be very useful in planning the future strategy of a company in all aspects, such as products, research and development, and management of resources.

## Blogs

Blogs are online, publicly accessible notebooks, analogous to traditional notice boards or diaries. Users, also known as bloggers, can publish their opinions, thoughts, and emotions, expressed in any form: text, images, and video. Other users can comment on the documents published and discuss. Due to the freedom of expression associated with the concept of blogs, there is much and growing interest in analyzing blog articles to extract condensed public opinion about a topic. Text in blogs is much easier to access than corporate pages, discussed previously, because the vast majority of blogs are hosted in a small number of blog sites, such as Wordpress, Blogger, and Tumblr. Blog articles vary largely in domains, languages, and style.

## Social Media

Social media, such as Twitter, Facebook, and Google+, allow users to briefly express and publish their thoughts, news, and emotions to all other users or groups of users that they participate in. Media have different approaches to groups of friends or interest groups related to each user. Each user apart from publishing is able to read the updates of users in the groups he or she participates, comment, or just express his or her emotion for them, e.g., Facebook "like." Moreover, users can republish an update of some other user so that it is visible to more people (Facebook "share," Twitter "retweet"). The content of user updates has different characteristics in the various media. For example, in Facebook, users can post text, links, images, and videos, while in Twitter each post is restricted to 140 characters, including posted links.

Mining social media text is a relatively new trend in the field of text processing. Strong interest has emerged about social media, due to their increasing popularity. Companies consider the habits, preferences, and views of users as very important toward improving the products and services they offer and also designing new products. Text in social media is written in many languages; however, less common are languages spoken in countries where the Internet is not used broadly.

There are several challenges relevant to social media text analysis [1]. First, due to the multitude of domains that can be observed in social media, it is challenging to determine which pieces of text are relevant to a domain. In contrast to publications and blogs, text in social media is often relevant to a number of different domains.

Second, the style of language in social media is significantly different than the style of any other type of text. Due to the length restrictions of posts, and also to increase typing speed, a very elliptical text style has evolved embracing all sorts of shortenings: emoticons, combinations of symbols with a special meaning (e.g., "xxx" and "<3"), words shortened to homophone letters (e.g., "cu" standing for "see you"), a new set of abbreviations (e.g., "lol", "rofl," and "omg"), and others. Moreover, spelling mistakes and other typos are more frequent in social media text than in other, more formal types of text.

Third and most importantly, the entire text published in social media is very impractical to process due to its immense size. Alternatively, text relevant to some topic is usually obtained by filtering either stored posts or the online stream of posts while they are being published. Filtering can take advantage of the text itself, by using keywords relevant to the topic of interest, or any accompanying metadata, such as the name of the author.

## News

Newswire and newspaper articles comprise a source of text easy to process. Usually text can be downloaded from news websites or feeds, i.e., streams of newswire posts structured in a standard manner. In addition, text is carefully written in a formal or colloquial style with very limited or no typos, grammar or syntax mistakes, and elliptical speech. The domain of articles is often clearly specified. If not, the title and keywords, if available, can be helpful in resolving it. Stored newswire and newspaper articles can be very useful to historians, since they are the trails of events, as they take place. In addition, advances and trends about economy and politics can be invaluable to business administration, management, and planning.

## Online Forums and Discussion Groups

Online forums and discussion groups provide a good source for strictly domain-specific text. Most of the forums and discussion groups are combined with programmatic access facilities, so that text can be downloaded easily. However, forums and groups are available for limited languages and topics and usually are addressed to a specialized scientific or technical audience. The style of text can range largely and depends on the topic discussed.

## Technical Specification Documents

Technical specifications are lengthy, domain-specific documents that describe the properties and function of special equipment or machinery, or discuss plans for industrial facilities. Technical specification documents are written in formal style and, due to their nature, are excellent sources of technical terminology. However, only a very limited amount of older technical specification documents are digitized.

## Newsgroups, Mailing Lists, Emails

Newsgroups are electronic thematic notice boards, very popular in the 1990s and 2000s. Users interested in the topic of a newsgroup are able to read notices posted by any member of the group, via specialized applications called newsgroup readers. Newsgroups are dominantly supported by a specialized communication protocol called Network News Transfer Protocol (NNTP). This protocol is used by newsgroup readers and also provides an interface that allows reading newsgroup contents programmatically. Newsgroups mainly contain domain-specific textual articles of formal or colloquial style.

Similarly to newsgroups, mailing lists are collections of email addresses of people interested in a topic. Users can publish emails related to the topic of the mailing list, informing other users about news, asking questions, or replying to the questions of other users. Access to the content of mailing lists can be implemented easily, since many mailing lists are archived and available online.

Apart from emails sent to specific mailing lists, emails in general can also be a valuable source of text. However, general emails are much more challenging to analyze than emails sent to mailing lists. Since general emails are not restricted to a specific topic, the domain of text is not known beforehand and should be captured while processing. Similarly to social media text, emails relevant to a specific topic can be retrieved from an email collection by filtering. Moreover, the text style in emails can range from formal and professional to really personal, condensed, and elliptical. Last but not least, access to general email can only be granted by approval of the administrator of the server where the corresponding email account is hosted or by the actual email account user. Lately, several collections of anonymized email text have been made available. Anonymization, apart from removing names, usually refers to the removal of other sensitive information, such as company names, account numbers, identity numbers, insurance numbers, etc.

## Legal Documentation

Lately, most countries and states make laws and other legal documentation available. Minutes of many governments, committees, and unions are also online indexed, usually after a standard period of time, 5 or 10 years. For example, the Europarl Corpus is a parallel corpus extracted from the proceedings of the European Parliament that includes versions in 21 European languages. Legal documentation is important for text processing as a large, domain-specific textual source for tasks such as topic recognition, extracting legal terminology, and events and others. In addition, legal documentation that comes with parallel translation is important for machine translation, multilingual term extraction, and other tasks that draw statistics on aligned text in more than one language.

## Wikipedia

Wikipedia, as a large, general purpose, online encyclopedia, is a valuable source of text, offering several handy properties for text processing. Wikipedia covers many, if not all, technical or scientific domains and also contains lemmas of the general domain. However, a subset of Wikipedia articles relevant to a specific domain can be easily retrieved by choosing entries whose titles contain terms of that particular domain. Moreover, Wikipedia comes with an interface that allows accessing its clean textual content programmatically. It covers a multitude of languages; however, it is not equally complete for all of them. The style of language is formal or colloquial. A unique disadvantage of the quality of text in Wikipedia stems from the fact that any user, with no previous certification, can submit his or her own articles or amendments to existing articles. An inherent feature of Wikipedia, called "Featured articles," can be used to select high-quality articles, in cost of massive loss of coverage.

## STRUCTURING TEXTUAL DATA

In the previous section, a number of diverse textual resources have been described with an emphasis on their fundamental linguistic properties: domain, language, and style. Some hints about the possible uses of the resources have been provided. In a further extent, some common examples of usage scenarios will be discussed in the "Applications" section. In this section, a few typical textual processing stages are introduced. The output of these processing stages can be applied to many domains and for various purposes.

## Term Recognition

Terms are words or sequences of words that verbally represent concepts of some specific domain of knowledge, usually scientific or technical. In other words, terms are lexical items closely related to a subject area, and their frequency in this area is significantly higher than in other subject areas. For example, some terms of the finance and economy domain are *inflation, interest rate, bonds,* and *derivatives,* while some terms of the domain of biology are *molecule, protein,* and *genetic code.* Recognizing terms in text can be useful for many processing tasks [4,7,8,12,20,24]. For example, neologisms in a domain, i.e., newly emerging terms, can designate advances in it. In addition, indexing using terms instead of just words can improve search performance [13].

Term recognition is the task of locating terms in domain-specific text collections. Approaches to term recognition can be classified as linguistic, dictionary based, statistical, and hybrid, depending on the different types of information that they consider. Linguistic approaches use morphological, grammatical, and syntactical knowledge to identify term candidates. Dictionary-based approaches employ various readily available repositories of known term representations, such as ontologies. Statistical approaches refer to the applications of various statistical tools, which receive as input frequency counts of words and sequences of words, co-occurrences of words, and features that capture the context of words or sequences of words, i.e., words that occur frequently before or after the target ones.

To provide a practical example of a simple term recognizer, we can consider a combination of parts of speech and frequency filtering. To capture term candidates that consist of adjectives and nouns, we apply a regular expression pattern on the output of a parts of speech tagger. Then, we compute the frequencies of term candidates and accept those that survive a given frequency threshold. This process is also described in pseudocode in Algorithm 11.1.

## Algorithm 11.1: A Simple Term Recognizer

Input: A textual document $t$.

Output: A list of terms, ordered according to frequency of occurrence.

1. Pass text $t$ to a part of speech tagger, and store its output, PoS($t$).
2. Apply the regular expression *(adj | noun)\* noun+* to PoS($t$), to identify TC, a set of $n$ term candidates.
3. Filter out terms in TC whose frequency is lower than 2 (or any other prespecified threshold value).
4. Store the terms in TC in a list, $L_{TC}$, in decreasing order of frequency.
5. Return $L_{TC}$.

Let's apply this simple term recognizer to a snippet taken from an answer of spokesman Josh Earnest to the press:

> There are a range of estimates out there about the economic impact of the pipeline, about how this pipeline would have an impact on our energy security. There are also estimates about how this pipeline may or may not contribute to some environmental factors. So there are a range of analyses and studies that have been generated by both sides of this debate [28].

Applying the regular expression of step 2 in Algorithm 11.1 to the above quote retrieves the term candidates below. The corresponding frequencies are shown within parentheses: *range* (2), *estimate* (2), *economic impact* (1), *pipeline* (3), *impact* (1), *energy security* (1), *environmental factor* (1), *analysis* (1), *study* (1), *side* (1), *debate* (1). Since the frequency threshold value specified in step 3 of Algorithm 11.1 is 2, the algorithm will output the following list of terms: [*pipeline* (3), *estimate* (2), *range* (2)].

## Named Entity Recognition

Named entities are terms associated with a specific class of concepts, i.e., a category, a type or kind of objects or things. For example, entity classes in the news domain are usually people, locations, and organizations. Some examples of biomedical entity classes are genes, proteins, organisms, and malignancies. The notion of named entities is very similar to the notion of terms. However, named entities cannot be defined independently of the corresponding named entity classes, while terms do not need to be classified.

Mostly, named entity recognizers use ontologies as their background knowledge [16,19]. Ontologies are domain-specific classifications of concepts in classes [5]. Each concept represents the notion of an object or thing and can usually be expressed in a variety of different verbal sequences. For example, in the domain of computers, the concept "hard disk drive" can be expressed as *Winchester drive, hard drive,* or just *disk.* Some ontologies have a tree-like structure, such that some classes are nested into other broader classes.

Named entity recognition methods attempt to recognize named entities of prespecified types in text and decide the type that they correspond to [3,6]. Baseline approaches do a direct matching of named entity realizations in the ontology to the text. Sophisticated approaches attempt to address several issues that hinder error-free recognition, such as

> The *variability* of named entities that is not covered by the ontology
>
> *Ambiguity*: Some named entities could be assigned to more than one class. For example, *Jordan* can be the name of a country or a famous basketball player, and *Kennedy* can refer to the former U.S. president or the airport named after him. To disambiguate a named entity, typically methods take into account the context in which it occurs.
>
> *Co-reference* is the phenomenon of multiple expressions in a sentence or document referring to the same concept. For example, suppose we have the following text: *John* walks slowly, because *he* has a bad knee. *His* son is standing by *him.* All words in italics refer to the same named entity, *John.* Ideally, a named entity recognizer should be able to recognize the pronouns and map them to the named entity, *John.*

To provide an example of a very simple named entity recognition approach, we would use a dictionary of named entities and then perform direct matching on the input text, as shown in Algorithm 11.2.

### Algorithm 11.2: A Simple Named Entity Recognizer

Input: A textual document $t$, a dictionary of named entities (NEs).
Output: Text $t$ with named entity annotations.
  1.  For ne ∈ NEs do {
  2.      If ne occurs in $t$ then
  3.          Add an annotation in $t$ for named entity ne
      }
  4.  Return text $t$ with named entity annotations

## Relation Extraction

In the previous section, named entities and the recognition method were introduced. The current section is about relations between previously recognized named entities and methods for recognition [17]. Semantic relations between named entities can be of various types, depending on the application that they will be used in succession. Some examples are

- *Is-a* relations: The general domain relations between a named entity of a semantic class to a named entity of a more general semantic class. For instance, from the phrases "*car* is a *vehicle*" and "*collagen* is a *protein*," the is-a relation pairs (*car, vehicle*) and (*collagen, protein*) can be extracted, respectively.
- *Interacts-with* relation: In the biology domain, these relations can be used to spot gene-disease and protein-protein interactions, useful for structuring biomedical documents semantically [2,22]. Examples are (*CIPK9, CBL3*) and (*FTO gene, apolipoprotein E*), which can be extracted from the phrases "*kinase CIPK9* interacts with *the calcium sensor CBL3*" and "*FTO gene* interacts with *apolipoprotein E*," respectively.

A simplistic method to identify semantic relations between named entities (NEs) is by applying patterns; for example, tuples of the *is-a* relations discussed above could be identified by the patterns: "[$NE_1$] is a [$NE_2$]," "[$NE_1$] is a type of [$NE_2$]," and "[$NE_1$], a [$NE_2$]" [10]. This method is able to extract a limited number of accurate tuples; in other words, it achieves high precision but low recall. The reason is that patterns accept instances strictly, allowing no variation on words other than the named entity slots. Using the parts of speech and lemmas of those parts can allow some minimal variation. Other approaches, more flexible to generalize, take into account the parsing tree of sentences and check if specific words or categories of words lie in certain positions [25]. Moreover, machine learners can be applied for this task, based on various features that capture the context of a candidate relation entity [27].

To illustrate how the pseudocode of a very simple relation extraction component would look, we provide Algorithm 11.3. The algorithm inputs a document accompanied with named entity annotations and applies a set of patterns to identify *is-a* relations.

**Algorithm 11.3: A Simple Relation Extractor**

Input: A textual document *t* with named entity annotations, a set of patterns:

P = {"NE1 is a NE2," "NE1 is a type of NE2," "NE1, a NE2"}

Output: Text *t* with named entity and relation annotations.
1. For *p* ∈ *P* do {
2.    If ne applies to *t* then
3.       Add an annotation in *t* for a *is-a* relation between $NE_1$ and $NE_2$
   }
4. Return text *t* with named entity and relation annotations

## Event Extraction

The notion of event in text mining is very similar to the common sense of events. Events are complex interactions of named entities, and they have a distinct, atomic meaning, separate from other events. Of course, events might be related, but each of them is complete and independent. Events are of different types and nature for different textual domains, for example:

- In the domain of *news*, events are incidents or happenings that took or will take place [26]. An event consists of complex relations between named entities that correspond to various aspects of it, such as time, place, people involved, etc. For instance, the sentence "*Mr. Westney* visited *New York* to present his program at Queens College" expresses a transportation event in the past, triggered by the verb *visit*. *New York* is a geopolitical entity (GPE) that plays the role of destination in this event, while the person *Mr. Westney* holds the subject position.
- In the domain of *biology*, events are structured descriptions of biological processes that involve complex relationships, such as *angiogenesis*, *metabolism*, and *reaction*, between biomedical entities. Events are usually initiated verbally by trigger words, which can be verbs, such as *inhibit*, or verb nominalizations, such as *inhibition*. The arguments of events are biomedical entities of specific types, such as *genes* and *proteins*, or other events, such as *regulation*. Events depend highly on the textual context in which they are expressed [18].

Similarly to relation extraction, event extraction can follow a number of simple or more sophisticated methods. Simpler methods recognize a set of trigger words and match specific patterns or apply standard rules. More sophisticated methods attempt to raise the constraints and shortcoming of simple approaches [11]. Bootstrapping approaches introduce iterations. They start with a standard set of trigger words and event extraction rules and iteratively expand these sets to recognize more instances. The procedure of enrichment is critical for the overall performance of this type of method. Machine learning approaches encode information about trigger words, named entity components, context, and probably other ad hoc observations as features, and then attempt to learn the ways that these features interact and correlate with the actual events. A trained learner can then be applied to raw text to extract events similar to the ones it was trained on. Machine learning methods usually perform better than pattern- and rule-based methods. However, extra performance comes at the cost of the expensive and laborious task of annotating training data manually.

As a simple example of an event extractor, we provide the pseudocode in Algorithm 11.4. The code is able to recognize transportation events similar to the one presented in the former bullet above.

**Algorithm 11.4: A Simple Event Extractor**

Input: A textual document $t$ with named entity annotations,

a set of trigger words: TW = {visit} and
a set of event patterns: P = {"NEperson trigger word NEGPE"}

Output: Text $t$ with event annotations.
1. For $p \in P$ do {
2.    For trigger_word ∈ T W do {
3.       If $p$(trigger_word) applies to $t$ then
4.          Add an annotation in $t$ for a transportation event expressed by NEperson, NEGPE, and trigger word.

     }

   }
5. Return text $t$ with named entity and event annotations

## Sentiment Analysis

Sentiment analysis is the task of assigning scores to considerable textual pieces, such as sentences, paragraphs, or documents that represent the attitude of the author with respect to some topic or the overall polarity of a document. Considering a single, coarse-grained sentimental dimension per textual piece, each is assigned a single score that represents positive, negative, or neutral sentiment [21]. A more complex model would consider more than one sentimental dimension, such as agreement, satisfaction, and happiness, assigning more than one score per text [14,23]. Moreover, the context of each text can be considered in more detail, so that a sentimental score is computed for each selected named entity. For example, a user review about a computer might be overall positive, but might be negative for some components, such as the speakers and the keyboard.

Similarly to named entity recognition, relation extraction, and event extraction, sentiment analysis is addressed in a domain-specific manner. In general, positive and negative sentiments are extracted by looking into domain-specific linguistic cues depicting agreement, disagreement, praise, negative slang, etc. [9]. Following a simple approach, a dictionary of preselected words associated with scores is used to aggregate the score of longer textual units. More sophisticated approaches can take into account lexical patterns, part of speech patterns, and shallow parsing results. Machine learning is also applicable to this task.

Algorithm 11.5 presents the pseudocode for a simple sentiment analyzer that considers a small lexicon of four words and aggregates an overall score for an input text. As an application example, feeding in the text "I like apples" would output the score +1, while feeding in "I hate bananas" would output the score –2. Evidently, this simplistic approach would perform badly in many cases. For example, "I don't like bananas" would output +1, while "I like love and I don't like hate" would output +2.

### Algorithm 11.5: A Simple Sentiment Analyzer

Input: A textual document $t$ and a lexicon of words associated with polarity scores:

$D = \{\text{love } (+2), \text{like } (+1), \text{dislike } (–1), \text{hate } (–2)\}$

Output: Text $t$ scored for sentiment analysis.
1. Score = 0

2.  For word ∈ D do {
3.      If word occurs *t* then
4.          Score = score + wordscore
    }
5.  Return *t*, score

## APPLICATIONS

This section describes several applications of structuring text in various domains, for diverse potential users and further usage.

### Web Analytics via Text Analysis in Blogs and Social Media

Web analytics focuses on collecting, measuring, analyzing, and interpreting web data in order to improve web usage and effectiveness for the interests of a person or an organization. Web analytics comprises an important tool for market research, business development, and measuring the effect of advertisement and promotional campaigns. Companies show increasing interest in monitoring the opinion of consumers about the products and services they offer. They are interested to know the effect of their activity both in general and to particular consumer groups.

Methods of web analytics can be classified as on-site and off-site. On-site methods consider statistics that can be collected from the target company website itself. Such statistics refer to traffic per time unit, number of visitors, and page views. Off-site web analytics methods concern measuring the impact of the activities of a company or an organization from web resources other than the website of that company or organization. Usually, web resources suitable for this purpose are online forums, blogs, electronic commerce websites, and social media.

Sentiment analysis is the most important tool in the process of assessing the attitude of posts toward products and services. As discussed above, sentiment analysis can be detailed enough to fit the analysis needs required by the user. However, the more detailed a sentiment analysis system is, the more training data is needed to achieve adequate performance. Apart from sentiment analysis, considering the terms occurring in posts related to the target organization, product, or service can give evidence about concepts that users consider as related. Recognizing the types of these terms, i.e., identifying them as named entities, would indicate how users think of the target products or services in comparison to other, probably competitive ones. Other metadata associated with social media posts, such as the author profiles, are useful to compile an analysis of the characteristics of users interested in the target organization, product, or service [1]. Often, companies are mainly interested in the ages and lifestyle or their customers. For the latter, the overall activity of users that posted about the target organization, product, or service should be analyzed.

Sentiment analysis and term recognition in conjunction with an analysis of user profiles can produce valuable decision-making results. Managers will be able to observe the levels of user satisfaction per profile attribute, such as age, gender, and location. Moreover, decisions can be based on the terms that occur in discussions of users per location or age group and the corresponding term importance scores.

## Linking Diverse Resources

For many domains, it is meaningful to merge together information coming from different resources. Examples from the domains of news and medicine are discussed below as indicative.

For a variety of interest groups and organizations the ability to observe the effect of advances in politics and economy as well as other decisions, events, and incidents is of invaluable importance. Having access to public opinion dynamics can be considered a form of immediate feedback, helpful in politics to form actions, measures, and policies. This aggregated knowledge can be compiled by linking together information for the same topic, coming from different resources: news articles, blogs, and social media. The process can be organized in four steps:

1. Clustering together news articles about the same topic
2. Retrieving blog and social media posts related to the topic of each cluster
3. Analyzing the opinion and sentiment in these posts
4. Aggregating sentiment and opinion mining outcomes per topic to be presented to the user

The entire process requires preprocessing all text to recognize terms, entities, relations, and events [26]. These metadata should be considered as features for clustering (first step), and also for constructing queries to retrieve relevant blog and social media posts in the second step. This analysis is valuable for decision makers as a feedback mechanism. For each decision made, they can observe the impact to the public or specific interest group in terms of sentiment, satisfaction, and opinions.

In the medical domain, while running a clinical trial, it is particularly laborious to locate patients that can participate taking into account the eligibility criteria specified [13]. This task can be automated up to some level to help doctors select matching candidates. Structured eligibility criteria of a clinical trial can be cross-checked with structured medical information from electronic health records of patients. The structuring necessary for this task refers to named entity recognition in both resources and identification of corresponding numerical indications and levels. Structuring will enable doctors to select patients that fulfill certain eligibility criteria automatically.

## Search via Semantic Metadata

Searching for documents with specific characteristics in large collections can be very tedious and costly. Document metadata can be used to improve searching and locating them much more efficiently. Semantic metadata, such as named entities, relations, and events, can contribute toward this purpose in addition to standard metadata accompanying the document. For example, in the newswire and newspaper domain, an article might be associated with inherent metadata about the name of the author, the name of the column it was published in, the date of publication and others, but also the named entities, relations among them, as well as events can be computed in the textual content of the article, as discussed in the "Structuring Textual Data" section.

As an example, suppose we have the *New York Times* article titled "New York May Use Money to Aid Children."* It was written by Raymond Hernandez, and published on Sunday, June 22, 1997, on the fourth column of page 14. The article belongs to the National Desk and is a part of the Tobacco Industry collection. All this information consists of the inherent metadata of the article.

Figure 11.1 presents an example workflow that can be applied to this particular article and others, to produce extra semantic metadata useful

---

* The article is available at http://www.nytimes.com/1997/06/22/us/new-york-may-use-money-to-aid-children.html and was last accessed on July 8, 2013.

**FIGURE 11.1**

Text mining workflow producing semantic annotations.

for search application. Term extraction applied on the content of this article can identify terms such as *children, tobacco industry, industry, federal government, attorney general, Richard Blumenthal, Connecticut, Dennis C. Vacco, Christine Todd Whitman, Friday night, George E. Pataki, healthcare,* and *healthcare expert.*

Forwarding the textual content of the article to a named entity will identify some of these terms as named entities: *Christine Todd Whitman, Dennis C. Vacco, George E. Pataki,* and *Richard Blumenthal* will be identified as people. *Democrats, Republicans, organization legislature,* and *federal government* will be identified as nationalities or religious or political (NORP) groups. Geopolitical entities (GPEs) are terms such as *Connecticut, New Jersey, New York,* and *Washington.* Similarly, a named entity recognizer would identify dates, such as *a year, 4 years from now, January 27,* and *6 months,* and money quantities, such as *$100 million, $400 billion,* and *$656.*

In the next processing step of the text mining workflow shown in Figure 11.1, complex events can be identified between the named entities recognized previously. For instance, an event of type "contact or meeting" is identified, triggered by the word *negotiations* and the GPE *Washington,* expressed in present tense and assertive mode. Moreover a "justice or sue" event is triggered by the words *lawsuit* and *sue,* and a "money transaction or transfer" event is triggered by the word *receive* and the money sum $400 million.

Metadata values for a specific kind of metadata, e.g., author name, can be presented collectively in the search environment to be used as search facets. This allows users to search the document collection in a different way than standard textual queries. They will be able to select a single value or a set of values for one or more metadata types and obtain as a result the documents that are associated with these specific data values only. Semantic metadata can be used in the very same way. For example, users can retrieve all news articles that were published on pages 10–20 in some newspaper and contain the geopolitical named entity *Washington,* a demonstration event and a movement event whose subject is *U.S. President Obama.* Using annotations as search tools improves search, because it allows us to easily locate documents of specific characteristics in large document collections.

Using metadata values as search facets can also be very valuable in many domains other than news. In the biological domain, it is very crucial for researchers to be able to retrieve all publications that refer to specific relations and events [15]. In the medical domain, within the procedure of running a clinical trial, doctors are obliged to retrieve and take into account all related previous clinical trials. Search using metadata as facets can be very helpful toward locating these trials quickly and precisely from collections containing a plethora of documents. Figure 11.2 shows a screenshot of the clinical trials search engine ASCOT [13], which indexes approximately 110K clinical trial documents. As it is visible close to the top of the screenshot, "selected categories," i.e., constraints applied to the search space, are *phase, phase 1; intervention type, drug; study type, observational;* and *termine term, blood pressure.* The former constraint considers clinical trails of phase 1 only. The second constraint restricts search to clinical trial protocols that study the effects of drugs, while the third restricts to observational studies. The last constraint requires for the term *blood pressure* to occur in the textual content of the protocols retrieved. These four constraints in combination are fulfilled by five clinical trial protocols

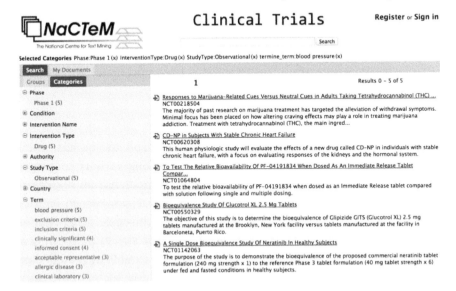

**FIGURE 11.2**
Screenshot of the clinical trails search engine ASCOT. (From Korkontzelos, I., Mu, T., and Ananiadou, S., *BMC Medical Informatics and Decision Making*, 12(Suppl. 1), S3+, 2012.)

only. They are shown on the right-hand side of the screenshot. Other constraints appearing on the left-hand side can be also selected. This example shows how metadata can provide an intuitive and user-friendly manner to search in vast document spaces. ASCOT also employs other methods for locating clinical trial protocols of interest, such as keyword search and clustering [13].

## Dictionary and Ontology Enrichment

In many domains, such as biology, chemistry, and technology, new terms are introduced constantly. Ontologies and other term dictionaries should be updated to keep up with advances, and this task is very expensive if performed manually [2,5]. Automatic term extraction applied to textual resources that contain neologisms, such as publications and forum discussions, can produce new term candidates. Checking these candidates only instead of reading the entire new publications is a much easier and less costly manual task.

Some ontologies hold translations of concepts in more than one language. It is common that multilingual ontologies are not equally developed in all the languages they offer. Bilingual term extraction can aid in enriching these ontologies, since it is able to extract pairs of terms for different languages [4]. In other words, bilingual term extraction can map the verbal sequences of existing ontology concepts to the sequences of the same concepts in other languages. This method of enriching multilingual ontologies requires a minimal cost for manual verification.

## Automatic Translation

Automatic word-by-word translation is a very difficult task because of the differences in syntax and sentence structure among various languages. For this reason, many machine translation methods use an alignment between semantic-bearing units of text, such as terms, named entities, and relations among them. The intuition behind this idea is that relation and events, that join entities together, retain their structure in any language. In addition, translations of terms tend to exhibit increased similarities across languages, especially in some domains, such as chemistry, biology, and medicine. Thus, identifying named entities, relations, and events can be helpful during translation. It is indicative that typical statistical machine translation systems operate by learning from the training data the translation of words or word sequences associated with probabilities, and then use these translation tables to translate unknown sentences.

## Forensics and Profiling

Forensics is the investigation of criminal activity by applying various sciences and technologies. Since blogging and social media comprise nowadays a significant part of communication for most people, investigating the online activity of criminals is worth investigating because it might reveal important aspects about their interests, plans, personality, way of living, and thinking. In other words, analyzing the activity of criminals in blogs and social media might provide more evidence about their profile in general.

Analyzing blog posts of somebody under investigation or comments that they might have submitted to other posts can reveal evidence about their ideas, background principles, and way of thinking. Toward processing this textual evidence, extracting terms and named entities as well as analyzing sentiment might be useful.

Apart from blog posts and comments, social media profiles and posts are useful for suspect profiling. The textual content of posts can be analyzed similarly to blog posts and comments. However, social media can provide extra information about the habits and acquaintances of a user. Specifically, the profile of each user in some social medium contains a set of friends. Analyzing the activity of each friend of a target user together with the relation between them might also be informative. Finally, some social media record information about the places that a user has logged in from. The time and place of these check-ins might be important for investigating criminal activity.

## Automatic Text Summarization

Text summarization is the process of producing a short version of a document that contains the most important point made in it. A summary produced by a human usually does not consist of the same sentences as the main document. Humans would synthesize the important parts of a document into new, more condensed sentences.

However, synthesizing a summary from scratch is a complex task to address automatically, because it requires a language generation step. Instead, typical automatic summarization methods concatenate the most important sentences of clauses extracted from the original document.

Specifically, automatic summarization methods typically assign an importance score to the sentences or clauses in the document to be summarized. Then, the sentences are sorted in order of decreasing importance, and only the top $N$ sentences of this list are presented as the document summary.

Toward the process of scoring document sentences or clauses, semantic metadata computed for the target document prior to summarization are of significant importance. Named entities and relations among them hold increased semantic meaning. Named entities, relations, and events in a document can be linked together to draw a skeleton of its meaning. Then, a summary should definitely contain the sentences that describe these interrelated events.

Automatic summarization of textual documents can be handy to present long text in a compact manner. Providing users with a condensed summary can be useful in a variety of applications, such as news, research publications in a specific domain, and advertisements of a product family.

## REFERENCES

1. E. Agichtein, C. Castillo, D. Donato, A. Gionis, and G. Mishne. Finding high-quality content in social media. In *Proceedings of the 2008 International Conference on Web Search and Data Mining: WSDM '08*, New York, NY, 2008, pp. 183–194.
2. S. Ananiadou and J. Mcnaught. *Text mining for biology and biomedicine*. Artech House, Norwood, MA, 2005.
3. M. Banko, M.J. Cafarella, S. Soderland, M. Broadhead, and O. Etzioni. Open information extraction from the web. In *Proceedings of IJCAI*, New York, 2007, pp. 68–74.
4. B. Daille, E. Gaussier, and J.M. Langé. Towards automatic extraction of monolingual and bilingual terminology. In *Proceedings of the 15th Conference on Computational Linguistics: COLING '94*, Morristown, NJ, 1994, pp. 515–521.
5. K. Englmeier, F. Murtagh, and J. Mothe. Domain ontology: Automatically extracting and structuring community language from texts. In *Proceedings of Applied Computing (IADIS)*, Salamanca, Spain, 2007. pp. 59–66.
6. O. Etzioni, M.J. Cafarella, D. Downey, A.-M. Popescu, T. Shaked, S. Soderland, D.S. Weld, and A. Yates. Unsupervised named-entity extraction from the web: An experimental study. *Artificial Intelligence*, 165(1):91–134, 2005.
7. K.T. Frantzi, S. Ananiadou, and H. Mima. Automatic recognition of multi-word terms: The C-value/NC-value method. *International Journal on Digital Libraries*, 3(2):115–130, 2000.
8. B. Georgantopoulos and S. Piperidis. A hybrid technique for automatic term extraction. In *Proceedings of ACIDCA 2000*, Monastir, Tunisia, 2000, pp. 124–128.
9. N. Godbole, M. Srinivasaiah, and S. Skiena. Large-scale sentiment analysis for news and blogs. In *Proceedings of the International Conference on Weblogs and Social Media (ICWSM)*, Boulder, Colorado, 2007.

10. M.A. Hearst. Automated discovery of WordNet relations. In *WordNet: An electronic lexical database*, ed. C. Fellbaum, pp. 131–153. MIT Press, Cambridge, MA, 1998.

11. H. Kilicoglu and S. Bergler. Syntactic dependency based heuristics for biological event extraction. In *Proceedings of the Workshop on Current Trends in Biomedical Natural Language Processing: Shared Task: BioNLP '09*, Stroudsburg, PA, 2009, pp. 119–127.

12. I. Korkontzelos, I.P. Klapaftis, and S. Manandhar. Reviewing and evaluating automatic term recognition techniques. In *Proceedings of GoTAL '08*, pp. 248–259. Springer-Verlag, Berlin, 2008.

13. I. Korkontzelos, T. Mu, and S. Ananiadou. ASCOT: A text mining-based web-service for efficient search and assisted creation of clinical trials. *BMC Medical Informatics and Decision Making*, 12(Suppl 1):S3+, 2012. Accessed from http://www.biomedcentral.com/1472-6947/12/S1/S3.

14. B. Liu. Sentiment analysis and subjectivity. In *Handbook of natural language processing*. 2nd ed. Taylor and Francis Group, Boca Raton, FL, 2010.

15. J.R. McEntyre, S. Ananiadou, S. Andrews, W.J. Black, R. Boulderstone, P. Buttery, D. Chaplin, S. Chevuru, N. Cobley, L.-A.A. Coleman, P. Davey, B. Gupta, L. Haji-Gholam, C. Hawkins, A. Horne, S.J. Hubbard, J.-H. H. Kim, I. Lewin, V. Lyte, R. MacIntyre, S. Mansoor, L. Mason, J. McNaught, E. Newbold, C. Nobata, E. Ong, S. Pillai, D. Rebholz-Schuhmann, H. Rosie, R. Rowbotham, C.J. Rupp, P. Stoehr, and P. Vaughan. UKPMC: A full text article resource for the life sciences. *Nucleic Acids Research*, 39:D58–D65, 2011.

16. G.A. Miller. WordNet: A lexical database for English. *Communications of the ACM*, 38(11):39–41, 1995.

17. M. Mintz, S. Bills, R. Snow, and D. Jurafsky. Distant supervision for relation extraction without labeled data. In *Proceedings of the Joint Conference of the 47th Annual Meeting of the ACL and the 4th International Joint Conference on Natural Language Processing of the AFNLP: ACL '09*, Stroudsburg, PA, 2009, vol. 2 pp. 1003–1011.

18. M. Miwa, P. Thompson, J. McNaught, D.B. Kell, and S. Ananiadou. Extracting semantically enriched events from biomedical literature. *BMC Bioinformatics*, 13(1):108+, 2012.

19. D. Nadeau, P.D. Turney, and S. Matwin. Unsupervised named-entity recognition: Generating gazetteers and resolving ambiguity. In *Proceedings of the 19th Canadian Conference on Artificial Intelligence*, Québec City, Québec, Canada, 2006, pp. 266–277.

20. H. Nakagawa. Automatic term recognition based on statistics of compound nouns. *Terminology*, 6(2):195–210, 2000.

21. T. Nasukawa and J. Yi. Sentiment analysis: Capturing favorability using natural language processing. In *Proceedings of the 2nd International Conference on Knowledge Capture: K-CAP '03*, New York, NY, 2003, pp. 70–77.

22. T. Ohta, T. Matsuzaki, N. Okazaki, M. Miwa, R. Saetre, S. Pyysalo, and J. Tsujii. Medie and Info-pubmed: 2010 update. *BMC Bioinformatics*, 11(Suppl 5):P7+, 2010.

23. B. Pang and L. Lee. Opinion mining and sentiment analysis. *Foundations and Trends in Information Retrieval* 2(1–2), Now Publishers, Hanover, Massachusetts, 2008, pp. 1–135.

24. X. Robitaille, Y. Sasaki, M. Tonoike, S. Sato, and T. Utsuro. Compiling French-Japanese terminologies from the web. In *Proceedings of the 11th Conference of the European Chapter of the Association for Computational Linguistics (EACL)*, Trento, Italy, 2006, pp. 225–232.

25. B. Rosario and M.A. Hearst. Classifying semantic relations in bioscience texts. In *Proceedings of the 42nd Annual Meeting on Association for Computational Linguistics (ACL)*, Barcelona, Spain, 2004, pp. 430–437.
26. H. Tanev, J. Piskorski, and M. Atkinson. Real-time news event extraction for global crisis monitoring. In *Proceedings of the 13th International Conference on Natural Language and Information Systems: NLDB '08*, pp. 207–218. Springer-Verlag, Berlin, 2008.
27. D. Zelenko, C. Aone, and A. Richardella. Kernel methods for relation extraction. *Journal of Machine Learning Research*, 3:1083–1106, 2003.
28. Kessler, G. President Obama's low-ball estimate for Keystone XL jobs. *The Washington Post,* July 2013. Accessed from http://www.washingtonpost.com/blogs/fact-checker/post/president-obamas-low-ball-estimate-for-keystone-xl-jobs/2013/07/29/ce886b1e-f897-11e2-afc1-c850c6ee5af8_blog.html.

# 12

## The New Medical Frontier: Real-Time Wireless Medical Data Acquisition for 21st-Century Healthcare and Data Mining Challenges

*David Lubliner and Stephan Kudyba*

## CONTENTS

## INTRODUCTION

Medical sensors, fixed, wireless, and implanted, are growing at an exponential rate. This trend is amplified by the growth of smartphones and tablets that provide the potential to provide real-time monitoring and proactive prevention. Cisco has estimated [3] that by 2015 mobile cellular traffic will reach an annual run rate of 75 exabytes, $10^{18}$ bytes or 1 billion gigabytes. This enormous amount of data doesn't even factor into the growth of this new emerging field of real-time wireless medical devices where studies have shown them to be a significant benefit to early detection and reduced acute emergency room visits. In 2012 the Federal Communications Commission allocated part of the spectrum for medical body area networks (MBANs), which will accelerate adoption of these technologies. Add to that genomic sequencing and the need to categorize, evaluate trends, mine data sets spanning large populations, and compress and store data that will potentially dwarf current storage architectures. The challenge is enormous but so too are the potential benefits. Kryder's law for data storage [15], an offshoot of Moore's law for microprocessors, shows similar patterns of growth of data storage systems, but may still not be enough to satisfy projections. New storage technologies utilizing molecular storage [9] may come to our rescue. We are at a critical inflection point where data, communications, processing power, and medical technologies have the potential to transform our ways of life. The real challenge is extracting meaning out of this torrent of information.

This chapter is a primer for those interested in exploring mining of medical data, in particular the challenges of extracting meaning from the new breed of wireless medical monitoring devices. The "Evolution of Modern Medicine: Background" section begins with a brief history of the quantification of medical practices and the advances that have led to the doubling of life expectancy in the past 100 years. The "Medical Data Standards" section introduces medical terminology that is crucial to developing a standard lexis of medical terms for data sharing. The "Data Acquisition: Medical Sensors and Body Scanners" section introduces medical data acquisition and the theory behind many popular sensors and medical scanners. The "Wireless Medical Devices" section introduces the communications and integration of these wireless sensor networks. The "Expert Systems Utilized to Evaluate Medical Data" section discusses expert systems, which is the first step in extracting meaning from medical data and provides techniques to make this data available to medical professionals and the public. The "Data Mining and Big Data" section discusses medical data mining and the new initiatives by the National Science Foundation (NSF), National Institutes of Health (NIH), and Department of Defense (DOD) to extract meaning from these big data sets in the petabyte ranges of $10^{15}$ to $2^{50}$.

We are entering into a brave new world of medical data acquisition. The potential benefits may transform healthcare from reactive to proactive treatment, reducing the burden of emergency rooms but increasing that on a new breed of medical informatics professionals. The challenge is to develop guidelines to ensure that privacy and support systems are constructed to provide preventive care to maximize the benefits and ensure equal access to these technologies.

## EVOLUTION OF MODERN MEDICINE: BACKGROUND

Medical knowledge has paralleled our perceptions of our place in the universe. When superstition dominated our discourse, illness and disease were predominantly attributed to forces beyond our control. Ancient Egyptian and Babylonians around 3300 BC began to quantify a system of medicine that included diagnosis and medical examination, but still included aspects of external forces as part of the equation. One of the first rational medical documents, the Edwin Smith Papyrus [19] on trauma and surgery, Egypt c. 1500 BC, details 48 cases of injury with a detailed diagnosis, examination, and treatment strategies. Treatment includes both suggested medication and spells to treat the condition. The text appears to be a transcribed copy attributed to Imhotep, a physician and high priest c. 3000 BC. The first hospitals, "Houses of Life," were also mentioned in this same era.

Babylonians, 1067–1046 BC, wrote a medical text *The Diagnostic Handbook* [8], by Esagil-kin-apli; it included patient symptoms and treatment through creams, pills, and bandages. In India, 600 BC, the "Complete Knowledge for Long Life" describes herbal remedies and appears to be linked to Buddhist practices. In China, 500 BC, "Yellow Emperors Inner Cannon" drew a parallel between the physical world and the spiritual aspects of disease. Another milestone in our quantification of medical practice was the Hippocratic Oath, Greece, c. 500 BC, where physicians were given guidelines on ethical practice and treatment. This oath incorporated treatises to external forces: "Apollo Physician and Asclepius and Hygeia and Panacea and All the Gods and Goddesses, Making Them My Witnesses, That I Will Fulfill according to My Ability and Judgment This Oath and This Covenant." Around this period the first Greek medical school in Cnidus, now part of Turkey, was established. The guiding philosophy was to restore the balance of humors in the body.

In the Middle Ages, 1200 AD, Islamic medical science advanced medicine in pharmacology, surgery, and ophthalmology guided by a systematic approach to medical practice. In the Renaissance, 1500 AD, experimental science in anatomy, neurology, and the circulatory system began our movement away from folklore. The first pharmaceutical text, *Antidotarium Florentine*, in 1542, was published by the Florence College of Medicine. By the early 1600s medicines were in common use in London. The College of Physicians issued guidelines for the preparation of drugs by authorized apothecaries. By 1750 an official pharmacological guide was published where only treatments sanctioned by a pharmacopeia committee were included.

Modern medicine truly began in the 1800s with anesthesia, the "germ theory of disease" [2], use of antiseptics, *Introduction to the Study of Experimental Medicine* by Claude Bernard in 1865 describing a scientific method of medical inquiry, bacteriology (Robert Koch), and many others. Nursing practice and education were quantified by Florence Nightingale with her book *Notes on Nursing* (1859). Her statistical analysis of infection and sanitation was influential in creating the public health service in India.

In the early part of the 20th century new diagnostic techniques, antimicrobial therapy, and evidence-based medicine such as triple-blind randomized trials accelerated medical knowledge and effectiveness. In the later part of the 20th century the exponential growth of medicine began: genomics, medical imaging, stem cell therapy, and modern surgery. The explosion of new microtechnology, gene therapies, transplants, and the World Wide Web of integrated knowledge sharing has put us on the threshold of this next great leap forward. As shown in Figure 12.1, there

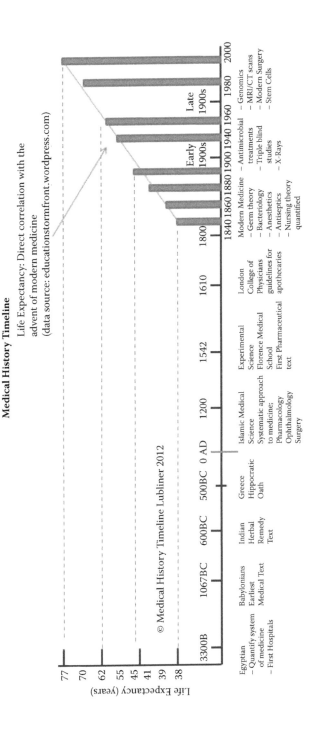

**FIGURE 12.1**

Evolution of medical science overlaid with life expectancy improvements.

has been a direct correlation with evidence-based medicine and the doubling of life expectancy.

With this exponential growth in medical knowledge comes enormous stores of data. The technology for genomic sequencing data has been reduced from a year to hours. This storehouse will continue to accelerate. The National Institutes of Health in 2012 released a genomic data store of 200 terabytes, soon to enter the petabyte range, $10^{15}$. With the advent of real-time wireless medical sensors, millions will be transmitting data. It's difficult to estimate the data volume, but in the first decade the terabyte–petabyte range is not unreasonable (see page 280). Data mining of medical data will present enormous challenges and benefits.

## MEDICAL DATA STANDARDS

A critical consideration in the analysis of medical data is to ensure all parties are using the same nomenclature. How can we extract usable information unless all parties adhere to international standards for data classification?

There are a number of national and international data standards that provide ubiquitous communications between doctors, health insurance companies, labs, and pharmacies, and for interoperability between electronic health records (EHRs).

The U.S. government in 1996 created a series of standards and specifications for electronic health records and data security. The National Institute of Standards is responsible for standards for federal agencies. The department responsible for health services is the Health and Human Services Department (HHS). In 1996 the Health Insurance Portability and Accountability Act of 1996 (HIPAA, Public Law 104-191) established guidelines for medical data and security of that information (Figure 12.2). These have been periodically updated, and a recent update to HIPAA Title II on data security [25] provides confidentiality, integrity, and availability (CIA) for medical information.

- Health Level Seven (www.HL.org), an organization started in 1987, has become the most popular international standard for data interoperability for medical practitioners (Figure 12.3). Collectively, it develops standards designed to increase the effectiveness, efficiency,

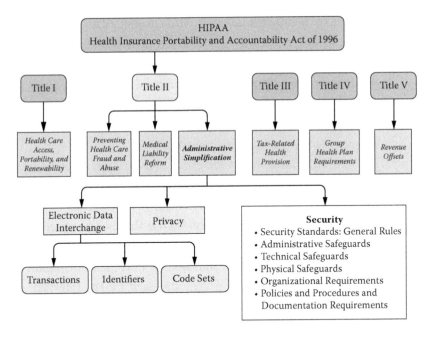

**FIGURE 12.2**

HIPPA standards created by the U.S. government in 1996. (From HHS, http://www.hhs.
gov/ocr/privacy/hipaa/administrative/securityrule/nist80066.pdf.)

| United States | Health Level 7 (HL7) and Healthcare Information and Management |
| --- | --- |
| | Systems Society (HIMSS) are involved in the standardization process for EHR in the U.S. |
| | The Certification Commission for Healthcare Information Technology (CCHIT) is a private not-for-profit organization founded to develop and evaluate the certification for EHRs and interoperable health informatics networks. |
| | The American Society for Testing and Materials (ASTM) |
| International | |
| Europe | CEN's TC/251 is responsible for EHR standards |
| | ISO TC215 produces standards for EHR requirements as well as accepting certain standards from other standards organizations. |
| | The openEHR Foundation develops and publishes EHR specifications and open source EHR implementations, which are currently being used in Australia and parts of Europe. |
| Canada | Canada Health Infoway (a private not-for-profit organization started with federal government seed money) is mandated to accelerate the development and adoption of electronic health information systems. |

**FIGURE 12.3**

Data interoperability standards.

and quality of healthcare delivery. HL7's primary mission is to create flexible, low-cost standards, guidelines, and methodologies to enable the exchange and interoperability of electronic health records. Such guidelines or data standards are an agreed-upon set of rules that allow information to be shared and processed in a uniform and consistent manner. Without data standards, healthcare organizations could not readily share clinical information.

- HL7 is an all-volunteer, not-for-profit organization involved in the development of international healthcare standards.
- Headquartered in Ann Arbor, Michigan, Health Level Seven is a standards developing organization (SDO) that is accredited by the American National Standards Institute (ANSI).
- Founded in 1987 to produce a standard for hospital information systems, HL7 is currently the selected standard for the interfacing of clinical data in most institutions.
- HL7 and its members provide a comprehensive framework (and related standards) for the exchange, integration, sharing, and retrieval of electronic health information.
- The standards, which support clinical practice and the management, delivery, and evaluation of health services, are the most commonly used in the world.

There are numerous other standards for data interoperability. The International Statistical Classification of Diseases (ICD-10) is a standard created by the World Health Organization (WHO) that contains over 14,000 names, codes, and descriptions of diseases so international medical practitioners can share findings using the same terminology. Another important standard is Systemized Nomenclature of Medicine (SNOMED) that provides a consistent way to describe medical diseases, diagnoses, and symptoms. Communicating and transmitting MRI, CT, x-rays, and PET scans utilizes the Digital Imaging and Communications in Medicine (DICOM) standard. The Institute of Electrical and Electronic Engineers (IEEE) standards association publishes approximately 200 standards. Examples are 802.11 for wireless medical device transmissions and 11073 for plug-and-play interoperability of medical devices [24].

# DATA ACQUISITION: MEDICAL SENSORS AND BODY SCANNERS

Medical data acquisition falls into a number of categories: electrical (EEG, EKG), electromagnetic, imaging (MRI, PET), chemical, biological (cultures), and genomic data sequencing. This section describes the theory behind some of those data acquisition technologies and also describes various medical sensors and scanners. A prerequisite for mining data and extracting meaning is a basic understanding of those technologies that generate this information.

## Sensors

Electrical: Current in nerve cells. At the highest level of abstraction current flows (electrons – valence electron [ve]) toward a positive potential; i.e., one side of a wire or nerve is positive. In a battery you have two chemical solutions initially both neutral; let's say for argument's sake that the atoms on each side of the battery have 10 protons and 10 electrons. When charging a battery you move electrons from one side to the other; i.e., one side has 9 electrons and the other 11 (Figure 12.4a). This provides a positive potential difference between the two sides of the battery; i.e., one side is more positive than the other. When connecting a wire between terminals of the battery the electrons, negative, move to the positive side. Once

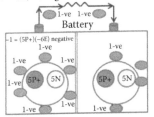

Resistance to regulate current flow
V = IR; Voltage = Current*resistance

1-ve  1-ve
Battery

–1 = (5P+)(–6E) negative
1-ve
1-ve        1-ve
1-ve  5P+  5N

1-ve
1-ve

1-ve        5P+  5N
1-ve
1-ve        1-ve

Potential difference, or voltage, between the two electrodes; i.e., one side is more positive than the other. We move -ve electrons, charge the battery, from one side to the other.
© Potential Difference Lubliner 2012

(a)

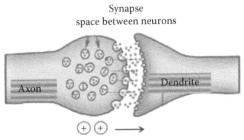

Synapse
space between neurons

Axon        Dendrite

(+) (+) ⟶

Positive ions moved across the gap making one side more positive, potential difference

(b)

**FIGURE 12.4**
(a) Potential difference in a battery. (b) Potential generated in synapse.

both sides are neutral, both have 10 protons, positive, and 10 electrons; the potential difference disappears and no current flows.

The same is true for electron flow in the body. In order for current to flo, a potential difference must be created from one synapse, the space between neurons, to the next. This is achieved by pumping positive ions across that gap between nerves. This is a sodium $(NA^+)$-potassium $(K^+)$ pump (Figure 12.4b).

## Electrical (EKG, EEG)

Electrocardiogram (EKG) measures the electrical activity of the cardiac muscle of the heart. When the sinoatrial (SA) node, the pacemaker of the heart located in the right atrium, initiates signals, it sends signals to the atria-ventricular node, then to the Purkinje fibers that propagate the signals to the rest of the heart.

In the SA node/pacemaker step (1), a large number of sodium ions $(NA^+)$ and a small number of potassium ions $(K^+)$ are migrating through the cell. Then in step 2, calcium $(CA^{2+})$ channels open up, creating an (action) potential, i.e., cell more positive generating a current (flow of electrons) in millivolts, a thousand volts (Figure 12.5). In step 3, a potassium channel opens up so more potassium ions flow out and the potential difference returns to negative, stopping the flow of current.

The action potential in cardiac muscle cells is initiated by a sodium spike that generates a calcium spike, which then produces muscle contraction (Figure 12.5). The voltage of a cell is usually measured in millivolts (mV), a thousand volts.

## Pulse Oximetry

Pulse oximetry is a method of monitoring oxygen saturation of a patient's hemoglobin. The process uses a pair of light-emitting diodes (LEDs) on one side of a finger and a photoreceptor on the other. There are two LEDs, one red at 660 nm wavelength and a second at 905–940 nm in the infrared range. The absorption at these wavelengths differs between their oxygenated (ox) hemoglobin and deoxygenated state. The ratio of the two can be calculated using the two frequencies. The absorption is calculated from the minimum vs. peak values, which makes simultaneously monitoring the pulse critical.

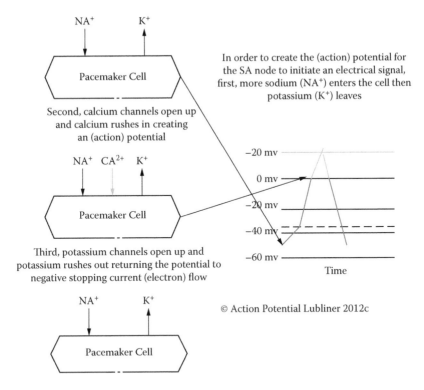

**FIGURE 12.5**
Action potential in cardiac nerves.

## Medical Scanners

Magnetic resonance imaging (MRI) is a noninvasive method used to render images of the inside of an object. It is primarily used in medical imaging to demonstrate pathological or other physiological alterations of living tissues.

### Magnetic Resonance Imagining vs. Computer Tomography (CT)

A computed tomography (CT), originally known as computed axial tomography (CAT), scanner, uses a type of ionizing radiation to acquire its images, making it a good tool for examining tissue composed of elements of a relatively higher atomic number than the tissue surrounding them (e.g., bone and calcifications [calcium based] within the body [carbon-based flesh] or structures [vessels, bowel] than the surrounding flesh [iodine, barium]). MRI, on the other hand, uses nonionizing

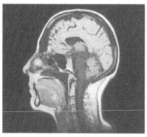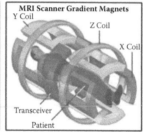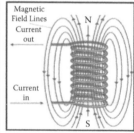

**FIGURE 12.6**

**(See color insert.)** MRI scan, schematic of scanner gradient magnets, and magnetic fields generated. (From the Magnetic High Magnetic Field Magnetic Laboratory, University of Florida, http://www.magnet.fsu.edu/education/tutorials/magnetacademy/mri/fullarticle.html.)

radio frequency (RF) signals to acquire its images and is best suited for noncalcified tissue (Figure 12.6).

- The magnet is the largest and most expensive component of the scanner, and the remainder of the scanner is built around the magnet. Just as important as the strength of the main magnet is its precision. The straightness of flux lines within the center or, as it is known, the isocenter of the magnet, needs to be almost perfect. Magnetic gradients are generated by three orthogonal coils, oriented in the $x$, $y$, and $z$ directions of the scanner. These are usually resistive electromagnets powered by sophisticated amplifiers that permit rapid and precise adjustments to their field strength and direction.
- In 1983 Ljunggren [15] and Tweig [22] independently introduced the $k$-space formalism, a technique that proved invaluable in unifying different MRI techniques. They showed that the demodulated MR signal $S(t)$ generated by freely precise nuclear spins in the presence of a linear magnetic field gradient $G$ equals the Fourier transform of the effective spin density, i.e.,

$$S(t) = \tilde{\rho}_{\text{effective}}\left(\vec{k}(t)\right) \equiv \int d^3x\, \rho(\vec{x}) \cdot e^{2\pi_2\, \vec{k}(t)\cdot\vec{x}}$$

MRI is essentially the manipulation of spins within a strong magnetic field, which then return to an equilibrium state. That a particle has spin is actually a mathematical description of the quantum mechanical nature of the particle—that happens to behave mathematically like spin—rather than a conceptual one (a sphere spinning on an axis). It is easy to imagine a positively charged sphere (e.g., the proton) of finite size (radius ~ $10^{-14}$ m), finite mass (~$10^{-27}$ kg), and a net electric charge (~$10^{-19}$ C) spinning, and therefore possessing a magnetic dipole moment.

### Positron Emission Tomography (PET)

Positron emission tomography (PET) is a nuclear medicine medical imaging technique that produces a three-dimensional image or map of functional processes or metabolic activities in the body. To conduct the scan, a short-lived radioactive tracer isotope, which decays by emitting a positron, which also has been chemically incorporated into a metabolically active molecule, is injected into the living subject (usually into blood circulation) (Figure 12.7).

The data set collected in PET is much poorer than that in CT, so reconstruction techniques are more difficult (see section below on image reconstruction of PET).

### Computed Tomography (CT)

Computed tomography (CT), originally known as computed axial tomography (CAT), is a medical imaging method employing tomography where digital geometry processing is used to generate a three-dimensional image of the internals of an object from a large series of two-dimensional x-ray images taken around a single axis of rotation. Cranial CT scans are shown in Figure 12.8. The bones are whiter than the surrounding area. Whiter means higher radio-density bones are whiter than the surrounding area. Whiter means higher radio density (i.e., the CT scan is designed to show higher-density structures).

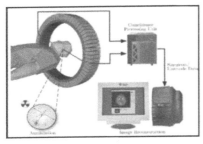 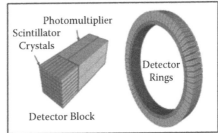

**FIGURE 12.7**
Positron emission tomography (PET) scan. (From the Max Planck Institute for Neurological Research, http://www.nf.mpg.de/index.php?id=78&L=1.)

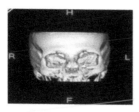 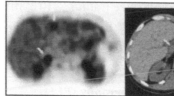

**FIGURE 12.8**

Pet scan vs. CT scan. (From RadioGraphics, http://radiographics.rsna.org/content/30/4/939/F37.expansion.html.)

### DICOM: Digital Imaging

Digital Imaging and Communications in Medicine (DICOM) is a format used for storing and sharing information between systems in medical imaging (also referred to as ISO 12052:2006) (Figure 12.9). It was developed in 1993 and is designed to ensure the interoperability of system sharing of medical images. The National Electrical Manufacturers Association (NEMA) holds the copyright to the standard (http://dicom.nema.org/).

## Imaging Informatics

Imaging informatics is the discipline associated with the acquisition, storage, knowledge base, mathematical modeling, and expert systems involved with the medical imaging field. A generic imaging system is described as a picture archiving and communication system (PACS), which communicates, stores, and analyzes data from multiple data formats and scanning technologies (e.g., Digital Imaging and Communications in Medicine [DICOM], ultrasound, endoscopy, and CT and MRI scanners). There are standard DICOM query protocols to transmit and retrieve images, CMOVE protocols, and a PACS [18] database using CQUERY. PACS links hospitals, imaging centers, and radiological groups to multiple hospitals. Hospitals access larger PACS systems through an internal radiological information system that includes patient tracking, patient scheduling, and workflow management.

As an example of an expert system used for the analysis and detection of cancer, it has been shown that the fractal dimension of 2D microvascular networks (Figure 12.10) can discriminate between normal vs. tumor tissue [6,7]. Research is continuing into fractal characteristics of 3D microvascular networks to determine if there is a correlation between the computed

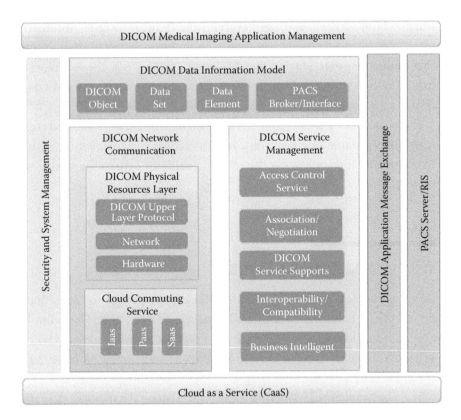

**FIGURE 12.9**
DICOM storage architecture and typical multiview DICOM storage. (From *Oracle®
Multimedia DICOM Developer's Guide*, http://docs.oracle.com/cd/B28359_01/appdev.111/
b28416/ch_cncpt.htm.)

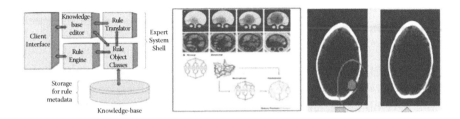

**FIGURE 12.10**
Expert system architecture, fractal capillary formation, and enhancement of tumors.
(From *Physiological Reviews*, http://physrev.physiology.org/content/91/3/1071.full.)

fractal characteristics and the nature of the tissue of origin. Automated assist and diagnosis software is approaching the quality of human experts that evaluate images. During the last decade (2000–2010), the reliability of expert system software, blue line, approached that of their human counterparts, i.e., radiologists.

The creation of a continuum from data collection, diagnosis, and treatment incorporated into electronic health records is transforming healthcare delivery and improving the overall quality of care in the healthcare system.

## WIRELESS MEDICAL DEVICES

Wireless medical devices can contain local data storage for subsequent download or transmit data in real time via various wireless technologies such as Bluetooth or protected wireless spectrums designated by the Federal Communications Commission (FCC), as indicated by 802.11b specifications.

These sensors are classified as either stand-alone devices or integrated in a sensor network where all devices share a common microprocessor controller that sends information as an integrated package. Both hospitals and individuals now currently utilize these devices. Research has indicated that this real-time data has reduced follow-up admissions. A new field is emerging where body sensor networks, an integrated suite of mobile medical monitors, are often integrated into clothing, which can be a significant aid to prevention of more serious conditions.

As wireless medical devices or body sensor webs become common, large real-time data streams are creating a new challenge in real-time data mining and big data, defined as extremely large data sets, to respond to possible life-threatening conditions in a timely matter. Some of these can be alleviated by locally intelligent processing; other issues will require a new breed of medical informatics professionals to analyze and develop protocols. As indicated in Figure 12.1, life expectancy has doubled in the last 100 years; the potential to match this rate of improvement using real-time wireless sensors integrated with smart devices/phones could be transformational.

## Bluetooth Wireless Communications

Bluetooth is one of the most accepted international wireless standards for wireless medical devices. It is characterized at short range, and recently in low-power variants with well-defined security protocols. It also contains specifications for personal area networks, piconets, of up to eight integrated devices.

There is an international organization/special interest working group (SIG) (https://www.bluetooth.org/apps/content/) that includes representatives from most medical equipment manufactures and publishes standards and holds regular seminars. The group also certifies testing laboratories to ensure Bluetooth standards meet local regulations. HL7, another international working group (www.HL7.org) that establishes EMR standards, closely works with this and other standards organizations, such as Healthcare Information and Management Systems Society (HIMSS), which is "focused on providing global leadership for the optimal use of information technology (IT) and management systems for the betterment of healthcare" (http://www.HIMSS.org).

## Body Sensor Networks (BNSs)

A body sensor network (Figure 12.11) is a series of medical devices, either external or implanted, worn by patients. The concept involves linking series of devices, using Bluetooth short-range communications, with a computer or smart device into an integrated packaged signal. Up to this point Bluetooth standard IEEE 802.15.4 has been a relatively inefficient system with higher transmission power required for communications. A new low-power Bluetooth called Wibree may provide longer battery life for these BSNs [20].

There are a number of standards for this evolving field to standardize these integrated systems:

- ISO/IEEE 11073: Low-level data standards for plug-and-play devices integrated into these BSNs that can contain a maximum of 10 connected devices.
- Integrating the Healthcare Enterprise (IHE) patient care domain (PDE): A joint effort by multiple medical sensor vendors to standardize interoperability between sensors and device interfaces. They are associated with Healthcare Information and Management Systems Society (HIMSS) and the American College of Clinical Engineering (ACCE).

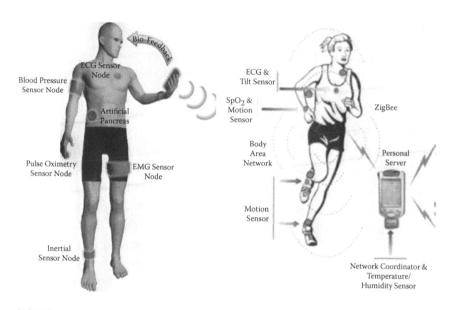

**FIGURE 12.11**

Body sensor networks. (From Robust Low Power VLSI Group, http://rlpvlsi.ece.virginia.edu/category/projects/body-sensor-networks.)

## Wireless Medical Device Protected Spectrum

In May 2012 the Federal Communications Commission (FCC) set aside part of the spectrum, 2360 to 2400 MHz, for use by low-power medical devices. The term for these low-power medical networks, typically used in hospital environments, is medical body area networks (MBANs). This spectrum was selected to prevent interference from Wi-Fi devices. Initially, this spectrum will be used by medical device manufacturers in relatively structured environments, but will evolve for all wireless medical devices.

## Integrated Data Capture Modeling for Wireless Medical Devices

There are several changes evolving in various areas of data generation. This includes more structured environments in fixed medical facilities, and less structured platforms (e.g., nonstructured private emergency care delivery and loosely structured technology-mediated monitoring); see Figure 12.12. This new model involves integrating multiple data sources into electronic medical records (EMRs), personal data records (PDRs), and continuity of care records (CCRs) and providing intelligent software to correlate data [16].

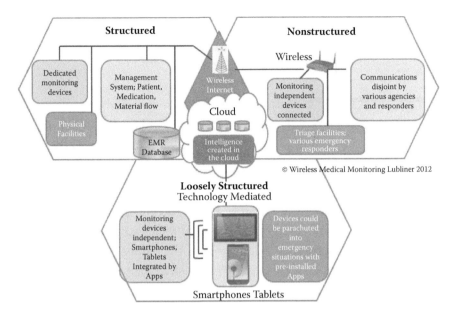

**FIGURE 12.12**
Structured, nonstructured, and loosely structured medical monitoring.

In structured environments the need to correlate patient data, common physiological monitoring parameters (CPMPs), blood pressure, heart rate, pulse oximetry, blood gases, etc., requires integration into a larger data repository, EMRs, which includes medications, lab tests, MRI/CT scans, and feedback from medical practitioners. Expert systems are evolving to manage and report on potential adverse scenarios.

In nonstructured environments, a disaster scenario involves $N$ number of patients with various levels of acuity and the need to coordinate response and transport based on acuity triage models. This can be divided into several subcategories:

Professional: Trained personnel entering the environment. FEMA, Red Cross city or federal services.
Volunteers: Local respondents responding to assist family or neighbors.
Possible automated devices: Dropped in methods to utilize the large base of wireless smart cell devices.

This typically involves personnel finding and deploying monitoring equipment. Since wireless devices are relatively short range, some temporary wireless network/monitoring structures need to be established that are linked into longer-range systems for coordination, point-to-point vs. wide area response. GPS and establishing patient ID also augment these systems.

## EXPERT SYSTEMS UTILIZED TO EVALUATE MEDICAL DATA

Expert systems can be referred to as computer based systems that provide decision support to users by incorporating hardware and software components and domain specific information to emulate human reasoning. The core components of an expert system are a *knowledge base*, composed of rules and facts, and an *inference engine*, supplied with data from a user, that selects the appropriate rules based on the data and calculates probabilities that the rules apply to a particular situation. An additional component is feedback from clinical data that cross-checks the validity of the rule/diagnosis, which then adds to the refinement of the expert system knowledge base (see Figure 12.13).

Once a basis framework has been selected, the inference engine asks a series of targeted questions proposed by the expert system to refine matches to the existing knowledge base. A list of probabilities are then generated; i.e., an example of a system used for determining heart arrhythmias states to the medical professional that 62% of arrhythmias are due to hypokalemia, a low potassium level, and 75% to hypomagnesemia, low magnesium, which might be making the patient more prone to arrhythmias. The system asks the individual to enter potassium and magnesium results from blood tests to validate or refute the hypothesis. This type of

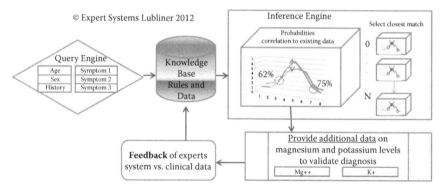

**FIGURE 12.13**
Expert system architecture.

feedback mechanism provides a more accurate diagnosis where additional data increases the probability of accuracy. This is an example of a rule-based (RB) expert system.

Other paradigms for medical expert systems are case-based reasoning (CBR), cognitive systems, and crowd-based expert systems. CBR utilizes an evolving library of cases where matches are made to the current case, rather than utilizing a standard rules-based engine; this is similar to the process of how doctors make a diagnosis. The process involves four steps: retrieve similar cases, reuse the case to solve similar problems, revise and modify the case, and retain the new case with updates for the case library (4Rs).

Cognitive systems [14,1] are a series of artificial intelligence paradigms with "the ability to engage in abstract thought that goes beyond immediate perceptions and actions." Originally comprehensive artificial intelligence (AI) systems attempted to model human consciousness, but due to their lack of success were modified for a more narrow expertise in specific domains of knowledge. An example is chess programs that are the equal of the best master-level chess players. Cognitive systems utilize structured representations and probabilistic models to support problem solving utilizing concepts from psychology, logic, and linguistics.

Crowd-based systems, wisdom of the crowds, provide a new method to extract large amounts of relevant data from the web on the assumption that large data sets may be more accurate than limited clinical data from the web. So far this approach has yet to be validated in the medical arena. This crowd-based approach has shown some success on social networking sites, where specific diseases are targeted and individuals supply anecdotal data.

## DATA MINING AND BIG DATA

Data mining can be defined as the process of finding previously unknown patterns and trends in databases and using that information to build predictive models [11]. In healthcare data mining focuses on detailed questions and outcomes. What symptoms, quantitative data, and clinical outcomes in combination lead to specific diagnoses and treatments? As discussed in the previous section, a combination of probabilistic and human-directed diagnoses evolves into a knowledge base. This works well with a finite data set, but with big data it can become difficult to process. Imagine millions of individuals with real-time wearable or implanted medical sensors sending data through smartphones. The data stream would certainly be in the terabyte range, but as these devices became ubiquitous, petabytes levels of data would not be unreasonable. Information can be summarized and evaluated locally on ever-evolving smartphones, but additional analysis and correlation, on a regional or global level, would require new stochastic techniques, i.e., algorithms to analyze random events. This seems like a contradiction in terms. Markov chains, random events, quantified as time series events or limited by a field space, or a finite geographical area or subpopulation can provide a deterministic function used to correlate or classify seemingly random events. Examples are plumes of breast cancer patients that appear to be random but with large enough data sets can create correlations, i.e., the butterfly effect, the concept that a butterfly flapping its wings in one area can create small finite effects over larger distances. Tracking the cause back to that original butterfly or a random mutation of flu virus anywhere in the world could predict and prevent epidemics.

## Genomic Mapping of Large Data Sets

Current genomic, genetic mapping, research has generated terabytes of data and is the focus of NSF and NIH research grants. The NIH in 2012 released its first genomic 200-terabyte data sets (equivalent to the size of the entire Library of Congress). This data set will grow exponentially as routine genetic mapping is a predictive medical diagnostic tool. If, for example, you have a 50% likelihood of developing breast cancer, proactive medical treatments will be prescribed decades before the first symptoms might arise. It may be possible to provide treatment in the womb to inhibit the activation of these epigenetic factors entirely. There is a new field of epigenetics that suggests either environmental or inherited factors are responsible for activating these genetic traits (i.e., the gene for breast cancer will remain dormant if the trigger that prevents the underlying inherited gene is not present). If removed, there is a low likelihood that these genetic traits will be expressed. In that case, genetic mapping, as technology reduces time and cost, most likely will become commonplace. The cost to map a single genetic sequence has gone down from $100 million in 2001 to $5000 in 2013, and from a year to a few hours (see Figure 12.14).

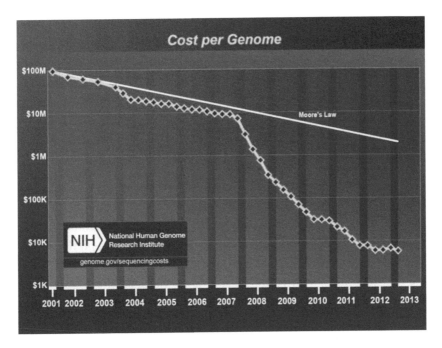

**FIGURE 12.14**

Reduction in costs of mapping a single genetic sequence. (From the NIH Human Genome Project.)

## FUTURE DIRECTIONS: MINING LARGE DATA SETS: NSF AND NIH RESEARCH INITIATIVES

This section describes initiatives underway to analyze the growing field of big data and provide significant research funds to enhance analysis of medical data and new methodologies that potentially may be utilized by other disciplines. NSF and NIH research is often a predictive indicator for future medical innovations, similar to previous DARPA investments that were responsible for many of today's computer advancements.

This field, big data, c. 2012 is the focus of support by several U.S. research agencies: the National Science Foundation (NSF), Department of Defense (DOD), and National Institutes of Health (NIH), committing $200 million to this big data initiative [26–29].

The following was a solicitation on an NSF page to researchers to submit grants:

The Obama Administration announced a "Big Data Research and Development Initiative." By improving our ability to extract knowledge and insights from large and complex collections of digital data, the initiative promises to help solve some of the Nation's most pressing challenges.

To launch the initiative, six Federal departments and agencies today, March 29th, 2012 announced more than $200 million in new commitments that, together, promise to greatly improve the tools and techniques needed to access, organize, and glean discoveries from huge volumes of digital data.

NIH also has dedicated significant funds to the analysis of larger data sets, specifically focused on genomic research. NIH announced in 2012 that the world's largest set of data on human genetic variation, produced by the international 1000 Genomes Project, was available on the Amazon Web Services (AWS) cloud at 200 terabytes, the equivalent of 16 million file cabinets filled with text. The source of the data, the 1000 Genomes Project data set is a prime example of big data, where data sets become so massive that few researchers have the computing power to make the best use of them. AWS is storing the 1000 Genomes Project as a publically available data set for free, and researchers only will pay for the computing services that they use.

Large data sets are also currently being generated by researchers in other fields. Some of those research initiatives are

- Earth Cube: A system that will allow geoscientists to access, analyze, and share information about our planet.
- The Defense Advanced Research Projects Agency (DARPA): An XDATA program to develop computational techniques and software tools for analyzing large volumes of data, both semistructured (e.g., tabular, relational, categorical, metadata) and unstructured (e.g., text documents, message traffic). Harness and utilize massive data in new ways and bring together sensing, perception, and decision support to make truly autonomous systems that can maneuver and make decisions on their own.
- The Smart Health and Wellbeing (SHB) program: By the NSF [22], the SHB's goal is the "transformation of healthcare from reactive and hospital-centered to preventive, proactive, evidence-based, person-centered and focused on wellbeing rather than disease." The categories of this effort include wireless medical sensors, networking,

machine learning, and integrating social and economic issues that affect medical outcomes.

The following is a representative funded research grant in the field of wireless medical device.

NSF award to utilize wireless medical sensors for chronic illnesses.
Telemedicine technologies offer the opportunity to frequently monitor patients' health and optimize management of chronic illnesses. Given the diversity of home telemedicine technologies, it is essential to compose heterogeneous telemedicine components and systems for a much larger patient population through systems of systems. The objective of this research is to thoroughly investigate the heterogeneity in large-scale telemedicine systems for cardiology patients. To accomplish this task, this research seeks to develop (i) a novel open source platform medical device interface adapter that can seamlessly interconnect medical devices that conform to interoperability standards, such as IEEE 11703, to smartphones for real-time data processing and delivery; (ii) a set of novel supporting technologies for wireless networking, data storage, and data integrity checking, and (iii) a learning-based early warning system that adaptively changes patient and disease models based on medical device readings and context.

The challenge of the above grant is to not just collect data, but build in sociological components, stress, economic conditions, etc., that might generate transient results. Results from previous studies have shown that filtering out unusual readings may result in more reliable data. Also, integrating smoking, drinking, etc., helps quantify the results. So apps that allow users to input data regarding their frame of mind or habits while the data is being monitored on the wireless medical devices can provide invaluable information for analysis of causal effects to physiological readings.

Assuming wireless mobile medical devices become common, estimates of data generated daily, with only a million users, range from 1 terabyte (TB) to 1 petabyte per/day (Figure 12.15). To put this in perspective, the digital storage for the Library of Congress is 200 terabytes. The population in 2012 is 300 million in the United States and 7 billion worldwide, and 50% of Americans have some type of smartphone or tablet. In the next 25 years 20% of the U.S. population will be over 65, making either wearable smart medical devices or those abilities directly embedded in smart devices likely to expand rapidly. This flood of potential data dwarfs all other applications. Data mining of this treasure trove of medical data will be the challenge of the decades to come.

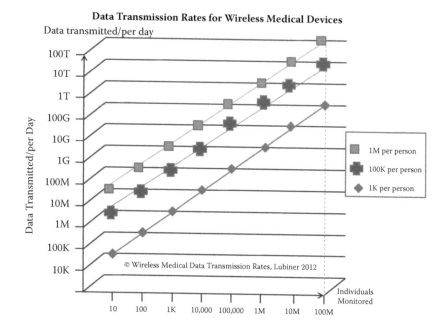

**FIGURE 12.15**

Smart Health data transmission projections as wireless medical sensors become commonplace.

# OTHER EVOLVING MINING AND ANALYTICS APPLICATIONS IN HEALTHCARE

Additional analytic applications that involve more basic business intelligence approaches of reporting and OLAP, optimization techniques to the more complex mining methods address three major areas that include: workflow activities of healthcare service provider organizations, risk stratification of a patient population, and enhancing patient treatment and outcomes with electronic health records data.

## Workflow Analytics of Provider Organizations

Large healthcare service providers (e.g., hospitals, healthcare systems, ACOs) are generating greater varieties of data resources that include metrics which measure the performance of numerous activities. Processes within these large service providers are continuously monitored to achieve greater efficiencies that ultimately can reduce costs and enhance patient outcomes. Some prominent performance measures which care providers seek to manage include the following:

- Patient Length of Stay at a Provider Facility
- Patient Satisfaction
- Capacity Utilization (e.g., bed utilization rates)
- Staffing (e.g., nurses to patient optimization)
- Patient Episode Cost Estimation
- ER throughput
- Estimating patient demand for services

These high-level metrics measure the performance of a diverse set of healthcare processes and require analysts to identify and manage a great variety of data variables to better understand the factors that impact or drive these measures. Provider organizations generate and record vast data resources in measuring activities at the patient level. One source of data is generated through the establishment and recording of time for activities. Time stamps that record the initiation and ending of corresponding subcomponents of workflow processes enable analysts to create duration variables according to various attributes of the process. For example, time stamps can facilitate the generation of the time that is required from initiating a lab test for a patient and receiving the results of that test (duration of patient test), which can play an important factor in affecting the LOS of a patient. Other variables that help provide descriptive power to analytic, decision support models involve the utilization of data according to standardization codes such as DRG, Physician Specialty, Treatment Area, etc., along with patient descriptive information [12].

- DRG of Patient
- Attending Physician Specialty
- Patient Descriptors (demographic, physiological)
- Treatment Descriptors (frequency of visits by nurses and doctors)
- Duration of workflow activities (time to receive lab results)

All these variables provide the building blocks to better understanding higher level performance metrics of care providers.

More basic analytic approaches (e.g., reporting, dashboards, cubes) can yield timely, actionable informative results, however these are more retrospective in nature (e.g., what has happened with a particular work-flow). More sophisticated quantitative, multivariate based approaches in the mining spectrum can identify patterns that depict relationships between descriptive and performance metrics and can provide more robust decision support capabilities.

Analytic approaches can be used to better understand additional per-formance metrics such as patient satisfaction rates, staffing optimization, etc. However, differences lie in the relevant data resources and availabil-ity of those resources that describe process activities. Some of these data resources may require additional administrative actions to be initiated in order to generate essential descriptive data, hence a greater variety of data. For example, patient surveys must be introduced to extract data variables to provide explanatory information as to what drives a patient's experience, not to mention the performance metric of how that experience is measured.

## Risk Stratification

Perhaps one of the most noteworthy concepts that addresses true suc-cess in healthcare, namely, achieving a healthier population with opti-mal resource management, is the idea of better identifying illnesses that are evolving in patients or identifying individuals at risk of developing serious, chronic illnesses and applying pre-emptive treatment in order to mitigate or avoid those illnesses. Risk stratifying patient populations has been a standard analytic application in the healthcare sector for years. Much analytic work has utilized financial, insurance claims based data as it involves patient based descriptors, diagnosis and treatment descriptors along with the important data of costs involved with corresponding ser-vice activities. Stratification techniques can include mathematic equations and weighting of corresponding variables, multivariate statistically based methods, and mining based approaches to determine the risk level of a patient developing a chronic illness.

The term "hot spotting" has received great attention recently when con-sidering the identification of high cost drivers in resource utilization of healthcare services [5]. Some enlightening information around this topic is the inclusion of such patient descriptors as geography and economic status when attempting to identify individuals that are high resource users of healthcare services, or more simply put, individuals that may become sicker than they otherwise would be because of the location of their resi-dence, inability to pay, and lack of access to care providers. All these new variables or "variety of data" plays an essential role in better understanding an individual's likelihood to develop serious illness and be high resource users of healthcare services. The ultimate result of robust analytic models that can more accurately identify those factors that lead to higher risk is the ability to mitigate those factors that lead to higher illness and cost driver rates. These factors may not only apply to diet and behavioral attributes, but simple logistics such as lack of access to transportation to reach a healthcare facility.

## Combining Structured and Unstructured Data for Patient Diagnosis and Treatment Outcomes

Electronic health records provide an essential data resource that provide descriptive information of a patient and various treatment activities they undergo. Some of this data is structured (e.g., demographics, physiological attributes), however, there is an unstructured portion to an EHR and this includes added notes or comments by attending physicians relevant to treatment activities. This latter information comes under the variety of big data and offers potential insights into how a patient may have reacted to certain procedures or why drug prescriptions had been changed, to name a few. This unstructured element introduces the potential for greater decision support information as to better treatment and outcomes or diagnosis.

An essential analytic method that can be utilized to unlock the potential value to the verbiage that is included in an EHR involves text mining that incorporates semantic rules. As was illustrated throughout this book (e.g., see Chapters 3, 10, and 11), text mining can provide structure to unstructured data that can then be analyzed with other mining methods to extract actionable information.

Some examples of the value of incorporating both structured and unstructured data in the case of EHRs can include insights such as the following:

- Avoiding possible adverse drug events as comments from attending physicians describe a patient's reaction to particular drugs or dosage of drugs.
- Optimizing diet or rehabilitation activities according to patient reactions to prescribed plans
- Considering psychological effects to applied treatments

We should reiterate the points made in Chapter 10 that the process of creating value from unstructured data is still a difficult task, however the benefits may warrant the effort. This provides a good segue to the following issue. A perplexing decision for many organizations in the evolving big data era is whether the value of pursuing big data initiatives warrants the costs involved. In the case of healthcare, the topic may be less of a conundrum given that many data attributes are already being recorded and the value can be substantial when considering the increase in quality to human life.

## SUMMARY

*Homo sapiens*, modern man, arrived on the scene, as indicated by the fossil record [17], around 200,000 years ago. Quantification of medical practices began around 5000 years ago in Egypt and soon after in China. But the true emergence of medical science arose only 200 years ago. Due to these advances, life expectancy has doubled from 38 to 77 in the past 100 years. We have reached a new milestone where science, technology, and communications have truly created one unified planet, at least scientifically. If we harness these recourses properly, this nexus of science and technological advances can lead to another doubling of life expectancy and reduce human suffering. The real challenge lies in extracting meaning, i.e., data mining this flood of information and making it readily available. I hope you are up to the challenge.

## REFERENCES

1. Brachman, R., and Lemnios, Z. (2002). DARPA's cognitive systems vision. *Computing Research News* 14: 1.
2. Crookshank, E. (1888). The history of the germ theory. *British Medical Journal* 1(1415): 312.
3. Dignan, L. (2011). Cisco predicts mobile data traffic explosion. http://seekingalpha.com/article/250005-cisco-predicts-mobile-data-traffic-explosion.
4. Englebardt, S.P., and Nelson, R. (2002). The role of expert systems in nursing and medicine. *Anti Essays*. Retrieved November 18, 2012, from http://www.antiessays.com/free-essays/185731.htmlp. 137.
5. Gawande, A. (2011). The Hot Spotters, *The New Yorker*, January.
6. Gazit, Y. Berk, D.A., Leuning, M., Baxter, L.T., and Jain, R.K. (1995). Scale-invariant behavior and vascular network formation in normal and tumor tissue. *Physical Review Letters* 75(12):2428–2431.

7. Gazit, Y., Baish, J., Safabakhsh, N., Leunig, M., Baxter, L. T., and Jain, R. K. (1997). Fractal characteristics of tumor vascular architecture during tumor growth and regression. *Microcirculation* 4(4): 395–402.

8. Geller, M.J. (2010). *Ancient Babylonian medicine: Theory and practice*. Oxford: Wiley-Blackwell.

9. Gopakumar, T.G. (2012). Switchable nano magnets may revolutionize data storage: Magnetism of individual molecules switched. Retrieved from http://www.science-daily.com/releases/2012/06/120614131049.htm.

10. Heckerman, D., and Shortliffe, E. (1992). From certainty factors to belief networks *Artificial Intelligence in Medicine* 4(1): 35–52. doi:10.1016/0933-3657(92)90036-O. http://research.microsoft.com/en-us/um/people/heckerman/HS91aim.pdf.

11. Kincade, K. (1998). Data mining: Digging for healthcare gold. *Insurance and Technology* 23(2): IM2–IM7.

12. Kudyba, S. and Gregorio, T. (2010). Identifying factors that impact patient length of stay metrics for healthcare providers with advanced analytics. *Health Informatics Journal* 16(4): 235–245.

13. Kusnetzky, D. What is big data? ZDNet, 2010, from http://www.zdnet.com/blog/virtualization/what-is-big-data/1708.

14. Langley, P. (2012). The cognitive systems paradigm. CogSys.org.

15. Ljunggren, S. (1983). A simple graphical representation of Fourier-based imaging methods. *Journal of Magnetic Resonance* 54(2): 338–348.

16. Mahn, T. (2010). Wireless medical technologies: Navigating government regulation in the new medical age. Retrieved from http://www.fr.com/files/uploads/attachments/FinalRegulatoryWhitePaperWirelessMedicalTechnologies.pdf.

17. McHenry, H.M. (2009). Human evolution In *Evolution: The first four billion years*, ed. M. Ruse and J. Travis, 265. Cambridge, MA: Belknap Press of Harvard University Press.

18. Oosterwijk, H. (2004). *PACS fundamentals*. Aubrey, TX: OTech.

19. Ritner, R.K. (2001). Magic. *The Oxford encyclopedia of ancient Egypt*. Oxford reference online, October 2011.

20. Ross, P.E. (2004, December). Managing care through the air. *IEEE Spectrum*, pp. 14–19.

21. Snijders, C., Matzat, U., and Reips, U. D. (2012). Big data: Big gaps of knowledge in the field of Internet science. *International Journal of Internet Science* 7(1): 1–5.

22. Twieg, D. (1983). The k-trajectory formulation of the NMR imaging process with applications in analysis and synthesis of imaging methods. *Medical Physics* 10(5): 610–612.

23. Walter, C. (2005, July 25). Kryder's law. *Scientific American*.

24. IEEE. (2012). Medical interoperability standards. Retrieved from www.IEEE.org/standards.

25. HHS.gov. HIPPA Title II regulations. Retrieved from http://www.hhs.gov/ocr/privacy/hipaa/administrative/securityrule/nist80066.pdf.

26. House.gov. (2012, March 29). Obama administration unveils "big data" initiative: Announces $200 million in new R&D investments. Retrieved from http://www.google.com/#hl=en&tbo=d&sclient=psy-ab&q=data±mining±healthcare±definition&oq=data±mining±healthcare±definition&gs_l=hp.3..33i29l4.1468.8265.0.8387.33.28.0.5.5.1.195.2325.26j2.28.0.les%3B..0.0...1c.1.JgQWyqlEaFc&pbx=1&bav=on.2,or.r_gc.r_pw.r_qf.&fp = 775112e853595b1e&bpcl=38897761&biw=908&bih=549.

27. NSF. (2012). Big data NSF funding. Retrieved from http://www.nsf.gov/funding/pgm_summ.jsp?pims_id = 504739.

28. NSF. (2011). Utilizing wireless medical sensors for chronic heart disease. Retrieved from http://www.nsf.gov/awardsearch/showAward?AWD_ID=1231680&Historical Awards=false.

29. NSF. Links to U.S. federal big data initiative 2010:

    a. NSF: http://www.nsf.gov/news/news_summ.jsp?cntn_id = 123607.

    b. HHS/NIH: http://www.nih.gov/news/health/mar2012/nhgri-29.htm.

    c. DOE: http://science.energy.gov/news/.

    d. DOD: www.DefenseInnovationMarketplace.mil.

    e. DARPA: http://www.darpa.mil/NewsEvents/Releases/2012/03/29.aspx.

    f. USGS: http://powellcenter.usgs.gov.

# Index

T - #0370 - 071024 - C4 - 234/156/15 - PB - 9780367378813 - Gloss Lamination